BAILOUT? BALONEY!

The Auto Bankruptcy Spin

Lou Lawrence

©copyright 2014 by Louis J. Lawrence Jr.

Fifth Edition June 2017

All rights reserved. No part of this book may be used or reproduced by any means, graphic, electronic, or mechanical, including photocopying, recording, taping or by any information storage retrieval system without the written permission of the author except in the case of brief quotations, embodied in critical articles and reviews.

Table of Contents

Foreword:	David Cole	5
Preface:	Chrysler & GM Bankruptcy	7
One:	Automobile Development	9
Two:	General Motors	57
Three:	Ford	115
Four:	Chrysler	185
Five:	UAW	221
Six:	Government	237
Seven:	Outlook	263

FOREWORD

David E. Cole
Chairman Emeritus Center for Automotive Research
University of Michigan

Those in the past who claimed, "We live in interesting times" surely would say the same about the past decade of chaos and change in the domestic automobile industry. We have seen some amazing things since the advent of the industry in the late 1890s; the rapid retooling in the early 1940s to build military vehicles and aircraft for World War II, to the highly sophisticated, technology-based vehicles of today, and the high-tech automobiles being developed for tomorrow. The "interesting times" perspective on the modern-era auto industry is embedded in Lou Lawrence's book, *BAILOUT? BALONEY!*

While we often talk about the "Great Recession" of 2008, most people don't realize that the auto industry actually experienced a depression. The recession caused a 40% decline in vehicle sales. In manufacturing, with its high fixed costs, the loss of such sales volume and the consequent reduction of revenue will cause catastrophic results in any industry. This problem is not unique to auto manufacturing, but is true whether we are making iPhones, bricks, refrigerators, or vehicles.

Many think that the 2008 financial disaster is related to normal recessions, but rather it is rooted in government legislation that promoted the idea that everyone should own a home, whether they could afford it or not. Government legislation led to a housing bubble that peaked in 2006, burst in 2007, and resulted in the 2008 Great Housing Recession. Many home mortgages went into bankruptcy, and other homeowners found themselves "under water" with their home loans, leading to a massive number of defaults and a collapse in property values. This was the trigger for the Great Recession. Unfortunately, the same legislation that caused the recession is still in place, as Lawrence notes in the chapter, "Government-Dysfunctional."

The Great Recession caused the bankruptcy of GM and Chrysler and Ford only avoided bankruptcy by using a $23 billion loan obtained in 2006 for restructuring. One important point made by Lawrence is that the liquidation of the car companies as many politicians demanded would have taken out the auto suppliers and resulted in a collapse of the entire industry. Because of the important role of the auto industry, a collapse would have precipitated a depression in the overall economy.

The government was quick to publicize its "heroic" role of saving the industry, but there was no bailout, only bankruptcy. Congress actually voted against a bailout, and $60 billion of the $79 billion loaned to automotive was used to pay the companies' bills while the Obama-Rattner study was in motion. The bankruptcy law was largely ignored; the union received 55% of Chrysler and the bondholders received nothing. The GM bondholders received 10% of their $30 billion investment while the UAW kept their pay, pension, and health care benefits.

As someone who was a part of the auto industry for many years, Lawrence brings a perspective based on a deep understanding of the most complex manufacturing industry on the planet. In addressing the various players – Chrysler, Ford, and GM, the United Auto Workers, and, finally, the government – he demonstrates this knowledge, and provides a review of the amazing history of the various organizations.

BAILOUT? BALONEY! gives us the other side of the story. It is a well-written and carefully researched story by an industry insider who has been around the auto-industry block.

PREFACE

Many wonder what caused the 2008 recession, but few know the recession was forty years in the making. Between 1968 and 2008, Congress passed twenty pieces of legislation to eliminate discrimination in housing. The White House also issued executive orders to increase home ownership for minorities and the poor. The legislation and presidential orders created a housing bubble in 2001-2006, that burst in 2007, and caused the Great Housing Recession that began in 2008.

The government *affordable housing* program eliminated key elements of mortgage loans; down payments, income checks, and credit ratings were eliminated; the only requirement was a signature. Politicians failed to recognize that many of the low-income families would not be able to make the mortgage payments and fifteen million foreclosures occurred. The program for *affordable housing* failed because of the foreclosures, and actually reduced home ownership for the poor.

When the foreclosures hit, politicians refused to accept any responsibility for the crisis; one senator reported *none of us had anything to due with the problem.* In addition to ignoring the probability of foreclosures, legislators failed to establish regulations to control the growth in housing, and controls of financial institutiions were ignored. Wall Street took advantage of the huge increase in mortgages, and issued mortgage bonds that included thousands of toxic subprime mortgages. The prospectus failed to mention the risk of the toxic mortgages, and investors did not know what they were buying. The foreclosures eliminated the bond income, and the securities were worthless. For the first time in history, Wall Street was facing bankruptcy.

Just as the politicians of the 1930s blamed business for the Great Depression, 2008 politicians blamed the housing recession on business management. The Washington blame game did little to help the 200,000 businesses that went bankrupt, including Chrysler and General Motors.

The government certainly bailed out Wall Street and banks, but ignored Main Street. According to the Treasury Center for Public Integrity, the government provided $14 trillion in the bailouts of 1065 financial institutions. However, the Treasury refused a $35 billion loan request by the auto companies, and Congress voted 52-35 *against* bailing out the auto industry. These facts have not received much attention by the media.

Another issue that has received little notice is the eight-month delay by politicians in making a decision on the auto problem. The Treasury studied the auto situation for a month; Congress studied the problem for two months, and the Obama-Rattner task force study required five months. Chrysler and GM were bankrupt in November 2008, and were burning working capital to keep the doors open during the *studies*. A total of $60 billion of working capital was used during the eight-months of political delays, which was 75% of the $79 billion loaned to Chrysler and General Motors. Ford avoided bankruptcy by using a $23 billion loan obtained in 2006 for working capital. Chrysler and GM were unable to obtain loans in 2008 since the banks were also bankrupt. The government was the only source of loans.

The eight-month delay, and the $60 billion cost of working capital have been missed by the media; it is almost as if it never happened. The lack of action and delay in decision-making by the government was appalling, but the government claim of an auto bailout was a sham. Regrettably, the media have echoed the fallacy, and the American public believes it to be true.

Bailout is providing help; bankruptcy is total failure. There was no auto bailout; there was only bankruptcy.

ONE

AUTOMOBILE DEVELOPMENT

1930 Cord Automobile

The automobile changed the world, but it was a long time coming. The Egyptians domesticated the horse in 2300 BC, but a self-propelled automobile was not in use until Karl Benz patented his *Motorwagen* in 1886. The development required nearly 200 years after the steam engine was invented in 1698, and 100,000 patents have been issued.

Since the beginning of mankind, obtaining a means of transportation has been a major objective. Horsepower was the only available form of transportation for over four thousand years. The spoke wheel was developed in 1900 BC, but a power source was required before another type of conveyance could be developed.

Leonardo da Vinci envisioned a self-propelled vehicle in the fifteenth century, and his drawings were similar to Karl Benz's first automobile patented in 1886 that was actually an engine mounted on a tricycle. Leonardo made several drawings of a vehicle, but all required manpoiwer or horsepower to make the vehicle move. Leonardo's *automobile* looked like a tricycle but lacked a power source.

Leonardo da Vinci Automobile

Before the invention of the engine, the development of railroads and the automobile, most of the populace lived on farms, and rarely traveled outside their home base. With the invention of the steam engine, the locomotive was developed, and railroads crossed the nation by the 1860s. Railroads permitted industry to expand, and allowed people to travel. The invention of the engine changed the world of transportation.

Steam energy was recognized over two thousand years ago, but it took nearly seventeen hundred years before a steam engine was developed. Dennis Papin, the French physicist, built a working model of a steam engine in 1679.

An engine is a device that converts energy into mechanical motion. The primary engines are heat engines, and both internal and external-combustion engines are heat engines. The internal-combustion engine creates heat inside the combustion chamber. Steam engines are classified as external because the heat is supplied by a separate source, the boiler. The energy in steam comes from the volume expansion when water is heated to its boiling point, turns into steam, and the volume expands 1600 times. The term "engine" is derived from the Latin word, *ingenium*, which means ability. The term "motor" comes from the Latin word, *motor*, which means mover.

Thomas Savery, an English mining engineer, invented and patented the first steam engine in 1698. Savery's design intent was to pump water from coalmines. Ropes and buckets had been used to haul the water from the mines. Savery started a company producing steam engines, with the primary applications being water pumps and water wheels.

The steam engine was the first mechanical motor to power industrial devices, and led to further applications for replacing manpower and horsepower for work. Prior to engine development, all work was done by hand and limited production. The steam engine completely changed industrial production.

Savery's Steam Engine 1698

The steam engine powered the Industrial Revolution of the late 1700s. However, Savery's steam engine had limited power, had several explosions, and obviously was not suitable for an automobile because of its size. James Watt, a Scottish engineer whose name is used for the unit of power, improved the steam-engine design by including a separate condenser, and later invented the rotary-motion steam engine in 1781.

The first steam-engine road vehicle was a military tractor built in 1769 by a French Army Captain named Nicolas-Joseph Cugnot. The design intent was to pull military artillery, but the steam vehicle was larger than the artillery. The French military cancelled the project, but Cugnot continued to work on steam-engine wagons. In 1781, one of Cugnot's steam vehicles ran into a stone wall, and the driver was killed. His financial backers pulled out, and money dried up for Cugnot's inventions. This was reported to be the first motor-vehicle accident in the world. Cugnot lost his army pension after the French Revolution and died in poverty in 1804 at age 79.

William John Rankine, the Scottish physicist, developed his theory of the steam engine in 1859, and the Rankine Cycle is still known as the basic cycle for steam engines. The invention of the steam engine was a scientific breakthrough that completely changed the methods of production. The Industrial Revolution involved the transition from horsepower to engine power in the 1760-1840 period, and improved industrial production.

While the early inventions and development work on steam engines occurred in England, scientists in America were also active in steam. In 1790, Oliver Evans of Delaware obtained a patent on a high-pressure steam engine, and had ideas of developing a steam-powered vehicle, but was unable to convince financial backers to support his project. He then turned his steam project to boats, and in 1804, built his first steam-powered boat. The boat weighed 4000 pounds, and most of the weight was the steam engine. In 1805, the Fulton Steam Works began developing steam-powered ships, and in 1807, Robert Fulton introduced the first steamship service between New York City and Albany, a distance of 150 miles. The trip required 30 hours.

The early steam engines were large, noisy, inefficient, and required considerable engineering development before they would be suitable for automobiles. The first use of steam engines for transportation was the locomotive. The negative factors of size and noise were not problems for the outdoor locomotives. The early steam engines were not suitable for automobiles, but worked for railways.

Richard Trevithick built the first steam locomotive in England in 1804. Trevithick continued his development work, and built the "Catch Me Who Can" locomotive in 1808. Evidently, it was popular to name the locomotives, because George Stephenson, another Englishman, built the "Locomotion," and started the first railway service in England in 1825. After 4200 years, the second means of land transportation was in use.

1808 Travithick Locomotive

Stephenson started a company to manufacture locomotives, and became the largest producer in the world. His company also manufactured locomotive components and developed cast-iron rails for railroads. In addition to producing locomotives for England, the company exported components. Rails and components were shipped to America before manufacturing facilities were constructed in the nation.

The first railroad in America was the Baltimore and Ohio system. In 1829, the B&O railroad, with its "Tom Thumb" locomotive, carried 26 passengers 13 miles. The trip required one hour and fifteen minutes, but was more comfortable than horseback. The first railway service in continental Europe was started in Belgium in 1835.

Between 1829 and the 1860s, railroads were constructed throughout the United States, and on May 10, 1869, Governor Stanford drove the final spike (the *Golden Spike*) to complete the transcontinental railway system at Promontory Summit, Utah. The railroads replaced the horse for long-distance travel, but the automobile had not been invented. Horses were still used for short travels, and transport people and goods from the railroad depots to town, so another means of transportation was needed.

Even though steam engine technology was being used for steamships and locomotives, the use of engines for automobiles had not been developed. The steam engines of the 1800s were too large for automobiles, but engineers were working to downsize the units. The lack of roads in America was another drawback. In the 1890s, there were hardly any paved roads in the U.S., and in 1900, there were only ten miles of paved roadways in the entire country.

Roads were better in Europe since the Romans had built stone roads 2000 years ago. Some of the Roman roads even had grooves to fit the wheels of the chariots and wagons to keep the vehicles on the road in the dark. Captured soldiers chiseled the grooves by hand, and many of the Roman roads still existed in Europe. Napoleon had also constructed roads during his reign, and the roadways throughout Europe were available for the self-propelled automobile.

Ancient Roman Road with Wagon Wheel Grooves

Engineers in England began mounting steam engines to carriages, and the first self-propelled land vehicles were in use in the 1830s. The large carriages carried passengers between towns in England. However, the farmers complained about the steam vehicles scaring animals, and others complained about the noise.

England passed the "Red Flag Act" in 1865 that required a rider to precede any steam vehicle, wave a red flag, and blow a horn, warning the populace that a steam vehicle was approaching. England could have been the first nation to start the automobile industry but failed to recognize the value of the new product.

In the United States, steam engines were being assembled to wagons and carriages by the 1870s. The first automobile race in the nation was held in 1878 between two steam-engine-powered vehicles. The state of Wisconsin was interested in providing an incentive to individuals to develop a self-propelled vehicle to replace the horse as a means of transportation. Wisconsin offered a $10,000 prize to the winner of a race between Madison and Green Bay, a distance of over 200 miles. The requirements were that the vehicles must be self-powered and average a speed of six miles per hour. Dr. J. W. Carhart, a professor of physics at the University of Wisconsin, had built a steam-engine vehicle and entered the event. The J.I. Case Company provided funds for the Carhart vehicle. There were only two steam-engine vehicles entered in the race. Carhart won when the other vehicle suffered a breakdown. Dr. Carhart thought of starting an automobile company but lacked the funds. The J.I. Case Company could have been the first automobile company in America, but the company failed to take advantage of the opportunity.

The development of a steam-engine vehicle came 140 years after the invention of the steam engine by Savery in 1698. The engineering and development work during this period provided the opportunity for engineers to apply the steam engine to a platform, wagon, or some other chassis for personal transportation. Since steam power had been recognized thousands of years ago, it was surprising that it took so long to develop a steam engine suitable for an automobile. However, communications at that time were poor, so developments in different parts of the world were not publicized or shared.

Steam engines power a vehicle by burning fuel that heats water in a boiler creating steam that expands 1600 times; the energy then pushes a piston, which turns a crankshaft that drives the wheels of the vehicle. The machine missing in Leonardo da Vinci's drawings was now in existence. The self-propelled vehicle offered the comfort, speed, and convenience that was not available with the horse or the railroad.

Once the steam engine was accepted as a safe means of power, there were unlimited applications for steam: steamships, railroads, printing presses, machine shops, even the elevators in the Eiffel Tower, and in the not-too-distant future, the automobile. Steam engines were the primary source of power from the time of the Savery invention in 1698, until the internal-combustion engine was invented in 1859.

The first automobiles were steam vehicles because the steam engine was the first engine invented. Even though steam engines had the disadvantage of a separate boiler, and required a continuous water supply, steam engine cars remained in production until mid-1920. In America, one of the most famous steam-vehicle companies was the Stanley Steamer Motor Carriage Company. Francis and Freeland Stanley founded the Stanley Steamer Company in Newton, Massachusetts in 1902. The company prided itself on safety, and there was never a reported explosion of a Stanley vehicle. The Stanley brothers built their first steam car in 1897, and the first automobiles consisted of a wood body mounted on a steel frame. The company was sold in 1918, but continued to build automobiles until 1924. By the mid-1920s, the internal-combustion engine vehicles had taken over the market because of price. The steam-engine cars cost $4000 ($54,000 today) in 1924, while the Ford Model T sold for $265 ($3600 today). In addition to the cost issue, steam-engine vehicles were noisy, and required a continuous water supply for the boiler. Gasoline was normally used to fire the boiler.

Stanley Steamer Automobile

The invention of the internal-combustion engine followed the steam engine by 161 years. French physicist Nicholas Carnot first developed the concept of the IC engine when he published his book on thermodynamics in 1824. It was not until 1859 that French engineer Jean-Joseph-Etinne Lenoir built the first internal-combustion engine. Lenoir patented a single-cylinder, two-cycle machine that used coal gas for fuel. In 1863, Lenoir mounted his engine on a carriage, and this vehicle would have been the world's first internal-combustion-engine automobile, had it worked. The engine was too small to power the carriage, and the project failed.

The Lenoir engine was too large for an automobile, and considerable redesign was required before the engine was suitable for a car. However, the internal-combustions engine did not require a boiler, and after design changes, was better suited for an automobile. Lenoir was a brilliant engineer who also invented the spark plug, and his plug design was the same as that used in today's spark plugs. Despite his inventions and patents, Lenoir died in poverty in 1900.

Lenoir Internal-Combustion Engine

The internal-combustion engine is a machine that produces power with the combustion of a fuel-air mixture. The IC engine powers a vehicle when combustion occurs. When fuel is combined with air and ignited, high-pressure gases apply force to a piston that turns the crankshaft, and the crankshaft drives the wheels of the vehicle

The Lenoir engine was too large for an automobile, so considerable development work was required before the engine could be used for many applications. Engineers recognized the advantages of higher power of the internal-combustion engine compared to steam engines, and they worked to improve the design of the IC engine.

In 1865, Karl Benz, a young engineering student in Germany, was given a leave of absence from university studies to assist in the installation of a Lenoir engine in a machine shop in Stuttgart. This was Benz's first experience with engines, and it led to his interest in engines and automobiles. Gottlieb Daimler, another German engineer and inventor, was also working on engines at that time. Daimler and Benz were the first to build an automobile.

Karl Benz 1844-1929

Gottlieb Daimler 1834-1900

In 1867, Nicholas Otto, the German engineer and inventor designed and patented a more efficient two-stroke-internal-combustion engine that required less fuel. The two-stroke engine utilizes two strokes for every power stroke, and a cycle is completed with two strokes of the piston. The steps include the compression stroke and the power stroke. Intake and exhaust strokes are not required since ports are used instead of valves. The first internal-combustion engines were two-stroke, spark-ignition machines. Diesel engines also used the two-stroke design.

Otto later designed a four-stroke IC engine, and the 1876 design became famous. The "Otto Cycle" design included four steps that repeated with every two revolutions. In the first step, the intake stroke, the piston moved down with fuel and air entering the combustion chamber. The second step, the compression stroke, involved the piston moving up, compressing the fuel-air mixture. In the third step, the power stroke, the spark plug ignited the fuel-air mixture when the piston reached a point near top dead center, and the expansion of gases caused by ignition produced power to turn the crankshaft, and drive the wheels of a vehicle. The fourth step, the exhaust stroke, involved the opening of the exhaust valves for exhaust. Otto used coal gas for fuel.

Nicholas Otto 1832-1891

Otto was awarded the gold medal for his engine design at the 1867 Paris Exposition, and he started an engine company in Deutz, Germany, near Cologne. The new "Otto Cycle" engine became famous, and Otto soon received a number of engine orders.
The Otto plant was poorly managed and was unable to fill the new engine orders. The plant was one of the first engine manufacturing facilities, so it was not surprising that it was not organized for production and could not fill the order backlog. Otto was a brilliant engineer, but a poor production manager. Otto's sales manager recognized the problem and was determined to fix the production problem that limited sales. He approached Gottlieb Daimler, a well-known engine engineer who had started the Daimler Engine Company in Germany. Daimler was having difficulty with his financial backers because he was spending most of his time designing and developing an automobile. The financial people wanted Daimler to focus on the profitable engine business and stop tinkering with the automobile.

Daimler accepted the production manager's job at Otto's engine company, but the sales manager had hired him, and not Otto. Gottlieb Daimler was an excellent production manager, as well as an outstanding engine engineer, and he soon corrected Otto's production problems. The new internal-combustion engine was more powerful, more efficient, and smaller than the steam engines at the time, so sales were increasing.

The first IC engines used coal gas as fuel since there was no gasoline before the 1860s. Gasoline became available after the development of the petroleum industry. Edwin Drake drilled the first oil well in 1859 in Titusville, Pennsylvania, and the industry grew due to the demand for kerosene for lamps. The fractional distillation process of petroleum started in the mid-1860s and produced oil for heating, kerosene for lighting, and gasoline. There was no demand for gasoline before the internal-combustion engine, and it was readily available and cheap.

Gasoline is more volatile than coal gas and offered more power. Gottlieb Daimler was the first to use gasoline for fuel. Otto and Karl Benz continued to use coal gas. While Daimler was working at the Otto plant, he changed Otto's engine design to use gasoline without Otto's approval, and was fired. Otto refused to use the new gasoline fuel. Daimler returned to his engine company, and the financial backers of his previous company allowed him to continue with his automobile development work. The Otto engine was historically significant because his four-stroke engine was the most practical power source for the automobile. Daimler developed a smaller, lighter, and more powerful four-stroke engine with the use of gasoline.

The internal-combustion engine became the primary source of power for vehicles. While steam and electric engines were the first used to power automobiles, the IC engine offered a more practical and powerful source of power. The availability of gasoline with the development of the petroleum industry in the 1860s offered more power for the engine because of gasoline's higher volatility. The petroleum industry and the internal- combustion engine were developed at the same time in history, and this certainly aided the development of the IC engine. The engine development for automobiles would have required much more time if gasoline had not been readily available. Coal gas had been used as fuel for years, but it is difficult to visualize coal gas stations as being practical.

Gottlieb Daimler and Karl Benz were born 60 miles apart in Germany, but their paths had never crossed. Both engineers were designing and developing engines in the 1870s, but their work was done independently. The Daimler and Benz companies were joined together in 1926, 26 years after Daimler's death. The German banks put the two companies together during the deep depression in Germany following World War I. Karl Benz was 82 at the time and not active in his company.

Daimler was the first to mount engines in a boat, a balloon, and a motorcycle, and as a result, designed a three-point star emblem to show his accomplishments on land, sea, and air. The three-point star is still used as the Mercedes emblem. Daimler believed that the age of the automobile was near, and he worked continually on vehicle development. Karl Benz's engine business produced engines not only for the German market, but also for the export business.

The Karl Benz financial backers demanded that he stop his automobile work, and concentrate on the engine business. The business partners in both Benz and Daimler's engine companies objected to the time spent on automobile development by the two pioneers and demanded that they focus on the profitable engine business. Both left their companies and continued to work on vehicle development in separate laboratories.

The financial backers of both companies were similar to the partners involved in Ransom Olds and Henry Ford's first companies two decades later. The financial people were interested in short-term profits and forced the auto pioneers out of their companies. The auto pioneers stayed with their automobile development plans and became famous and wealthy, while the financial backers went broke.

Daimler and Benz were developing their automobiles in their manufacturing plants by mounting engines on different platforms to produce a self-propelled vehicle. Gottlieb Daimler's development work was done with four-wheel carriages, but Benz was mounting engines on tricycles. Karl Benz continued to use coal gas for fuel, while Gottlieb Daimler had changed his engine design to use gasoline.

Some people in America believe Henry Ford with his Model T started the automobile industry. Some schoolbooks actually taught this misconception. However, the automobile industry began in Europe, because the engine was invented in Europe.

Karl Benz, still working with a tricycle, mounted his two-cylinder engine on a velocipede, and began testing the unit on the roads in Germany. The "vehicle" had no top, had a small coach seat, 36-inch wheels in the rear, and a 20-inch wheel in front. The engine was mounted behind the driver, and a tiller was used for steering. A hand brake was used for stopping, but there was no reverse. Benz was granted a patent for the first internal-combustion engine automobile on January 29, 1886, and he called the vehicle the *Motorwagen*. Karl Benz worked for a bicycle company after graduating as a mechanical engineer, and this led him to work with tricycles rather than a four-wheel carriage.

Karl Benz 1886 Motorwagen

If Gottlieb Daimler had simply mounted his larger four-cylinder engine on any available wagon or carriage, he could have been the first to the patent office. However, Daimler designed a custom coach, and Wimpf and Sons, a German coach company, required nine months to build the coach. On August 28, 1886, seven months after Benz's patent, Gottlieb Daimler patented a four-cylinder engine automobile. Benz's car looked similar to Leonardo da Vinci's sketches, but included the key element of the engine. Daimler's car looked more like an automobile.

Gottlieb Daimler's Automobile

The internal-combustion engine automobile had finally been invented, and after thousands of years of waiting, a practical means of personal transportation was available. The next problem was how to sell the product, because there was little publicity for the new automobile. By the 1860s, half the sailing ships had been converted to steam powered vessels, and steam locomotives were transporting people in most countries, but the automobile had yet to find its place in the transportation market.

The Daimler automobile company was selling only three vehicles a year during the nine-year period between 1886 and 1895, so the new invention had not created a huge sales drive. In an attempt to stimulate interest, Gottlieb Daimler went into the taxi business. However, once he started sending vehicles to cities in Germany to start his taxi business, the city of Munich passed an ordinance limiting the number of vehicles in the city to 25. This was an example of the public's fear of the new vehicles. Other cities were more lenient, and his taxi business was successful. Daimler's taxi drivers dressed in formal clothes and demonstrated the value and safety of the new vehicles, and the public began to accept the automobile. The Daimler and Benz company sales increased and the new automobile was on its way.

Karl Benz finally designed a four-wheel vehicle to replace his tricycle, but the vehicle was smaller than the Daimler cars. Size and power were the main differences between the early Daimler and Benz vehicles.

In 1896, Gottlieb Daimler was restricted to bed because of a weak heart, but he continued to run his company. After years of development, Daimler was convinced that the "Automobile Age" was near. In 1899, Kaiser Wilheim II requested a review of the Daimler vehicles, and Daimler's son, Adolf, organized an expedition of twelve Daimler models, and drove the cars past Daimler's house so Daimler could see his automobiles. Two weeks later, on March 6, 1900, Gottlieb Daimler died, eleven days short of his 66th birthday.

Wilhelm Maybach was Daimler's chief engineer, and he took over the Daimler Company. An entrepreneur named Emil Jellinek wintered on the Riviera and owned a Daimler. He regularly raced with his friends and often bragged about his automobile. Jellinek sometimes sold his cars to his competitors, and he continued to order new Daimlers. Since the Daimler cars were more powerful than his competition, Jellinek won more races and continued to sell his cars. He saw an opportunity to sell Daimlers, and he ordered 36 new vehicles with larger engines and redesigned body styles. This was the largest order in the history of the business – 550,000 marks, which would be equivalent to $3.5 million today.

Even though Maybach was concerned about the major redesign, he could not afford to turn down the order. Jellinek also demanded that the engine be mounted in the front, because "that's where the horse used to be." Prior to this, the Daimler engine was mounted in the middle of the vehicle. Jellinek's other demands were that he be granted the sales rights for most of Europe, and that the automobiles be named Mercedes, the name of his eleven- year old daughter. Maybach agreed to the terms and proceeded to redesign the Daimlers into the Mercedes. The Daimler vehicles would forever be named Mercedes.

The new design required a new engine and chassis, but Maybach was an outstanding engineer and he completed the redesign to Jellinek's specifications, and on time for his major race in Nice. The new "Mercedes" was half the weight of the prior design at 2200 pounds, and could reach 55 mph. The design and development work of Maybach in such a short time frame was truly remarkable. The new Mercedes received considerable publicity after the Nice race, and by 1901 it was outselling the Benz, whose sales had fallen by 40%.

Karl Benz, similar to Henry Ford two decades later, was stubborn, and continued to stay with his two-cylinder, small Benz design. Benz's sons, who were active in the company, and his sales manager, disagreed, and started designing a new, larger Benz vehicle without Karl Benz's approval. The new design included a new engine, and a new transmission replacing the belt drive. The new car was named the "Parsifal," and Benz sales soon recovered.

Despite the success of the new product, Karl Benz objected to the takeover of his responsibilities and removed himself from an active role in the company. The stubborn attitude of Karl Benz, in which he ignored the changes in the market, would be duplicated by Henry Ford 25 years later, with Ford's refusal to accept the fact that the Model T was obsolete. Benz lost sales in Germany, and Henry Ford lost sales in America because of the failure to accept the customer demands. In both cases, the companies suffered financial losses and a loss of market share. The difference between Benz and Ford was that Henry Ford refused to give up control of his company, while Karl Benz retreated to a minor role.

The Daimler and the Benz auto companies were the largest in Europe, and were strong competitors. The Daimler automobiles served the large vehicle market, and Benz models focused on the small-car market. It is surprising that Daimler and Benz failed to join toigether. Their companies were not far apart in Germany, but the two automobile pioneers never met each other.

The U.S. automobile industry began ten years after Benz patented the automobile. Karl Benz had obtained the world's first patent for the automobile in 1886, and in America, George Selden, a patent attorney, obtained the first U.S. automobile patent in 1895. Selden saw an opportunity to obtain royalty fees for the new automobile and charged a fee of 0.75% for every vehicle produced. Lawers were also *ambulance chasers* in 1895. Henry Ford refused to pay and filed suit. The courts first agreed with Selden, but the appeals court ruled the Selden patent invalid in 1911.

The first car company in America was the Durea Motor Wagon Company in Springfield, Massachusetts – not Detroit. The Durea brothers, Charles and Frank, built their first automobile in 1893, and started their company in 1895. They sold their first automobile in March 1896, and the car was involved in the first automobile accident in the nation two months later. The driver spent the night in jail. The company closed in 1898 because of a personal disagreement between the Durea brothers.

Alexander Winton, owner of a bicycle company, founded the second American car company, the Winton Motor Carriage Company, on March 15, 1897 in Cleveland, Ohio. Ransom Olds started his first company, the Olds Motor Vehicle Company, August 21, 1897 in Lansing, Michigan. The first three U.S. car companies were located outside Detroit, which today is called "Motor City." Henry Ford's first company, the Detroit Automobile Company, was started on August 15, 1899, but was closed fourteen months later due to a lack of a vehicle design. Ford started his second company, the Henry Ford Company, in November 1901, but the company also closed four months later because of a lack of a saleable vehicle. Ford was finally successful with his third company, the Ford Motor Company that was started June 16, 1903 in Detroit. Historians have ignored that Henry Ford failed with his first two companies because Ford did not have a product ready for production until 1903.

Steam and electric vehicles dominated the market at the turn of the twentieth century, and the market was one for the wealthy because of the high prices of vehicles. The lowest-priced steam car cost $3700 ($100,000 today), and the price of an electric car was $3200 ($86,000 today). There were 90,000 automobiles on the road in 1900 with 40% being steam, 38% electric, and 22% internal-combustion engine vehicles. Internal combustion, or gasoline-engine, cars were not yet in volume production.

The Winton Motor Carriage Company was producing 100 cars a year by 1900, and unbelievably, was the largest producer of gasoline-engine automobiles in the nation. The Winton company sales fell during the 1920-1921 recession, and the company closed in 1924.

Ransom Olds was an automobile pioneer and many believe that Olds was the father of the U.S. auto industry. However, Henry Ford has received far more credit. Olds held 34 patents and was the only one of the world automotive pioneers that worked with all three-power sources – steam, electric, and gasoline. Ransom Olds was also the first to develop the moving assembly process by using wheeled carts to transfer vehicles down the assembly line in 1901. Prior to this change, the chassis remained in one location, and workers brought parts to the vehicle for assembly. If you can imagine the assembly operations with workers standing around waiting for their turn to assemble their components, it had to be a mess. In Ransom Olds' new process, the chassis was mounted on a wheeled cart and pushed down a line of workers who remained at their workstations. The workers assembled their components and pushed the chassis to the next workstation. Sounds simple, but the wheeled-cart, moving-assembly process was a major improvement and reduced assembly time by 90%.

Henry Ford has been given credit for inventing the moving assembly line, but Ransom Olds was the first to make the change from a stationary-assembly operation to a moving-assembly process, and he did this twelve years before Henry Ford. Ford changed to a rope-and-pulley system in 1908, in which the chassis was pulled through the assembly operations. Ford improved the process by using a moving conveyor in 1913, and assembly time was reduced from 12.5 hours to 1.5 hours. Ford engineers copied the conveyor system used in a Chicago slaughterhouse.

Ransom Olds started his career by building steam-engine vehicles in his father's machine shop in the early 1890s. In 1904, one of his steam vehicles was exported to India, and this was the first automobile exported from the United States. Olds began to develop gasoline-engine vehicles, and he patented his first internal-combustion-engine vehicle in 1896. He started the Olds Motor Vehicle Company on August 21, 1897, about 100 miles northwest of Detroit in Lansing, Michigan, his hometown. The company was in financial trouble in 1900, and was purchased by Samuel Smith, a copper baron, who renamed the company the Olds Motor Works, and relocated the plant to Detroit. Ransom Olds remained as general manager. After working with the three different power sources, Olds determined that the gasoline-fueled internal-combustion engine was the engine of the future.

Ransom Olds designed and developed the Curved Dash Oldsmobile in 1901. The name came from the front panel of the car. Early automobiles had a panel at the front of the vehicle instead of a grille used in today's cars. The panel was similar to the front panel of a horse carriage that was called the "dash" because it prevented the carriage driver from being "dashed" by flying stones thrown up by the horses. Even today, the instrument panel of an automobile is often called the *dashboard.*

The Olds Detroit plant burned to the ground on March 9, 1901, and Olds moved his assembly operations to a nearby foundry building. He ordered engines from Henry Leyland's company, and other parts from the Dodge brother's plant. The Dodges supplied every part for Henry Ford's cars except for the tires and seats.

The Machinist Union went on strike in June 1901 and caused violence in the Olds Plant. As a result, Olds moved his operations back to Lansing. The first Oldsmobiles were produced in Detroit, but after the union violence, Oldsmobiles were produced in Lansing. Olds used the wheeled-cart process in Lansing.

The new assembly process allowed Olds to increase production to 20 vehicles a day, which was the highest rate of production in the industry. The Curved Dash Oldsmobile was a stylish two-seat vehicle, with a single-cylinder engine mounted below the driver's seat. A hand-crank mechanism was also located under the seat. All gasoline-engine cars were started with a hand crank until 1912. Steering was with a hand tiller, and the car sold for $650 ($17,500 today). Ransom Olds was actually the first to price cars for the average buyer although Henry Ford has been given credit for this. The car was small but could reach 25 mph, which was adequate for the roads at that time.

1901 Curved Dash Oldsmobile

The low-priced 1901 Oldsmobile completely changed the market – the average person could afford to buy a car. The Olds sales volume increased and by 1903, the Olds Motor Works was the largest producer of automobiles in the world. However, Samuel Smith, the owner, demanded that Olds develop a larger vehicle to gain additional profits; Olds refused, and was forced out of the company in January 1904. This was similar to the situations with Gottlieb Daimler and Karl Benz two decades earlier, and a few years later with Henry Ford.

Olds continued to build automobiles by starting the REO Company (his initials) which he founded in August 1904. The REO Company was also located in Lansing, and the REO name was used because Smith threatened a lawsuit if Olds used his name. With Olds' engineering and manufacturing abilities the REO Company soon produced more vehicles than the Olds Motor Works. When Samuel Smith fired Ransom Olds he lost the genius who made the company successful, and Smith had to sell the company to GM in 1908 due to financial difficulties.

Ransom Olds continued to run the REO Company until 1915 when he retired at age 51. He purchased over 37,000 acres of property near Tampa, and the city of Oldsmar was named after him. Olds started a land development project in Florida that failed, and he lost over $40 million in today's dollars.

REO failed to compete with Ford's Model T that was introduced in 1908, and became a minor player in the market. The company was in financial trouble in the 1930's due to the Great Depression, and Olds returned to the company for a short time in 1933 in an attempt to save the business. The attempt was not successful and REO car production ended in 1936. The company continued to build trucks until 1975. Olds left the auto business for good in 1936, and retired in Lansing, Michigan. He died on August 26, 1950 at age 86. Ransom Olds was a true pioneer in the U.S. automobile business, and many claim he was its founder.

Olds has never received the recognition he deserved. He obtained 34 patents including the design of the 1901 Curved Dash vehicle, and the moving-chassis assembly line. He also created a mass market for automobiles with his 1901 Oldsmobile. He built his first steam car at age 30, and assembled both electric and gasoline-engine automobiles as well. The Curved Dash Oldsmobile was publicized in the 1905 song *The Merry Oldsmobile.*

Ransom Olds 1864-1950

Henry Ford started his first automobile company on August 5, 1899, and named it the Detroit Automobile Company. In 1896, Ford mounted his engine on a wood platform with four bicycle wheels, and knocked down a part of his garage-laboratory to get the vehicle outside. He road tested the Quadricycle and made several design changes. Ford found three investors - Mayor of Detroit William Mayberry, Senator Thomas Palmer, and lumber baron William Murphy, and started his first auto company.

Henry Ford 1863-1947

The Quadricycle was a prototype vehicle and not suitable for sale, and Ford had considerable design and development work to do before he could go into production. Before long, his investors were interested in shipping cars, not development work, so they pressed him to ship a product for sale. Ford launched a delivery truck and shipped the vehicles. The trucks were difficult to assemble, and had msny quality problems. Henry Ford later said the delivery truck was rushed into production. In reality, Ford started his company too soon, and did not have a product ready for production. The Detroit Automobile Company was closed fourteen months later and the three investors lost $90,000 ($2.5 million today).

The Detroit Automobile Company did not have a product, but did have a product catalog. The brochure presented a cost analysis comparing the cost of owning a horse versus an automobile over a five-year period. The analysis showed that if an individual bought horse for $500, the annual upkeep over the five-year period, plus the depreciation of the horse, would be greater than the total cost of the automobile, including gasoline and a new paint job. Possibly the horse was "His Eminence," winner of the 1901 Kentucky Derby.

Henry Ford's Quadricycle

David Dunbar Buick started the Buick Auto-Vim and Power Company in Detroit in 1899 to build engines. David Buick was a brilliant engineer who invented the overhead valve engine, and developed the Buick automobile. However, Buick was a craftsman and could never stop designing and start production. He ran out of money, and evidently did not have Henry Ford's perseverance, because he sold his company to James Whiting. Whiting moved the company to his hometown of Flint, Michigan, about 60 miles north of Detroit. David Buick accepted a severance of $100,000 ($2.6 million today) in 1906. He left his engineering skills behind and invested in oil and real estate, but lost most of his money. If he had kept his stock, Buick would have had over $100 million, but he died in poverty at age 75 in 1929. His last job was as an inspector at a Detroit trade school. It was a truly tragic ending for an auto industry pioneer.

Henry Ford found a new group of financial backers and started his second company, the Henry Ford Company, on November 20, 1901. The company was new, but Ford's new vehicle was still not ready for production. Ford must have been a super salesman with a pitch that convinced financial people to back his product, because he was always able to find people to back his plans and ideas. The Henry Ford Company was his second company and the third was yet to come. However, his new vehicle was still not ready for production, and he again had a problem with the financial backers. Henry Ford had built his Quadricycle in 1896, and five years later, he still did not have a production product. Historians have ignored that Ford's Quadricycle was only a prototype vehicle. His first production vehicle, the Model A, was not introduced until 1903 in his third company. Henry Ford left the Henry Ford Company in March 1902, four months after incorporation, because the financial backers demanded that he ship a vehicle, and his new automobile was not ready for production.

The financial backers were unhappy with Ford's lack of a production vehicle and decided to liquidate the Henry Ford Company. They hired Henry Leyland, an engine company owner, to evaluate the company. Leyland reviewed the facilities, and recommended the company be reorganized rather than liquidated. Leyland bought the Henry Ford Company, and changed the name to the Cadillac Motor Company. Historians have failed to report that the first Cadillac was assembled in the former Henry Ford Company, and the vehicle included Ford's inventory of parts.

Leyland was a machinist who invented the electric barber clippers, and was president of the Leyland, Faulconer, and Norton Company that supplied engines to the Olds Motor Works. He was a capable engineer and production manager, and he could see the opportunities available with the tooling, facilities, and inventory available in the Henry Ford Company. He installed a new engine in the Ford chassis, assembled most of Ford's components, and started production. The first Cadillac was shipped four months after Leyland bought Ford's company. Leyland's Cadillac looked very similar to Henry Ford's first vehicle built in his third company, the Ford Motor Company, since Ford had designed both cars. Both automobiles were named the Model A.

It is interesting that Ford Motor Company, General Motors, Cadillac, and automobile historians have ignored the fact that the first Cadillac was actually designed by Henry Ford, and most of the parts in the vehicle were from Henry Ford's inventory. Henry Leyland later sold Cadillac to General Motors, and the brand has been a competitor to Ford Motor Company for 110 years.

Henry Leyland with his first Cadillac

Henry Ford never forgave Leyland for acquiring the Henry Ford Company. Ford probably could have won a lawsuit against Leyland for stealing his automobile design and using his components to build the Cadillac, but in 1902, the legal profession was less populated.

Persistence was Henry Ford's strong suit, and he found eleven new financial backers and formed the Ford Motor Company on July 16, 1903, sixteen months after leaving the Henry Ford Company. Henry Leyland was shipping Cadillacs out of his prior company, but Ford had yet to ship a production automobile. The fact that Henry Ford failed with his first two companies has not been well publicized, and over seven years of development work were required to complete his redesign after the Quadricycle.

Henry Ford's determination and persistence enabled him to stay with his plan to start an automobile company, in spite of the many obstacles that stood in his way. David Buick had the engineering ability, possibly even more than Ford, but evidently did not have Ford's perseverance.

Ford finally completed the development of his first automobile, and shipped his first Model A within a month of starting Ford Motor Company. The seven-year wait was over, and Henry Ford was a successful entrepreneur. The Model A had no top, and had a bench seat for two people. It had an eight-horsepower engine and could reach 45 mph. The car sold for $850 ($21,750 today), and 1750 were produced between 1903 and 1905.

1903 Ford Model A

In the early 1900s, electric cars were in the competitive race for vehicle production, and they offered the advantages of quick starting and quiet operation. The problems of cost, low power, limited distance, and the lack of charging stations limited sales. Electric vehicles started in Europe in 1832, but there was a lack of efficient batteries. Thomas Davenport, a blacksmith from Vermont, developed a direct-current motor in 1834, and mounted the motor on a carriage. This was the first electric vehicle in America. A French physicist, Gaston Plante, invented the rechargeable battery in 1856, and the invention led to further development of electric vehicles. Andreas Flocken, a German engineer, built the first battery-powered vehicle in 1888.

1906 Baker Electric Car

Walter Baker of Cleveland, Ohio, began working on battery-powered electric vehicles in the early 1890s, and founded the Baker Motor Vehicle Company in 1899. The first Baker electric automobile was a two-seat model priced at $850 ($23,200 today). By 1906, Baker was the largest electric car producer, and a Baker car was in the White House fleet. However, the Ford Model T gasoline-engine car introduced in 1908 took over the vehicle market, and the Baker Company closed its doors in 1916.

Gasoline-engine vehicles began to take the market away from electrics because of price. The price of electric cars was more than double the internal-combustion-engine automobiles. In 1916, the cost of the Ford Model T was $8360, and the cost of a Baker Electric was $19.380 in today's dollars. Many gasoline-engine cars included the electric starter by 1913, eliminating the hand crank for starting, which had been an advantage of electric vehicles. The cost of batteries was the main problem, and this has plagued the electric-vehicle market for a century. The battery cost, along with the limited power and distance capability, has prevented the electric vehicle from becoming a major factor in the market.

Hybrid vehicles have become popular recently due to better fuel economy and lower vehicle emissions. The hybrid car is primarily a gasoline-engine vehicle with assist from an electric motor. While most think the hybrid is new technology, the first hybrid car was pattened in 1905 by Henri Piper, a German inventor.

In an attempt to force electric vehicles into the market, the Federal Government granted tax incentives to buyers of electric cars in 2009. The tax incentive was significant ($9000), but the buying public still refused to purchase electric cars (the dog would not eat the dog food). The problems of cost, power, and distance that forced electric cars out of the market 100 years ago still prevailed. The government also increased the vehicle fuel-economy requirements (CAFE) in an attempt to stimulate the sales of electric vehicles, but customers still refused to buy electrics.

Steam-powered automobiles were originally popular since steam preceded gasoline-engine vehicles. As mentioned earlier, 40% of the automobiles on the road at the turn of the twentieth century were steam-engine vehicles. As gasoline-engine automobiles developed, they were cheaper and more powerful, so steam vehicles began to lose market share, and by the 1920s, most steam-vehicle companies had closed their doors. The internal-combustion vehicles had taken the market.

After James Whiting moved the Buick Motor Company from Detroit to Flint in 1903, he hired William Crapo (Billy) Durant as the general manager. Durant was the owner of a carriage company located in Flint that supplied components to the automobile manufacturers. A former cigar salesman, Billy Durant was an entrepreneur who had grown his carriage company to be one of the largest in the world. Buick Motor Company was small when Durant took over, and it had sold fewer than 50 cars. Durant used his sales abilities when he took the Buick car to the New York Auto Show, and he returned to Flint with orders for 1100 automobiles. This was not only an amazing achievement, but also probably the largest automobile order in history at that time.

Durant could see that the automobile would be the future mode of transportation, so he gave up a profitable carriage business to take the job at Buick. He had the foresight to see the elimination of the carriage business when automobiles became popular.

William C. *Billy* Durant 1861-1947

Buick's production of automobiles increased when Oldsmobile faltered after Ransom Olds was fired. Buick was highly profitable, and Durant formed General Motors Corporation on September 16, 1908. Unfortunately, one hundred years later Lehman Brothers filed for bankruptcy, the 2008 housing recession began, and GM was heading for bankruptcy. Vehicle sales declined because of the recession. GM was unable to reduce costs and ran out of cash to pay their bills.

Henry Ford continued to develop new vehicles and he named each new model in alphabetical order. The 1907 Model N was the last right-hand-drive model. A new assembly process was started in 1908 using ropes and pulleys to drag the chassis thru assembly, with workers remaining at their workstations and assembling components as the chassis passed by. The rope-and- pulley process was the forerunner of Ford's moving conveyor line that was started in 1913. The conveyor process was similar to the slaughterhouse conveyor system used by meat processors.

Ford and C. Harold Wills designed the Model T, and started production of the famous automobile in late 1908. By May of 1909, production could not keep up with sales. The Model T was an open-air, left- hand-drive vehicle, with a 20 hp four-cylinder engine, and could reach 45mph. The base price was $825, which would be $22,000 today. Ford's Model T sales increased to 35.000 units by 1911. After starting three automobile companies Henry Ford finally developed a production vehicle in 1903, and the 1908 Model T would make him famous and wealthy. Ford developed several models between 1903 and 1908, but the Model T would soon take 50% of the U.S. market.

Henry Ford's dream of producing an automobile for the masses had come true. Ford never finished high school, but his technical abilities led him to develop the prototype Quadricycle in 1896. His perseverance permitted him to continue with his work and his salesmanship allowed him to obtain financial investors.

1908 Ford Model T

There were hundreds of engineers and entrepreneurs building automobiles in the early 1900s, including my grandfather, John Henry Lawrence, an engineering instructor at Vanderbilt University. He built his first car in 1904, and obtained a Tennessee registration on June 26, 1905, for one dollar ($25 today). Unfortunately, he was not interested in starting an automobile company, so there was no Lawrencemobile.

Henry Leyland had acquired Henry Ford's second company, the Henry Ford Company, in 1902, and started producing the Cadillac. The Henry Ford Company failed because Henry Ford had not completed his first auto design, and was unable to produce a car. The financial backers decided to liquidate the company, and Henry Leyland bought the company. Ford never forgave Leyland for *stealing* his company. Leyland installed a new engine, and used Ford components to launch the first Cadilac in October 1902.

Leyland sold Cadillac to General Motors in 1908, but he remained with GM. Leyland had a disagreement with Billy Durant and founded Lincoln Motor Company in 1917. Lincoln ran into financial trouble and went into receivership in 1922. Henry Ford made an offer of $5 million for Lincoln, and was the only bidder. Lincoln's facilities and tooling were appraised at $16 million, and the court demanded that Ford pay $8 million for Lincoln Motor Company. Henry Ford got his revenge over Leyland to the tune of $8 million, which would be $100 million today.

In 1911, Ford moved assembly operations to a new facility designed by Albert Kahn. The plant was located in Highland Park, a small city completely bordered by Detroit. The new conveyor assembly process was installed, and assembly time was reduced from 12.5 hours to 1.5 hours, an amazing reduction. With the new styling in 1911, Ford's volume was double the prior year's production, and the company captured 35% of the U.S. market. The Model T was becoming the largest selling automobile, and soon would take over 50% of the U.S. market.

1911 Ford Highland Park Plant

In 1914, Henry Ford announced a historic wage increase for employees. Wages were doubled to $5 dollars a day, and the workweek was reduced to 40 hours. The workweek was 60 hours in many industries. The new wage rate for an eight-hour day would amount to $14.30 per hour in today's dollars, twice the current minimum wage, and equal to a new autoworker's starting hourly rate today. Absenteeism had become a problem at Ford, and the new wage rate and workweek reduced the absenteeism problem.

Billy Durant took advantage of the Olds' weak financial condition and acquired the company in late 1908. Olds was the first of Durant's many acquisitions after starting General Motors. In 1909 Durant acquired Cadillac, Oakland (later Pontiac), Cartercar, Rapid Motor Vehicle Company (later GMC), and additional smaller companies. Durant even tried to buy Ford Motor Company, but the deal fell through because Henry Ford demanded eight million in cash, and GM was short of cash.

The two-year acquisition spree by Durant was amazing, but it cost him his job. Durant consolidated 13 car companies and 10 parts-manufacturing companies into General Motors. Operating capital was almost non-existent, and the debt accumulated with the acquisitions put General Motors in deep financial trouble. The board fired Billy Durant in 1910. However, Durant would assume control of General Motor six years later.

William Crapo Durant had the vision to see that his profitable carriage business would go the way of the buggy whip when automobiles replaced wagons and carriages. Durant took a general manager's job at a small automobile company (Buick), and this must have been a difficult decision for Durant because he left his profitable worldwide carriage firm to join Buick.

Buick had sold only 37 cars before Durant took over. His salesmanship and drive moved Buick to the top of the auto world, and his vision for the auto business drove him to create the largest automobile company in the world, General Motors.

William *Billy* Durant was an entrepreneur, a visionary, and a super salesman, but he lacked the ability to organize a company. He failed to build an organization to support his acquisitions and this led to his termination as president of General Motors. Billy Durant's 23 acquisitions were historic but he was unable to integrate the acquired companies into a cohesive organization. Even though Durant was successful with his carriage company, the firm only manufactured one product, and did not have a multitude of brands. He simply did not have the experience to organize and manage a large corporation.

The GM board appointed Charles William Nash, the president of Buick, to succeed Durant as the new president of General Motors, and Walter Chrysler took over Buick. Nash had the task of organizing GM into one company. As Durant was not strong on organization, there was little direction from the top of the corporation.

The loss of the top job at General Motors failed to deter Billy Durant, and on November 3, 1911, he joined Louis Chevrolet to form the Chevrolet Motor Company. Durant knew Chevrolet when he was at Buick, and he had hired Chevrolet as his racecar driver. The company was successful and began to take an increasing share of the market. Durant and Chevrolet had a disagreement on how to run the business, and Durant bought out Louis Chevrolet in 1914. Durant took his share of the profits and acquired a controlling interest in General Motors. He fired Charles Nash as president and took control of GM again in 1916.

By 1916, Henry Ford had accumulated $60 million in cash ($1.26 billion today). Ford wanted to use the cash to build new manufacturing and assembly facilities to increase Model T capacity, so he stopped paying dividends to stockholders. Ford also objected to the Dodge brothers starting a car company in 1914 with Ford dividends, even though the Dodges had put $10,000 of the $49,000 initial capital into the start-up of the Ford Motor Company. The Dodge brothers were given 10% of the stock, but the $10,000 should have given them 20% of the company, and this discrepancy has never been explained. However, the Dodges filed a lawsuit to obtain dividends. The Michigan Supreme Court ruled in 1919 that a business corporation was organized primarily for the stockholders, and made the decision that Henry Ford should pay stockholders $19.3 million. Ford threatened to start a new company, resigned as president, and made his son, Edsel, president of Ford Motor Company. Edsel negotiated with the stockholders, and Henry Ford was able to buy all the stock. Henry Ford became the sole owner of the Ford Motor Company. In the relatively short period of 16 years, Henry Ford had progressed from a 25% owner of a new start-up automobile company to a 100% owner of the largest auto company in the country. There were over 200 companies producing cars during this period. Henry Ford succeeded, and most others failed.

When Billy Durant assumed control of General Motors for the second time in 1916, GM was still a disorganized company. Organization was not Durant's strong suit, and when the 1920-1921 recession hit, GM was near bankruptcy. The GM board again fired Durant, and Pierre du Pont took over as president.

The government caused a severe recession in 1920 when the Federal Reserve raised interest rates in 1919. The interest rate was increased to 7%, which was the highest rate in any period except for the Jimmy Carter era in the 1970s. The 1920 recession was sometimes called a depression because of the 47% decline in the stock market and the increase in unemployment from 5% to 12%. The number of business failures tripled, vehicles sales dropped and 76 auto companies closed their doors.

Paved roadways had been a serious deterrent to automobile growth since the beginning of the auto industry. The government finally did something about the problem in 1916 when the Federal Road Act was passed providing $75 million for new roadways.

Despite Durant's lack of organization, he was able to keep Alfred Sloan as a vice president of General Motors after Durant acquired his company. Sloan may have been Durant's most important acquisition. Alfred Sloan was appointed president of GM in 1923, and he began to install a strong financial system and create a decentralized organization. Sloan was president of the Hyatt Roller Bearing Company that was acquired by Durant in 1916, and he remained with General Motors as a vice-president.

Sloan would remain with General Motors for his entire career first as a vice president, then president, then CEO, and finally chairman from 1937, until his retirement in 1956. When Sloan took over as president, General Motors was still being run by the previous owners of the acquired companies, with little direction from the top of the corporation. Many of the GM brands competed with each other in the marketplace. Sloan reorganized the brands and created a brand ladder, with Chevrolet at the bottom of the ladder, Cadillac at the top, and Pontiac, Oldsmobile, and Buick in between. The Sloan restructure of the brands was the first attempt to establish brand loyalty for an automotive company. The Sloan strategy was to sell a customer a low-end Chevrolet as the first car, and offer higher-priced and larger brands as customers increased their income. Ideally, the customer would remain a GM owner up to the Cadillac level.

Even though the Ford Model T led in sales, GM with Buick, Oldsmobile, and Cadillac began to increase market share. The Model T was a huge success and sold over fifteen million vehicles, but Ford did not offer brands to compete with General Motors. The Lincoln was at the top of Ford's brand ladder, but Ford had no brands between the Model T and the Lincoln. The lack of Ford brands between the low-priced Model T and the luxury Lincoln would limit sales until the present day.

Henry Ford failed to read the tealeaves to see the market changes. He believed that his Model T would continue to cover the market, and remain the number-one seller. In fact, Ford was planning a large expansion of production facilities in the Dearborn Rouge area for additional production capacity for the Model T.

Rather than develop new models to replace the Model T, Henry Ford reduced prices to maintain volume production. However, in 1927, Model T production fell 75%, and GM produced almost five times the Ford volume. GM had also introduced the annual model change, but Ford did not. The Model T was finally obsolete.

Walter Chrysler, the former president of Buick, formed Chrysler in 1925. Chrysler left General Motors in 1919 and ran Willys-Overland for two years. His next venture was to acquire the troubled Maxwell Motor Company. He stopped Maxwell production and started building the Chrysler automobile in 1924. Chrysler launched the Plymouth and DeSoto brands, and acquired the Dodge Motor Company in 1928. The Dodge Motor Company had been started in 1914 and was a larger company than Chrysler, and Walter Chrysler had a major reorganization change to merge the two companies into one corporation.

The Dodge brothers, John and Horace started as machinists and started a machine shop in the Detroit area. They were soon manufacturing transmissions and other auto components for Ransom Olds and Henry Ford. The Dodges supplied component parts for all carmakers, and produced every part for Ford cars except for the tires and seats.

Henry Ford was unable to pay for his component-part purchases in the Henry Ford Company. When Ford Motor Company was started in 1903, Henry Ford owed the Dodge brothers $7,000 ($175,000 today). The Dodges gave Ford an additional $3000 ($75,000 today) for a total of $10,000 for 10% of the company. Ford declared a 10% dividend in the first year of production, so the brothers got some of their money back in less than a year. The Dodges terminated their Ford business in 1914 and started the Dodge Motor Company. The Dodge brothers, Horace and John, were capable engineers and managers, and the Dodge Motor Companyy was immediately successful, and was noted for engineering and quality.

With the start-up of Chrysler in 1925, the Big Three had finally been established. The shakeout of over 200 automobile companies had resulted in General Motors, Ford, and Chrysler becoming the largest and most successful car companies.

By 1927, Ford's market share had fallen below 15%, and the company closed for six months to launch the new Model A. Henry Ford had refused to accept that the Model T was obsolete. Ford had ignored his son Edsel's plans for a new model vehicle, similar to Karl Benz three decades earlier, when Benz had ignored the market changes, and failed to listen to his sons' request for a new vehicle. In both cases, their companies suffered a dramatic loss of market share. When Edsel Ford presented a new vehicle prototype for Henry Ford's approval, the elder Ford destroyed the car to show who was boss. The failure of Henry Ford to recognize the market change, which made the Model T obsolete, was a tragic mistake and caused the Ford Motor Company to lose market share. His stubbornness and strong management style would eventually lead his company toward bankruptcy at the time of his death.

The Model T had changed the automotive market from a rich person's toy, to one in which the average person could own a car. The famous vehicle completely changed the U.S. market, and was the largest seller for nearly nineteen years.

The new Model A was a scaled-down Lincoln, and was a stylish automobile, but bumpers were extra and cost $15 ($200 today). Since the Model T sales had dropped below 15%, the Ford Motor Company was completely closed for six months, until a new model was in production. The model that replaced the Model T was labeled the Model A, the identical brand name of Ford's first production car in 1903. It was amazing that Ford engineers could develop and launch a completely new car in six months. The six-month shutdown put pressure on Ford to launch the new car; the Model A was rushed into production, and had customer quality problems that would have caused recalls today. Car buyers were less critical in 1928, and sales of the Model A soared. The vehicle was in production from 1928-1931 and total sales exceeded twenty million, five million more than the Model T.

1928 Ford Model A

The six-month shutdown of the Ford Motor Company was costly in both financial terms and market share, and GM and Chrysler gained share from Ford. Many customers gained permanent loyalty to GM and Chrysler, resulting in Ford dropping to third place in market sales a few years later.

Ford was also investing heavily in the famous Rouge manufacturing complex in Dearborn, Michigan. The Rouge facilities included new manufacturing plants and an assembly plant. Ford started producing steel and glass in the new plants, as well as engines, stampings, and tooling. Raw material for steel was shipped in by boat through the Detroit River. The Rouge facilities were located fifteen miles west of Detroit, and the huge undertaking resulted in the world's first independent cluster of automotive manufacturing plants in one location. The Rouge complex would be a fixed-cost burden for the company when the Great Depression hit two years later.

The original concept for the new manufacturing facility was to provide additional capacity for the Model T, and Henry Ford had developed the plan ten years earlier when he stopped paying dividends to stockholders to save cash for the investment. During that ten-year period, the market changed and the Model T became obsolete. When production ceased for the famous Model T, newspapers pictured the Model T with wings flying into heaven. The Model T sales exceeded fifteen million vehicles during its nineteen-year history.

The growth of the automobile industry continued throughout the *Roaring Twenties,* and annual vehicle production increased to five million units by 1929. The five-million mark was more than twice the 1921 volume of two million units. Gasoline-engine vehicles had taken over the market with more engine power and lower prices. Steam and electric vehicle manufacturers were unable to compete with IC-engine autos, and most had closed their doors by the late 1920s. Due to the refusal of Henry Ford to accept that the Model T was obsolete, General Motors and Chrysler had increased market share. Chrysler added the Plymouth and DeSoto brands and was increasing sales. Chrysler had acquired Dodge Motors and was merging the two companies. Dodge was larger than Chrysler was, so the acquisition was a major undertaking.

The automobile industry had become the largest single industry in the country by 1928, employing over 500,000 workers in auto plants, and the same number in affiliated industries. The U.S. automobile business had progressed from its birth in 1896, through its infancy in the early 1900s, and the growth spurt in the 1920s, to become a huge industry. The development of the automobile had required nearly 200 years after the steam engine was invented, but the wait was worth it. The automobile had given people the long needed mode of personal transportation. The self-propelled vehicle completely changed the world; people could travel at will, and not be concerned by train schedules or horseback problems.

The rapid growth of the auto business came to a sudden halt with the Great Depression, and all but nine automobile firms closed their doors. The government caused the Great Depression of 1929 when the Federal Reserve raised interest rates in 1928, and the depression was a severe economic downturn that lasted eleven years. The industrial production for World War II finally ended the disaster that was the longest, deepest, and worst economic period in the 20th century.

Great Depression by Dorthea Lange

The Great Depression was devastating for the country, with unemployment reaching 25% - one in four families was out of work. Stock investors were jumping from hotel windows, families lost their homes, farmers lost their farms, and the unemployed sold apples on street corners. GDP fell 35%, industrial production fell 47%, 9000 banks failed, and the government caused the economic debacle.

Economists and other experts have differed on the cause of the Great Depression, but the economist Milton Friedman and Ben Bernanke of the Federal Reserve have agreed publicly that the cause was the interest-rate increase by the Federal Reserve in 1928. The increase in interest rates resulted in a tight money condition, and the Federal Reserve failed to control the money supply. On "Black Thursday," October 24, 1929, the sale of 13 million shares started the stock market decline, and the following Tuesday, over 16 million shares were sold. Over $30 billion ($400 billion today) was lost in a one-month period.

Unemployment increased from 3% to 25%, and more than 50% of families were living below the minimum subsistence level. Automobile sales dropped, and over 90% of the auto companies went out of business. American families suffered the most – they were unable to feed their children.

The Great Depression was a terrible disaster, and our government caused it. The tragic thing was that politicians failed to recognize the cause, and as a result had no idea of how to correct it. The New Deal has been touted as the solution to the Great Depression, but if an analysis is made of the 42 government agencies created by President Roosevelt, the New Deal failed to fix the depression. The 1976 Nobel Prize winner in economics, Milton Friedman, worked in the government on the New Deal in the mid-1930s, and his conclusion was, *the New Deal was the wrong cure for the wrong disease.*

The government was at a loss to determine the cause of the Great Depression, and as a result, failed to correct the errors by the Federal Reserve. Congress made the futile attempt to correct the problem with the infamous Smoot-Hawley Act, but the legislation made the problem worse. Even President Roosevelt failed to understand the cause of the depression. Roosevelt blamed business monopolies for the rise in unemployment. The Fed continued to raise interest rates throughout the 1930s resulting in the depression lasting until the military production for World War II finally ended the economic debacle. The failure of the entire government to recognize the cause of the depression is truly amazing. However, it is typical of politicians to spend all their time blaming someone else for a problem, rather than correcting the situation.

The generally accepted explanation of the Great Depression is that the cause of the depression was stock-market speculation, and that the New Deal corrected the problem. Nothing could be further from the truth. Milton Friedman insisted for years that the Federal Reserve interest rate increase in 1928 caused the depression and Ben Bernanke, the Federal Reserve chair, agreed with Friedman during his retirement party. The Federal Reserve has done a terrible job in its attempt to control the economy and some economists have stated that the agency should be abolished. The models and metrics used by the Federal Reserve are obsolete.

The Great Depression changed the automobile industry from a healthy business that was hiring thousands of workers to a group of near-bankrupt companies closing their doors. There were 108 automobile companies producing vehicles in the nation before the depression but only nine survived. General Motors, Ford, Chrysler, Hudson, Nash, Packard, Studebaker, Crosley, and Willys were able to stay in business, but all others failed. Over 32,000 other businesses went bankrupt during the Great Depression and 9000 banks failed. The Great Depression was a tragic time for everyone and our government caused the economic disaster.

The media failed to analyze the cause of the Great Depression and accepted the government's excuses. Politicians never did determine the cause and correct the problem, and the depression lasted until World War II production ended the debacle. The identical scenario occurred with the 2008 Great Housing Recession. The media never fully analyzed the cause of the 2008 financial disaster, and only reported the government excuses for the housing crisis.

TWO

GENERAL MOTORS

General Motors Headquarters in Detroit

William Crapo (Billy) Durant founded General Motors on September 16, 1908 in Flint, Michigan, 60 miles north of Detroit. While most auto companies were started by engineers, GM was started by a former cigar salesman. On September 15, 2008, 100 years later, Lehman Brothers filed for bankruptcy and the Great Housing Recession began. Vehicle sales declined dramatically, and the drop in revenue created a working-capital problem. GM could not pay its bills and asked the government for a loan. The Senate voted 52-35 against a bailout of General Motors and drove the company into bankruptcy. There was no bailout, just bankruptcy. The 100th anniversary of GM was not a happy day.

Born in Boston on December 8, 1863, Billy Durant was the grandson of former Michigan governor Henry Crapo. Durant dropped out of high school to work in his grandfather's lumberyard, but soon started selling cigars. He moved on to carriage sales, and in 1885, at age 22, started the Coldwater Road Cart Company in Flint. The company was successful, and Durant parlayed a $2000 investment into a $2 million business ($60 million today). He partnered with Josiah Dort, and the Durant-Dort Carriage Company became one of the largest in the world.

The Buick Motor Company was started in Detroit by David Dunbar Buick in 1899 and was the fourth U.S. auto company, with Durea, Olds, and Ford preceding Buick. James Whiting, a lumber baron, purchased Buick in 1903 and moved the company to Flint, his hometown. David Buick was an auto pioneer who invented several engine components and developed the Buick automobile. Unfortunately, he could never stop designing and go into production. He ran out of money and sold his company to James Whiting. Buick was an outstanding engineer and craftsman, but his inability to develop a vehicle for production and sale cost him his company.

James Whiting made the best decision of his career when he hired Durant as general manager of Buick in 1904. Durant was a highly successful owner of a carriage company in Flint, but he evidently could see that the automobile would replace the horse carriage, and he decided to go into the automobile business.

The Buick Motor Company had produced only 37 vehicles when Durant was hired, but he used his salesmanship almost immediately. Durant entered the Buick car in the New York Show and obtained orders for over 1100 new cars, which was the largest group of orders in history. With the new orders, Buick prospered, and began to take volume from the Olds Company. The Olds Motor Works was located in Lansing, Michigan, and was the nation's largest auto producer in 1903.

Samuel Smith, the owner of the Olds Company, forced founder Ransom Olds out of the company in January 1904. Smith had purchased the Olds Company from Ransom Olds and he demanded that the company produce luxury cars for higher profit margins. Ransom Olds refused and left the company. Olds had started the Olds Company on August 21, 1897, developed the 1901 Curved Dash Oldsmobile, invented the moving-assembly process, and made Oldsmobile the largest producer of automobiles by 1903. Olds went on to start another car company named REO (his initials), and out-produced the Olds Company in two years.

Samuel Smith's decision to force Ransom Olds out of his company turned out to be a major mistake. Olds was not only a brilliant engineer and innovator, but also a capable production manager. Olds Motor Works vehicle production declined after Ransom Olds left the company, and by 1906, sales had dropped 75%. The Olds Motor Works sales continued to decline whithout Ransom Olds running the company, and Smith was forced to sell the firm to Billy Durant of General Motors in 1908.

Durant brought Charles Nash, a supervisor at his Durant-Dort Carriage Company, into Buick as general manager. Durant, with Nash's help, increased production and sales of Buick, GM's first company, and the newly acquired Olds Company.

Samuel McLaughlin founded the McLaughlin Motor Car Company in Canada on November 20, 1907. Durant collaborated with McLaughlin to produce the McLaughlin-Buick car in Canada, and shortly afterward, the partners started General Motors Holding Company in Flint on September 16, 1908. The former cigar salesman had founded the automobile company that was to become the largest car company in the world.

Robert Samuel McLaughlin has not been recognized in the U.S. as a pioneer in the automotive business, but he had a distinguished career in the business. McLaughlin was born in Ontario, Canada on September 8, 1871, and worked in his father's carriage company. He became a director of General Motors in 1910 and remained on the board for over 50 years, the longest- serving board member in history. He was CEO of General Motors Canada until his retirement in 1945. Samuel McLaughlin died on January 6, 1972, at the ripe old age of 100.

Buick was initially the only brand produced by General Motors, but Durant would soon change that. He began an acquisition spree by purchasing the financially strapped Olds Motor Works shortly after starting GM in 1908, and he acquired Cadillac, Oakland (later Pontiac), Rapid Motor Vehicle Company (later GMC), Cartercar, Elmore, Ewing, and Reliance Motor company. The Welch and Rainier companies were acquired in 1910. Durant acquired 13 car companies and 10 automobile component companies in a little over two years.

A single acquisition normally requires two years of reorganization to absorb the new company. The acquisition of 23 companies in a two-year period caused havoc in General Motors. Durant had even attempted to buy Ford Motor Company, a little-known fact. The deal fell through when Henry Ford demanded $8 million in cash ($200 million today), and General Motors was short of cash. The acquisitions had created working capital and debt problems for the company, and the GM board fired Durant in 1910. Charles Nash took over as president of General Motors. Walter Chrysler had joined Buick as production manager, and followed Nash as president of Buick.

Billy Durant had the drive and initiative to acquire companies, but he failed to integrate the companies into General Motors. Durant had started GM in 1908 with the Buick brand, and two years later had eleven brands, most of which competed in the same market segments. There was little management structure in the company, little financial control, and definitely no organization control. That GM survived the acquisitions was amazing, but Billy Durant did not survive.

Billy Durant had not lost his drive. He joined with Louis Chevrolet, the former French race driver, and investors William Little, and Dr. Edwin Campbell, Durant's son-in-law, to form the Chevrolet Motor Company on November 3, 1911, in Lansing, Michigan. Durant knew Louis Chevrolet from earlier years when Durant had hired Chevrolet as a race driver for Buick. Durant and Louis Chevrolet had a disagreement, and Durant bought out Chevrolet in 1914.

An interesting note: Durant supposedly saw a bow tie in the wallpaper of a French hotel, and he was inspired to adopt the bow tie as the emblem for the Chevrolet vehicles. The emblem is still used today. The Chevrolet Motor Company was profitable, and Durant took his share of the profits and acquired over 50% of GM stock. He was able to gain controlling interest in GM in 1916.

Charles Nash left GM when Durant took over. Some reports say that Durant was miffed at Nash because he became president of General Motors when Durant was fired in 1910. Other reports indicated that Nash resigned from GM because he could not get along with Durant, although Nash had worked for Durant in his carriage company. Nash vowed to never work for anyone again, and he bought the Thomas B. Jeffery Motor Company in Kenosha, Wisconsin in 1916, and changed the name to Nash Motors. The Jeffery Company had been started in 1900, and was second to Oldsmobile in total automobile production in 1903. Nash also acquired LaFayette Motors of Milwaukee, the Mitchell Car Company in Racine, Wisconsin, and Kelvinator, a leading manufacturer of kitchen appliances. Evidently, Charles Nash had learned the acquisition technique while working for Billy Durant.

Nash led Nash-Kelvinator until he retired in 1936. Charles William Nash died in Beverly Hills, California in 1948 at age 84. Unfortunately, he did not live to see the success of the Nash Rambler that was introduced in 1950 as a small car. The Rambler was a hit in the market and it was unfortunate the other U.S.

carmakers did not see the need for small cars. The nation's car market was changing, and the small car segment would later grow to be the largest single section of the U.S market. The lack of competitive compact and sub-compact vehicles by the Big Three would eventually result in the loss of over 50% of the market.

Durant took over as president of General Motors in 1916, but the company had not completed its reorganization after the 23 acquisitions. Financial controls were still lacking, and when the sharp recession of 1920 hit, sales dropped, and the company was again in financial trouble. The 1920 recession was caused by the Federal Reserve interest-rate increase. The GM board fired Billy Durant on November 30, 1920, for the last time, and Pierre du Pont, a large stockholder, took over as president.

Durant was still determined to be in the auto business, and he started Durant Motors in 1921 in Lansing. The company was moderately successful, but the sales decline in automobiles during the Great Depression caused Durant Motors to close its doors in 1933. Durant had been active in the stock market, and the 1929 crash cost him most of his money. He was close to bankruptcy by mid-1930, and he lived on a small pension provided by Alfred Sloan of General Motors. After being on top of the world as an international automobile executive, his last job was managing a bowling alley in Flint, Michigan. William Crapo Durant, the auto pioneer who created General Motors, died in 1947 at age 85.

The Durant era at General Motors was remarkable. A carriage company owner, and former cigar salesman, with no knowledge of engines, transmissions, or automobiles, joined the automobile industry as general manager of Buick. When Durant joined Buick, the company had sold only 37 automobiles. He immediately increased sales when he obtained orders for 1100 cars at the New York Auto Show. Durant made Buick profitable, started General Motors, and acquired 23 companies, and all of this was accomplished in a four-year period.

Billy Durant started in the auto business at exactly the right time, but had never managed a large intergrated business. He was successful in the carriage business, but had never *worked in the pits* to gain the experience necessary to run the largest automobile company in the world. General Motors was in disarray from the beginning, and he obviously had little time to run the business with his acquisition efforts. The big question is why he did not see the lack of organization when he took over GM the second time in 1916, and correct the problem. The answer was probably that Durant was a salesman and entrepreneur who did not understand the need for organization.

Pierre du Pont recognized he needed help in the operating side of the business, and Alfred Sloan was appointed president of General Motors in 1923. Sloan was an electrical engineer from MIT and the former owner of Hyatt Roller Bearing Company. Hyatt was part of United Motors, which was acquired by Durant in 1916, and Alfred Sloan had remained with GM as a vice president.

Sloan organized GM into one company and established the brand ladder in which each brand targeted one segment of the market, with Cadillac at the top of the ladder with high-priced vehicles, and Chevrolet at the lower end of the ladder with lower-priced cars. The Pontiac, Oldsmobile, and Buick brands were positioned at the middle steps of the ladder.

The brand ladder ended the acquired companies competing with each other in the same market segments. The overlap in market segments had been going on for 13 years, because the owners of the ten auto companies acquired by Durant in the 1908-1910 period had continued to run their businesses as they had done before the General Motors acquisition. Sloan's concept was that buyers would remain in the GM "family" by moving up the ladder as their income increased. Ideally, customers would remain loyal to GM and continue to purchase GM vehicles. The brand ladder continues today, although with fewer brands.

Alfred Sloan was the first to use financial statistics, such as return on investment, to measure performance, and the financial controls Sloan established were recognized to be the best in the industry. These financial controls would later save GM during the Great Depression.

Alfred P. Sloan Jr. of GM

Henry Ford was still producing the Model T with few changes, although Ford finally added the electric starter in 1919. The electric starter was a major improvement in internal- combustion vehicles because it eliminated the need for the hand crank, which was a safety problem. Hand cranks caused injuries and even death when malfunctions occurred. Henry Leyland of Cadillac demanded electric starters after a friend was killed by a hand-crank mechanism when the engine backfired.

General Motors began targeting all segments of the vehicle market with their brand ladder of automobiles. The automotive market in the 1920s was more sophisticated than the early years. Customers demanded more than the basic vehicle that Ford offered with the Model T. GM produced different brands in different colors. Ford was still the largest producer but the Model T was only offered in black because of a paint-curing problem. GM began to take an increasing share of the market.

The Ford Model T had dominated the industry for nineteen years, and sales of the unit exceeded fifteen million vehicles, but Henry Ford was complacent and failed to read the tealeaves. The market had changed and the Model T was finally obsolete by 1927. Ford Motor Company sales had dropped 75%, and General Motors took over as the largest producer of vehicles in the world. GM's success resulted from the brand ladder, which met customer demands in all segments of the market. The reorganization of General Motors by Alfred Sloan was a remarkable feat at a time when business management was in its infancy. The GM market success was aided by Henry Ford's refusal to accept that the market had changed.

In the mid-1920s, General Motors purchased a stake in Greyhound Corporation and Yellow Coach Bus Company. To increase sales, GM purchased a majority interest in National City Lines that built rail transit lines in various cities. GM began to replace rail transit with buses. This led to the "Great American Streetcar Swindle" scandal, and a lawsuit. General Motors was found guilty of violating the anti-trust law.

In 1925, GM bought Vauxhall in England, and in 1926 purchased Hertz Drive-Ur-Self System, and Yellow Cab Manufacturing Company. John D. Hertz would later buy back the rental car business in 1953. The company continued its acquisitions with Opel of Germany in 1929, and Holden of Australia in 1931.

Styling of General Motors vehicles took a major step forward when the company introduced the Cadillac La Salle in 1927. The styling was by Harley Earl, who continued as vice president of the design studio until his retirement in 1959. As demand for automobiles continued to rise, GM's organization was the best of the Big Three, and the company continued to increase sales.

The Great Depression struck in October 1929 after the Federal Reserve increased interest rates in 1928 and created a tight money condition. Vehicle sales fell nearly 80% between 1929 and 1932, and unemployment rose to 25%. The depression was a disaster for automakers; 90% went out of business. The luxury and high-priced market practically disappeared, and famous brands such as Cord, Duesenberg, and Pierce Arrow closed down. In addition to the terrible plight of Americans during the Great Depression, the automobile business suffered a shakeout of carmakers that added thousands to the unemployment rolls. The depression changed the automobile industry from a healthy growing business to a group of near-bankrupt companies. Annual auto production fell from 5.6 million units to 1.4 million, and 99 auto companies closed their doors.

Unemployment rose to 25%, while the rate of unemployment before the depression was 3%. The economic debacle could have been avoided if the Federal Reserve had not raised interest rates in 1928, and had kept its hands off the economy. The fact that the government caused the Great Depression has received little media attention. With Alfred Sloan's leadership and financial controls, General Motors survived the Great Depression and remained profitable throughout the 12-year depression debacle, an amazing accomplishment.

Chrysler was in a start-up mode at the onset of the depression. The company was started in 1925, acquired Dodge Motors, a larger company, in 1928, and was launching the new Plymouth and De Soto product lines when the depression hit. With Walter

Chrysler's leadership, the company lost money in only one year of the Great Depression. Ford struggled during the depression because of the high fixed costs of the new Rouge manufacturing complex, and Henry Ford's lack of financial controls.

General Motors cut costs sharply during the depression by closing plants, laying off workers, and reducing purchased-part material costs by working with their suppliers. GM also completely changed their marketing strategy by reducing prices on the Cadillac, Buick, and Oldsmobile brands, to stimulate sales of their higher-priced models. In some cases, the price reductions were as high as 70%. Chevrolet, the lower-priced brand, increased market share because the demand for low-cost vehicles dominated the market. These changes demonstrated Alfred Sloan's ability to adapt to the changing market.

Walter Chrysler demanded a 30% cost reduction and reduced the selling price of all models. Chrysler also increased productivity in manufacturing and became the low-cost producer. Chrysler increased their market share from 8% to 27% during the Great Depression, the largest gain in history. Walter Chrysler did an outstanding job in managing the company through the Great Depression, but he has received little credit for his performance.

Henry Ford attempted to raise vehicle prices to offset the loss of volume, but the price increase failed. Henry Ford had never installed an accounting system, and the company was not able to reduce costs to meet the loss of volume. Ford Motor Company lost 12 percentage points in market share during the depression, and Chrysler increased their share of the market by 19 points.

The Big Three survived the Great Depression with General Motors and Chrysler increasing market share. Ford survived, but Henry Ford's stubbornness in attempting to maintain the Model T cost the company dearly. Henry Ford would not live to see his company rise to the top again. He died in 1945, and the company was in third place in sales and near bankruptcy.

General Motors continued with acquisitions despite the Great Depression. Relatively unknown acquisitions by General Motors were the Fokker and Berliner-Joyce aircraft companies in 1930. GM joined the two into the General Aviation Manufacturing Company. The corporation also acquired North American Aviation, and GM was in the airplane business. The market for aircraft was slow due to the depression, but GM held on to the aviation business until 1948. Ford was also in the aircraft business, producing the Ford Tri-motor. The auto companies would later produce aircraft for the nation during World War II.

General Motors acquired Electro Motive Corporation and engine supplier, Winton, in 1930 to create the Electromotive Division, which supplied most of the diesel engines for locomotives. The division also manufactured engines for ships during World War II. General Motors sold the division in 2005, when the corporation was in a desperate need of cash.

The United Auto Workers (UAW) union was formed in 1935 and quickly began efforts to organize the Big Three. Union organizers were able to convince workers that the companies were the cause of the job losses, and promised jobs if they would join the union. The UAW started sit-down strikes to gain union organization. The sit-down strike tactic involved workers sitting down at their workstations and stopping production. The first sit-down strike was at a General Motors plant in Atlanta, Georgia, in 1936, but the most famous sit-down strike was at a GM plant in Flint, Michigan, and started on December 29, 1936. The UAW workers occupied the plant and production ceased. When police attempted to break up the strike, the workers threw auto parts from the windows of the plant, forcing the police to withdraw. This was known as the "running of the bulls" in union halls. The Flint sit-down strike lasted through January 1937, and the workers stayed in the plant, disregarding the absence of heat, lights, and water. The wives of the workers brought meals, water, and probably other liquid refreshments, and passed them through the windows of the plant. The governor of Michigan, Frank Murphy, acted as a mediator and brought the two sides together. General Motors accepted the UAW union on February 11, 1937. After the UAW organized General Motors, there were a large number of "wildcat" strikes that shut down production. The wildcat strikes were called by the local plant UAW representatives, and not authorized by union management, but the strikes stopped production.

World War II finally ended the Great Depression when industrial production for war material increased employment. The war was a terrible and tragic event, but with the Federal Government stumbling through eleven years of legislation that created more problems than solutions, it is doubtful that politicians would have ever found a solution.

Alfred Sloan's restructure of General Motors and his quick reaction to the financial crisis of the Great Depression, saved the corporation. Sloan's financial controls enabled major cost reductions, and he directed a dramatic change in marketing strategy. GM survived the depression without losing money, and actually gained market share – a historic accomplishment.

Alfred Sloan ran General Motors from 1923 until his retirement on April 2, 1956. His 33 years of managing the largest auto company in the world included firsts in developing annual styling change, brand-ladder pricing, strict financial controls, and the complete reorganization of the company into a decentralized structure. While Ransom Olds and Henry Ford were called the fathers of the automobile industry, Alfred Sloan was the father of management. Alfred Sloan died in 1966 at age 90.

After World War II started, General Motors stopped commercial automobile design and assembly and changed over to military production. GM produced airplanes for the military in their aircraft division, all types of military vehicles, including tanks, on their assembly lines, and armaments in their parts plants.

The automotive industry received accolades for its amazing work during World War II, but this effort has been ignored over the last 50 years. In the 2008 Congressional Hearings, Congress praised the Japanese and German auto companies during the hearings, while criticizing GM, Ford, and Chrysler. The Obama-Rattner task force even gave Chrysler to Fiat, an Italian auto company.

When the war ended, the UAW was quick to renew its strike policy. The union called a 113-day strike against General Motors in November 1945, three months after the end of the war. The UAW had gained power in Washington with its large lobby office. In the 1945 labor contract negotiations with General Motors as the strike target, the UAW not only demanded a 30% wage increase, but also demanded the authority to set the prices of vehicles – an amazing and unheard-of demand. Other unions in the auto industry undermined the UAW's 30% wage demand by settling for a lesser increase, and the UAW was forced to agree to the smaller wage amount. At the end of the 113-day strike, GM refused to allow the UAW to set prices.

Walter Reuther's famous statement "too old to work, but too young to die" was his motto to gain company-paid pensions in the 1947 contract negotiations. The companies' position was that Social Security was the system for retirement, and since the workers were no longer employees, the company was not obligated to pay them wages for retirement. Today's pension plans have reverted to this thinking, in that most companies do not offer a guaranteed pension plan, but offer a 401k. The settlement reached in the 1947 contract with GM included a major wage increase in that the cost-of-living benefit was added. This COLA benefit was the first in industry and would add to the labor cost in future years. Walter Reuther was determined to gain guaranteed pensions, and the 1949 contract negotiation would turn out to be an industry-changing event.

The UAW picked Ford as the strike target in 1949. The Ford Motor Company was in a financial crisis in the 1940s, and a long strike would have been disastrous, possibly even fatal. The company was near bankruptcy in 1945 when Henry Ford II took over, and was in the middle of a reorganization. The new post-war models had been introduced a month before the negotiations, and Ford was still in third place in sales. The company was in financial trouble but on the brink of a comeback. Ford agreed to the UAW pension demands, and for the first time in history, unions gained guaranteed pensions. Pattern bargaining had gained a historic benefit that would ultimately lead to bankruptcy.

The UAW pattern-bargaining strategy worked, and established a model for future negotiations. In pattern bargaining the union demanded that all labor contracts in the industry be identical, or at least similar. The problem was that the Big Three companies were dissimilar in size. General Motors was three times the size of Chrysler, and twice the size of Ford. Pattern bargaining in automotive gave the union a huge advantage because the union could afford a long strike, but the auto companies could not. The UAW used its strike fund to support the workers during a strike. The strike fund was accumulated by using part of the worker's weekly union dues to build up the fund between contracts. The union strike fund provided workers with enough money to pay the rent, and put food on the table during a strike, similar to unemployment benefits. The UAW collected strike-fund money from all car manufacturers during the period between contracts. The strike fund was large enough to pay workers during a strike because all companies paid into the fund, but the union called a strike against only one company.

A prolonged strike is almost fatal to a car company because of huge financial losses, usually in the billions of dollars, and a loss of market share. The loss of market share is critical because volume is so important in the capital-intensive auto business. The car companies are at a distinct disadvantage in the labor negotiations since the companies realize they are unable to survive a long strike. The union strike target, the first car firm picked for contract negotiations, is forced to accept the UAW demands to avoid a long strike.

Chrysler disagreed with Ford's 1949 contract because of the pension, and refused to accept the company-paid pension benefit. The UAW called a 104-day strike that cost a loss in profits and a loss of market share. Chrysler finally agreed to the company-paid pension in order to end the strike, but the effects of the 104-day shutdown changed the company from a viable business to a near-bankrupt company. The financial loss was huge, but the loss of market share was disasterous. The market-share loss caused Chrysler to fall to third place in sales volume. Production volume was near the break-even point and the company became borderline profitable. When recessions caused industry volume to decline, Chrysler lost money. The poor financial position due to lower volume also limited the capital that could be used for the annual model changes, and this problem caused the company to lose even more sales. The 1949 UAW contract was a disaster for the Chrysler Corporation, and UAW pattern bargaining forever changed the U.S. automobile industry.

Chrysler was unable to recover the lost volume primarily because of the limited cash for annual styling changes and product innovations. The near-bankruptcy situation in 1979 due to the recession was a direct cause of the low Chrysler volume caused by the loss of market share after the 1949 strike.

It is amazing that the media have not reported on the importance of the unfair labor tactic of pattern bargaining. Congress certainly does not understand the UAW advantage with pattern bargaining in labor negotiations since legislators continually asked the auto CEOs why "they gave away the store" to the union in the 2008 Congressional Hearings.

After the Chrysler strike, General Motors accepted the pension benefit, and the UAW gained the historic "Treaty of Detroit" agreement in the 1949 negotiations with GM. To avoid the long strike that Chrysler had endured, GM agreed to the UAW demand for the company funded pension plan, and agreed to hospitalization and medical benefits – the first in industry. This historic contract, along with other UAW benefits such as "30 and out" and the infamous "jobs bank," would drive the annual cost of pensions and health care to a level that would force GM and Chrysler into bankruptcy six decades later. The pattern bargaining technique had forced all of the Big Three to lose the contract negotiation battle.

Pattern bargaining is the root cause of the high labor and fringe costs in the auto industry, and it is amazing that the media and historians have ignored the situation. The topic is never mentioned when contract negotiations are in process, and the car companies never complain about the union tactic. This is a colossal blunder by automotive management; it is as if management refuses to accept the problem. When interviewing auto executives the reason given for ignoring the pattern bargaining issue was that management felt that the benefits gained by the UAW would be the same for all companies and not give an advantage to any one company. Obviously, this thinking was wrong because the total industry was forced into bankruptcy because of pattern bargaining.

Chevrolet sales increased after WW II and in 1950 sales were 300,000 units higher than Ford. However, General Motors management believed the brand to be an "old man's car," and decided to change the customer image to attract younger buyers. The chief engineer of Cadillac, Ed Cole, and his assistant, Harry Barr, were transferred to Chevrolet with the direction to make a change. These two designed and developed a new small-block V-8 engine that became famous. The new 265 (CID) "Turbo-Fire" engine with the 8:1 compression ratio could reach 180 hp with a four-barrel carburetor. The engine was lighter and more powerful than other GM engines and was a hit with young hot-rod drivers. The small-block V-8 was later used on all GM vehicles except the Saturn. Ed Cole's engine knowledge was the key element.

Edward Nicholas Cole 1909-1977

    In addition to the small-block V-8 engine, Ed Cole was the driver behind the Corvair, GM's first successful compact car. GM began the developmet of compact vehicles in the 1960s to compete in the small-car market, but except for the Corvair, most were smaller versions of GM's large cars, with six and eight cylinder engines, and all the extras for profit.
    The Corvair had an air-cooled rear engine, independent suspension, and was the first unibody vehicle produced by Fisher Body. The 1960 Corvair was named "Car of the Year" by *Motor Trend* magazine, and was produced between 1960 and 1969.

In the 1960s, the Big Three began developing new compact models to compete in the small car market, but most were not competitive with the Volkswagen Beetle. The VW Beetle was imported into the U.S. in the 1950s, and by the 1960s was taking an increasing share of the small-car market. The small two-door, four-passenger, rear-engine car was popular.

1960 Corvair

The Corvair sales were over 250,000 in 1960 and 337,000 in 1961. However, the handling characteristics of the early Corvairs received negative publicity in Ralph Nader's 1965 book, *Unsafe at Any Speed*. Nader reported that GM had removed a roll bar from the design for cost-reduction reasons, and without the roll bar, the Corvair would roll over under certain conditions. GM had not deleted the roll bar; they had just not added it. Engineers proposed the roll bar as an option, but management had rejected it as a production option.

Even though Porsche, VW, and Mercedes used similar designs, and the NHTSA tests found that the Corvair was equal to competing designs, General Motors had over a 100 lawsuits pending because of Corvair crashes. John DeLorean, a former GM vice president, stated in his book, *On a Clear Day You Can See General Motors*, that Nader's claims were accurate.

General Motors knew of the rollover problem because of the lawsuits involving Corvair accidents, and a similar situation would occur 50 years later when there were 100 lawsuits on the ignition-switch problem. In both cases, GM failed to recall the problem vehicles until years after the problems were first reported.

Nader, who in 1964 was an unknown attorney working for the labor department on automobile safety, continued his attack on the Corvair. In the first sentence of his book, Nader stated, "For over a half century, the automobile has brought death, injury, sorrow, and deprivation to millions of people." This opening statement demonstrated his bias and was indicative of his negative attitude toward the automobile industry.

Nader's book may have passed into oblivion if General Motors had not hired private investigators to investigage Ralph Nader. Nader discovered the investigation and complained to the media, and evidently, the government got involved because he worked in the labor department. Before long, the Nader book was front-page news, and Congress called a hearing in which GM management apologized to Nader. Nader filed a lawsuit that continued for years, and finally GM settled for $425,000 ($2.5 million today).

General Motors handled the Nader problem poorly with the private eye business and the refusal to correct the rollover problem. The failure to settle Nader's lawsuit added to the negative publicity. The bad publicity created a serious problem for the Corvair, and the entire automobile industry. GM added the roll bar to the 1964 models, but sales declined dramatically. Corvair sales fell over 50% in 1966, and only 27,253 were produced in 1967, a drop of 92% from the peak year of 1961. GM sold only 6000 Corvairs in 1969, and the model was eliminated.

If GM had included the roll bar in the initial design, the rollover problem would not have happened; the Corvair would have survived, and Nader would have continued as a non-descript attorney in the government.

The Corvair was the first compact car that competed with foreign imports, and it unfortunate that the rollover problem caused the cancellation of the brand. Possibly Ford and Chrysler would have recognized the need for competitive small cars, and developed vehicles that met the competition. If the Nader issue had not occurred, the Big Three may have been able to avoid the huge loss of the small-vehicle market.

Ed Cole was named president of General Motors in 1967, retired in 1974, and became CEO of the taxicab manufacturer Checker Motors. Tragically, he was killed when his small plane crashed on May 2, 1977 on the way to a Checker meeting in Kalamazoo, Michigan. Edward Nicholas Cole was elected to the *Automotive Hall of Fame* in 1977.

The compact vehicles introduced by the Big Three were designed for profit rather than competitiveness, and as a result were too large and had too many extras. Many models had six-passenger seating and six-cylinder engines. Automotive management finally recognized the import threat, but the drive for profit steered their compact designs toward larger vehicles. For this reason, the Big Three never have been able to design and build a small car that is competitive with imports. The Nash Rambler introduced in 1950 was a small car, but much larger than the VW Beetle, and the design was a carryover from the Nash small vehicles. The market was demanding small cars, and the Rambler became the third-largest-selling automobile in the U.S. however, management hubris and the desire for the added profit of large cars prevented a change to competitive small vehicles.

The first attempt at compact cars in the 1960s resulted in the Chevrolet Corvair, Ford Falcon, and Chrysler's Valiant. The "Pony" cars like the Mustang were highly successful, but were in the specialty market, not the compact market. Regrettably, the profit objective was stronger than the market share objective by Big Three management.

Auto management evidently believed they could recover the lost market share with American-type compacts with added content for profit, but the concept failed. The failure of U.S. manufacturers to meet the compact competition was the main reason for their loss of market share to foreign imports.

The UAW flexed its muscles again in 1970, even though Walter Reuther had died in a plane crash in May, before the contract negotiations started. The UAW called a 67-day strike against General Motors, and the union obtained a 13% wage increase in addition to the famous "30 and out" pension benefit, which allowed workers to retire with an annual company-paid pension of $6000 a year ($42,500 today) after 30 years of service. This historic pension benefit would later be one of the reasons that General Motors filed for bankruptcy. In the 2009 Congressional Hearings the political "business experts" asked GM CEO Rick Wagoner why management had "stupidly" allowed the UAW contracts to explode with huge wage increases, and even greater benefit increases. Obviously, Congress knew nothing of pattern bargaining. Unfortunately Wagoner did not have an answer, but the answer should have been pattern bargaining, and possibly the bankruptcy court would have outlawed this UAW tactic.

In 1970, General Motors was still the largest producer of automobiles in the world, and the UAW was strong with 400,000 workers in GM alone. In later years, GM would be second to Toyota in production and near bankruptcy, and the UAW would lose over half their members. Foreign automakers would soon produce over 50% of the vehicles in the U.S. market.

The Big Three launched a new generation of sub-compact models in the 1970s to meet the import threat. General Motors introduced the Vega, and Ford, the Pinto. Unfortunately, both vehicles made the "worst car ever" list. Ford's infamous Pinto burst into flames in rear end collisions, and the Chevrolet Vega had numerous engineering and quality problems.

The new small-car products launched by General Motors in the 1960s and 1970s (Corvair and Vega) were well intentioned, but failed because of product problems. The problems should have been detected during the engineering testing, and corrected. Instead, the defects were shipped to customers, resulting in lawsuits and customer complaints. GM's reputation was damaged and customers rushed to the Japanese imports.

In addition to the functional problems, customers complained about poor paint and rust. The Big Three did have a rust problem in the 1970s. As a quality director at Ford in 1973, I attended a dealer meeting with most of the vice presidents of Ford in attendance. The chairman of the Ford dealer group started the meeting by throwing a Ford fender on the conference table. Rust and coffee cups flew everywhere, and the problem was the fender was from a current model vehicle. Quality was not a measurement used by the Big Three for bonus performance, but certainly should have been. One of the financial measurements used for an assembly plant manager's bonus was material usage. If a plant used less material for paint, management received a larger bonus. There was something wrong with using only financial statistics for performance measurements, but in my years at Ford, quality was never a part of manufacturing or engineering performance objectives. Quality was considered the responsibility of the quality department, but quality engineers do not design or manufacture the product. The quality function is similar to finance; both measure performance, but are not responsible for performance. The metrics for individual performance were financial; quality was not included, however an occasional human resource objective was added for performance reviews.

Japanese imports gained a reputation for outstanding quality, and the problems with the Vega and Pinto added to the criticism of U.S. vehicles. Customers would no longer accept poor quality and Big Three management failed to recognize the seriousness of the problem. For years, each of the Big Three companies used production counts as the measurement of success, and quality problems caused a loss of production. Each company had an outstanding quality system, but management closed one eye to quality when problems hit the production floor. The Japanese had copied the Big Three quality systems, but the difference was that Japanese management paid attention to quality and adhered to the quality system with strict controls. When defects were found in Japan, production operators had the authority to immediately stop the assembly line by pulling a cord. The line would not be started until all defects were found and removed from the area. Big Three management did not trust the UAW workers to stop production, and refused to allow the assembly line to stop when defects were found. The quality inspectors were given the job of "sorting" for defects as production continued. Sorting was not effective, and vehicles were shipped with quality problems. Neither GM, nor the other members of the Big Three, had adopted the "zero defect" system used in Japan. Financial measurements were more important than quality in the U.S. because finance failed to recognize the loss of sales due to quality problems. As a result, the Japanese outperformed U.S automakers in quality.

    Vehicle safety became an issue in the 1960s when more than 90,000 deaths were attributed to vehicle accidents. Nader's 1965 book on the Corvair problem gained a lot of publicity, and in 1966, the government passed the Motor Vehicle Safety Act. The Safety Act was necessary since the auto industry, including foreign manufacturers, had not established firm safety procedures. The Corvair rollover problem could have been corrected before vehicles were in production if a strict procedure were in place to address potential safety issues. The lack of a disciplined safety procedure would later cause another serious safety problem with General Motors in 2014. The ignition-switch problem was first detected in 2002, but was ignored until the recalls.

Customers share the safety responsibility, and the lack of customer attention to safety was apparent with seat belts. Drivers disconnected seat belts after the Safety Act was passed in 1966 because of the belt discomfort. Seat belts, although valuable for safety, did not get full use until state laws required drivers to buckle up or pay a traffic ticket.

Next in safety regulations were the requirements for head restraints, energy-absorbing steering columns, ignition-key warning systems, anti-theft locks, side-marker lights, padded interiors, and bumpers for the 5-mph-impact requirement. These features were immediately added to the vehicles by auto engineers, and were costly, but safety came first.

Vehicle-emission requirements were added when the Clean Air Act was passed in 1963 to control smog. Engine engineers worked around the clock to develop engine calibrations that met the emission requirements. The Federal Government demanded that the Big Three engineers work independently, and threatened jail time if car companies shared technical information. The Japanese government formed a consortium, allowing joint effort in Japanese companies to develop engine solutions for smog, resulting in faster and less-costly development. The government under the Anti-Trust Law threatened the engineers in the U.S. if they worked together with the competition. The government control added cost and caused a time delay in implementing smog-control and emmission development.

By 1970, Japan had emerged as the second-largest automobile producer in the world with 5.3 million units. The U.S. was still first with 8.3 million units, but the Japanese rate of increase was remarkable. Japan's auto production in 1960 was 482,000 vehicles, and in ten years, it had increased to 5.3 million. The Japanese government supported their auto industry, and limited auto imports into Japan with strict laws. By 1975, Japan's output had increased to 6.9 million vehicles, a 30% increase in the five-year period, while U.S. production remained the same. In 1980, Japan became the largest producer of vehicles in the world with 11 million units, and took 28.5% of the world market. U.S. production had slipped to 8 million units. Japan remained the largest auto producer until 2009, when China became the number-one producer of vehicles in the world.

In the twenty years between 1960 and 1980, Japan's auto production had increased from 482,000 to over 11 million units, while U.S. production had remained at the 8 million level. This did not happen by accident; it happened because of outstanding support by the Japanese government, excellent vehicles, hubris of Big Three management, and the failure of the U.S. government to support an industry that employed three million workers.

The Federal Government controls the automobile business, and the Federal Reserve attempts to control the economy, but if their performance is measured by the Great Depression, and causing 50% of the recessions since World War II, along with Congress causing the 2008 housing recession, the report card would show a failing grade. The lack of support for the auto industry was demonstrated during the 2008 Congressional Hearings when Congress voted *against* bailing out the carmakers.

Internal-combustion automobile engines are fueled with gasoline, and gasoline is refined from crude oil. The foreign imports gained market share in the U.S. when OPEC created the oil shortages in 1973 and 1979, causing gasoline prices to soar to record levels. The Federal Government should have eliminated drilling restrictions to allow U.S. oil companies to drill for more oil. The nation has sufficient oil reserves to be independent of OPEC, but the government refused to allow drilling. The lack of an energy policy has plagued the country for over 40 years. Instead of the government allowing more drilling, Congress passed the Corporate Average Fuel Economy (CAFE) law in 1975 that required an increase in vehicle fuel economy. Instead of allowing increased oil drilling, the government pushed the responsibility for oil consumption to the automobile companies. The CAFE law ignored the fact that the number of vehicles increased every year, and as a result there was no way that increasing fuel economy in automobiles would make the country independent of foreign oil imports. Imported oil made up 35% of U.S. usage before the CAFE law was passed, and despite the increase in vehicle fuel economy, oil imports jumped to over 50%. The government ignored the increase in the number of vehicles. The oil industry has developed a new shale oil process that has increased oil production, but the environmental lobby is against the new process, and the lobby has politicians in its pocket, so oil exploration has been suppressed.

In 1973, OPEC increased oil prices to penalize the U.S. for aiding Israel in the 1967 war with Egypt, and in 1979 Iran responded to Jimmy Carter by shutting off oil supply. Gasoline prices soared, and the economy turned south, with interest rates over 20%, high inflation, and high unemployment, and the Big Three suffered huge losses. Chrysler was headed for bankruptcy, and the new CEO, Lee Iacocca, asked Congress for $1.5 billion in loan guarantees to keep the company afloat. Congress passed the Chrysler Corporation Loan Guarantee Act on December 20, 1979. Iacocca turned Chrysler around, and in 1983, Chrysler repaid the bank loans five years ahead of schedule and the government made $500 million. The government profit received little media attention.

The OPEC and Iranian oil crises changed the U.S. auto market dramatically. Before the OPEC action, there was a big demand for large cars, and delivery time for a Cadillac was 12 weeks. After OPEC, dealer lots were full of large cars since customers were demanding small, fuel-efficient vehicles. The Big Three had done a poor job in meeting the competition in the small car market, and had no products available. Foreign imports took the market.

1973 was not a good year for the Big Three. In addition to OPEC, the UAW gained additional wage and benefit increases in the 1973 contract. The UAW retirement benefits increased, and the "30 and out" benefit was revised to allow workers to retire after 30 years, regardless of age. A family dental plan was added along with seven additional holidays. The first pension benefit was negotiated in 1949 at Ford, next came 30 and out, and the latest was 30 and out with no age limit. Thirty percent of the GM workers who retired in 1976 were under the age of 55. The cost of retirement benefits for GM had doubled by 1973.

The cost of government-mandated safety and environmental requirements, along with the increase in UAW worker pay and benefits, caused the Big Three to raise prices to cover the costs. Vehicle prices increased 20% between 1970 and 1973.

The increasing market share loss by General Motors, Ford, and Chrysler caused an overcapacity problem for all the automakers. Instead of downsizing by closing plants that were no longer required because of lower production volumes, General Motors management refused to accept that the company could suffer a permanent loss of market share. GM continually predicted sales increases in their annual budgets, which showed the need for capacity, even though sales continued to decline.

GM used the "hockey stick" method in establishing budget volumes. The hockey stick is flat for a short distance, and then turns upward, and this unfortunately was the method used by GM to establish budget volumes. By using this forecast method, it was unnecessary to close plants since the company was predicting that future sales increases would require added capacity.

Budget volume in automotive is extremely critical because it establishes the cost base. If volume goes up, more people and tooling are required, and costs go up. If budget volume goes down, people are laid off, and capital expidentures are cut, and costs go down. By predicting higher volumes in the future, GM did not match budget volumes to actual production and sales volumes, and costs per vehicle increased since the company was losing market share. This budget volume problem has received no attention by the auto media, but was one of the problems that led General Motors into bankruptcy.

General Motors finance allowed this ridiculous method of budgeting to go on for years despite actual sales never reaching the budget volumes. Finance failed to correct the management idea that refused to accept that GM would continue to lose volume to foreign imports. This mistake would kill the company in later years when the jobs bank would prevent GM from closing plants because labor became fixed costs with the jobs bank.

The finance area of GM had long been recognized as the best in the U.S. automobile industry, so the failure to force plant closures to match capacity with actual volumes was unbelievable. It was even more unbelievable since the CEO of GM usually came from the finance area. The sales and marketing groups were certainly overconfident in their sales forecasts, and allowed their optimism to factor into their volume predictions. However, the finance group had the responsibility to question, and change the budget volumes. The failure to establish realistic budget volumes caused excessive overhead costs that would one of the major factors that caused the bankruptcy.

The Japanese had not gained the 30% market share in the U.S. without criticism. Lee Iacocca was the loudest critic of Japan's advantage and demanded a "level playing field," and Michigan legislators were also critical of the Japanese government's influence in the market. In 1981, the Japanese companies agreed to a voluntary trade agreement with the United States that limited the number of imported vehicles to 1.68 million a year. This agreement appeared to be a concession by the Japanese, but in reality, it fit with the strategy of the Japanese carmakers. The Japanese companies launched their premium brand vehicles,

Toyota's Lexus, Honda's Acura, and Nissan's Infiniti, and started building assembly plants in the U.S. The voluntary trade agreement was obviously a planned strategy to give Washington's politicians a carrot, with no basic change.

General Motors continued to develop new vehicles in the attempt to increase volume. A complete line of new vehicles was launched in the early 1980s, most of which had the front-wheel-drive design, which was to become the main powertrain system in the industry. The new designs were technical innovations that were remarkable, but the new vehicles failed to stem the market share loss.

On January 1, 1981, Roger Smith was appointed CEO of General Motors, succeeding Thomas Murphy. Smith was a 1947 graduate of the University of Michigan, and he received an MBA from Michigan in 1953. He started his GM career as an accounting clerk in 1949. He was named treasurer in 1970 and a vice president in 1971. Smith was made executive vice president in charge of finance, public relations, and government relations in 1974. Roger Smith's experience with GM prior to being named CEO was in staff assignments, and much of his career was in the New York office, away from the dirty job of making cars and trucks. He had no experience in the operations side of the business, and evidently could not see from New York the benefits of Alfred Sloan's decentralized organization. Smith believed that everything should be run from the top of the corporation, and as a result, his first major decision as CEO was to change General Motors from a decentralized company to a centralized structure. Sloan had put the decentralized organization in place in 1923, and it had worked for 60 years. Roger Smith's background in New York led him to take a different approach, and he changed an organization that successfully managed the Great Depression crisis, and was the leader in world automotive. His top down centralized management idea started GM's downfall.

Roger Smith 1925-2007

The first organization change took the assembly plants from the brand divisions, which had run the plants since the 1920s, and created the General Motors Assembly Division. The Fisher Body Division was eliminated, and this organization had run the body shops. The result of the reorganization was that Alfred Sloan's brand-profit-center system was changed, and the new organization required new executives, new managers, and new supervisors, many of whom were inexperienced in their new assignments. For example, old-school supervisors who had run the plant operations for years ran Fisher Body. When the new centralized organization took place, the GMAD people were unable to run the body shops, because the experienced Fisher Body supervisors were retired early to get them out of the way of the new organization. A disaster occurred when production operations failed to operate. The reorganization was poorly planned, probably because the company had been run with a decentralized structure for nearly 60 years. GMAD required two years to correct their organization problems. The two-year organization change caused quality problems at a time when the U.S. auto industry was struggling to regain public acceptance in quality.

The next organization change was the CPC-BOC reorganization (Chevrolet, Pontiac, Canada - Buick, Oldsmobile, and Cadillac). Pundits questioned this organization change, and even people inside GM did not understand the need for the change. The CPC-BOC change moved people around, and caused inefficiency in most opoerations. When Roger Smith later created a completely separate business unit for Saturn, there were huge organization changes throughout the company and more inefficiency.

When major organization changes continue for years, people move up and down the organization, and new bosses walk in the door every day. Nobody knows who their next boss will be, and employees tend to jump into their foxholes, pull their helmets down over their ears, and wait for the dust to settle. People do not want to make waves, or be noticed, afraid they will lose their jobs. The major organization changes cause morale problems and a loss of productivity. The Roger Smith organization changes were a disaster, and completely changed the way General Motors was managed, or was not managed.

The reorganizations were enough to keep management busy, but the labor contract of 1984 was on the table. Unfortunately, for the auto industry, General Motors agreed to the infamous *jobs bank* in the negotiations. Roger Smith approved the contract, but the jobs bank would prove to be not only costly, but a major deterrent to adjusting plant capacity to actual sales volumes. With all the financial expertise at General Motors, management must have recognized that with the jobs bank, direct and indirect labor costs became fixed rather than variable. The jobs bank was to prove disastrous for GM and the automobile industry. In the jobs bank, workers were paid 95% of their wages and 100% of their fringes - vacation, health care, and retirement - if they were laid off. The only requirement of workers was to report to a local GM facility and sign that they were available for work. They would then sit around all day, and report the following day, while drawing their pay. Why GM would ever agree to the jobs bank is a question that has never been answered, but it was one of the reasons that General Motors was forced into bankruptcy. The jobs bank was costing GM a billion dollars a year by 2005.

The jobs bank also affected how GM management ran the business. The company could not downsize to match the declining volume due to losses in market share because the jobs bank required the company to continue to pay laid off workers. An example of the jobs bank problem occurred in 1988, when Chevrolet was launching a new compact car. The underbody of the car would not allow a normal-size steel fuel tank. The steel tank supplied by the GM plant in Lansing would accept only 10 gallons of fuel, giving the owner the concept of poor fuel economy.

The solution to the problem was to use a plastic fuel tank, which could be molded to fit the crevices in the underbody, and gain an additional five gallons of fuel, which was a fifty percent increase in fuel capacity, and acceptable. General Motors did not have the technology to produce plastic fuel tanks, so Chevrolet gave an outside supplier, a New York Stock Exchange company, a five-year contract to produce the plastic tanks. This created a problem for the GM division producing steel tanks, since the loss of the Chevrolet business meant the plant must lay off workers, but still pay them in the jobs bank. The outside supplier had invested in a multi-million-dollar plastics research center, and had built two new manufacturing plants to handle the Chevrolet business.

GM management made the decision to obtain the plastics technology by copying the supplier's tooling and processes, and manufacturing the plastic fuel tanks in General Motors. This would avoid the layoff problem. The supplier discovered that GM had ordered duplicate tooling from its tool suppliers when one of the tooling companies asked which set of tools should be shipped first – GM's, or the supplier's.

Executives from the supplier company immediately met with GM management at the vice president level, accusing GM of stealing its technology and violating the five-year contract. The GM vice president claimed he knew nothing about the problem although he had signed the financial appropriation for the multi-million dollar tooling project. Even though Chevrolet had signed a five-year contract with the supplier, GM had decided that they would take over the plastic fuel-tank business to avoid the layoff of hundreds of workers at the steel fuel-tank plant and paying them in the jobs bank. Neither the signed contract nor the illegal copying of the supplier's process and tooling bothered General Motors.

This is just one example of how the jobs bank changed General Motors management decisions. The supplier lost their five-year contract and GM copied the supplier manufacturing process and used the supplier-designed tooling. The supplier later sold their plastics business and moved out of the Detroit area.

There were many similar problems with General Motors and their suppliers later with CEO Jack Smith and Jose Ignacio Lopez, Smith's purchasing czar. Lopez shopped the world for lower prices even though many suppliers had multi-year contracts, and in some cases had proprietary designs or processes. Lopez paid little attention to those technicalities.

GM's market share continued to decline in the 1980s, and the annual budgets continued to project an increase in sales. This ridiculous assumption of sales increases failed to recognize that the company was losing market share every year and was the main reason that the company failed to close plants. Once the jobs bank became a part of the labor contract in 1984, GM was unable to match capacity to sales volume because workers laid off in any plant closing would move into the jobs bank and continue to be paid. How General Motors management could ever agree to the jobs bank is unbelievable, and the sales increase in the annual budgets only compounded the problem.

The Roger Smith reorganizations continued to shake up General Motors, and were not complete when GM announced the Saturn program on January 7, 1985. The Saturn originally was intended to be a small car, and included in the existing brand divisions. General Motors certainly needed a new subcompact product to compete with the Japanese, but somewhere along the way, the Saturn became an all-new vehicle, with new facilities and a complete new organization.

Instead of launching the new vehicle in one of the car divisions, Saturn was established as a subsidiary, and was set up to operate independently from the GM organization. The Saturn reorganization was not only unusual for General Motors, but Saturn employees were trained in the Japanese methods because the idea behind Saturn was to copy the Japanese systems. Whoever dreamed up this idea failed to consider the effect on the remainder of the GM organization. The people transferred into Saturn assumed a special attitude, many thinking the "old GM" was obsolete. This did not sit well with the other GM employees, including executives at the vice president level. The Saturn organization was poorly planned, but the idea of improving worker involvement in operations was an excellent concept. The worker involvement idea was limited to Saturn, and the remainder of GM plants continued to operate as business as usual.

The Japanese management system included the unions working with management. In America, the UAW had worked against management from its inception, and every UAW president had preached the hardline approach since Walter Reuther. The average UAW worker heard only about the negative side of management, and local union representatives preached the anti-management behavior.

UAW General Motor's vice president Donald Ephlin was unique in the UAW organization in that he believed the union should work with, rather than against, management. The infamous

"Memorandum of Understanding" was signed, which included several different elements from the normal UAW contracts. The UAW workers were to be paid 80% of the normal contract rate, but were part of a profit-sharing program, and work rules were flexible, similar to the Japanese work rules. Despite being granted a UAW labor contract by General Motors in a right-to-work state, UAW management was not pleased with the unique contract, afraid that it would set a precedent. The Memorandum of Understanding was doomed when Stephen Yokich, a hotheaded militant, was elected president of the UAW in 1993. Yokich worked behind the scenes to eliminate the separate agreement and contract, and by 2003, Saturn workers rejected the agreement, and the UAW went back to its normal anti-management policy.

Roger Smith approved the Saturn program in 1985 despite the company's excess capacity. The project included new engine, stamping, and assembly plants in Spring Hill, Tennessee, south of Nashville. GM had 30% excess capacity, but finance approved the $6 billion project. The company also set up a completely separate dealer organization which required added costs for GM, and the new Saturn dealers were required to build completely new dealer operations across the country. Creating a new GM division is similar to creating a new company. A new organization was established, and management personnel were transferred into Saturn from other General Motors divisions, which created a massive change in people throughout the company.

The Saturn plan changed from a small car to a new, separate brand, which was not only unnecessary, but a duplication in the brand ladder. GM's market share was 46% when Smith assumed the CEO position, but it was declining every year. General Motors had too many brands for their market share, and the last thing the company needed was a new brand that competed with other GM brands in the marketplace. The addition of new plants in a new location was also a major mistake.

There were simply too many "new" elements in Saturn. The plan included an all-new vehicle, new organization, new people, new labor contract, new plants, new location, new dealer organization, and new management. It was an all-new plan that was destined to fail. Smith's inexperience in operations led to bad decisions, and his strong personality led him to ignore more-experienced executives.

Initial sales of Saturn vehicles were high, but GM's total sales continued to decline, so the Saturn sales took volume away from other GM brands, and were not incremental volume. Market share continued to decline.

With the financial problems of General Motors in the early 1990s, the company did not update the Saturn product line, and sales began to drop. Whether Saturn was ever profitable depends on the allocation of overhead, but with the huge investment in land, facilities, and tooling, if the costs were allocated properly, Saturn had to be a big loser. Saturn will go down in history as a major mistake by General Motors, similar to Ford's Edsel three decades earlier.

The Saturn brand was eliminated in the 2009 GM bankruptcy. Saturn was an idealistic venture by General Motors, and ignored the overcapacity problem in the company. The Saturn program was destined to fail since the UAW never bought into the concept that Saturn was a separate company, and that workers should work with management. General Motors should never have launched the Saturn, and the surprising thing was that Roger Smith, a financial expert, not only approved the project, but also championed it throughout his tenure as CEO.

The next major move by Roger Smith was the acquisition of Electronic Data Systems (EDS). GM acquired EDS in 1984 for $2.6 billion, and unfortunately for Smith, Ross Perot, the EDS CEO, came with the deal. Perot received a billion dollars in cash and stock, and was given a seat on the GM board since he became the largest single shareholder. The objective of the acquisition was to improve GM's information technology for the future. The problem was that GM paid too much for EDS, and Ross Perot out-negotiated Smith. EDS was granted special stock, and given a cost-plus pricing arrangement within GM. In the auto companies, as in most companies, a transfer price is used to transfer products from one division to another. For example, when the engine division ships an engine to the assembly division, the engine is shipped, or transferred, at a transfer price, which is established by accounting. The transfer price is based on cost and the price of the product from competitive sources. The outside estimated cost is always in question. Perot negotiated a transfer price agreement favorable to EDS. As a result the EDS costs charged to the using GM divisions was not competitive with outside systems companies, and the using GM divisions ended up paying too much. The new GM EDS division turned out record internal profits, resulting in excessive bonus payments for the new GM-EDS people, which upset the other GM executives.

After the GM acquisition of EDS, it was not uncommon for systems companies outside GM to quote business to the GM divisions at half the EDS transfer price. As a result, many systems projects were outsourced. The divisions purchasing and paying for the EDS services found the transfer prices were not competitive. The buying divisions were paying more to EDS than they would have paid if the services were bought outside the company. The transfer-price problem continued for the time that Perot was on the GM board, and continues today to a lesser degree. Roger Smith's lack of experience in operations again caused a serious mistake, but the transfer price problem was only the tip of the iceberg.

As a member of the General Motors board, Ross Perot soon began to express his opinions on how the company was managed. Unluckily for Roger Smith, Perot's opinion was that General Motors was mismanaged, and the problem started at the top of the company. Perot continued his attacks on Roger Smith in board meetings, and the board was not used to criticism by a fellow board member. Normally the CEO controlled board meetings, with the board quietly agreeing to everything recommended by the chairman. Ross Perot reported, "Revitalizing GM is like teaching an elephant to tap dance." Smith finally had enough of Perot and asked him to resign. General Motors paid Ross Perot $750 million to go away.

Roger Smith's tenure as GM's CEO was a rollercoaster, from the big losses in the early 1980s, through the good years in the mid-1980s, and finally to the huge losses in the late 1980s. GM's market share declined from 46% to 35% during his time as CEO, an utter disaster, and for some reason Smith, a career financial expert, allowed his finance department to approve the "hockey stick" budget volumes throughout his ten years as CEO. The hockey stick budget volumes exceeded the actual volumes and not only prevented downsizing the company to actual volumes, but added huge costs. The jobs bank, Saturn, EDS, and the multiple organization changes happened on his watch, all of which damaged General Motors. Smith retired July 31, 1990. In 2013, *Fortune Magazine* listed the ten worst auto CEOs in history, and Roger Smith was number five on the list; Henry Ford was first because of his refusal to accept that the Model T was obsolete.

Roger Smith's pension of a million dollars a year received considerable negative press when he retired, and he was forced to reduce the amount because of stockholder complaints and negative publicity. Roger Smith died on November 27, 2007, 18 months before General Motors filed for bankruptcy.

The financial section of General Motors is considered by most to be the best in the industry, and normally the CEO comes from the financial sector. It is therefore difficult to understand how finance allowed the budget volumes to exceed the actual volumes during the 1970s and 1980s. The Japanese and other imports took an ever-increasing share of the U.S. market, and GM was the biggest loser. By budgeting unrealistic volumes, the company retained facilities (assembly, stamping, and engine plants) that were no longer required. These plants amounted to billions in investment, and thousands of workers. While the plant closures would have been painful, and sadly would have put many workers out of work, the move was necessary to save the company. Instead of adapting to the changing market as GM had done under Alfred Sloan during the Great Depression, GM management continued to hope for higher volumes, but actual volumes declined year after year. It was unbelievable that the largest auto company in the world continued to ignore the market changes. The Saturn project added plants when GM should have been reducing facilities, which is even more difficult to understand.

In an attempt to reduce costs, GM finance demanded the use of "common" parts across all brands. This probably sounded like a good idea, but unfortunately, many of the "common" parts turned out to be exterior sheet-metal components. Using the same sheet metal across brands resulted in most GM brands looking alike. One of Ford's commercials showed a valet parking cars at a hotel, and as the GM cars were driven by, hotel patrons would say: "it's a Cadillac, no, it's an Oldsmobile, no, it's a Chevrolet." There was little difference in appearance for most of the GM brands, and as a result, sales fell even further. Finance should have stayed in the green-eyeshade part of the business and stayed out of styling. Rick Wagoner, the CEO from 2000 to 2009, admitted that finance had made a mistake in interfering with design decisions.

Robert C. (Bob) Stempel followed Roger Smith as CEO in August 1990, and inherited a magnitude of problems: huge losses, quality problems, and a GM market share of 35%, which was the lowest in over 60 years. Fixed costs were out of control, and excess capacity exceeded 30%. Like they say, "other than that, the company was in great shape."

Stempel was under considerable pressure to do something, and unfortunately, he elected to make a presentation on television that was not well thought out, and obviously had little planning behind it. During the televised speech, he outlined a plan to close plants, but he had no specifics on which plants, when they were to be closed, or the effects of the closures. Stempel obviously had no plan, but was attempting to show that GM was working on something. He should have waited until a real plan was developed that considered all elements of the equation such as the total cost, the UAW, the jobs bank, and the effects of the massive layoffs.

The Stempel speech did not address the dramatic loss of market share by General Motors or the effect of the jobs bank. He was attempting to present a positive outlook for GM, but this was an impossible task because of the financial situation of the company. The jobs bank was not mentioned by Stempel, but neither GM nor the UAW had disclosed the jobs bank when the 1984 contract was announced, so the media and the public knew nothing about it.

On November 2, 1992, Bob Stempel was relieved of his duties as CEO, and replaced by John F. (Jack) Smith. Smith started as a payroll clerk and spent time in the GM financial office in New York. He later served as president of GM Europe and was known as a cost cutter, but had no experience in operations. His first move as CEO was to bring in Jose Ignacio Lopez as vice president of purchasing for North America. GM management had ignored the over-capacity problem, had not corrected its quality problems, and had no plan to fix the company. Smith took the approach of demanding suppliers help fix GM's cost problems. Lopez was certainly the person to make it happen. The Smith-Lopez team completely changed the GM purchasing policies by shopping the world for cheaper prices, and existing contracts with their current suppliers did not stand in their way. The tactic was unethical, but got results. However, many long-term auto suppliers refused to accept GM's ruthless price demands such as an immediate price reduction of 20%, and a 5% price reduction every year, and gave up their automotive business. The auto supplier business was a low return business, and large companies elected to drop out.

However, the General Motors volume is so large that it is not difficult to find some other supplier to accept the low return business. Unfortunately, for automobile buyers, many of the new Lopez suppliers had never heard of six sigma, and GM quality suffered. The quality problems did not get a lot of attention from Lopez, because he was only interested in lower purchased-part prices. The quality problems were shipped to customers because cost reduction was the objective.

When Volkswagen offered Lopez a job in Europe, Jack Smith promoted Lopez to president of GM's U.S. operations, a position for which Lopez was totally unqualified. How the experienced GM executives who deserved that job felt has never been discussed, but fortunately for GM and the U.S. automobile industry, Lopez decided to take the Volkswagen job.

General Motors accused Lopez and three GM executives of stealing over 50 boxes of GM documents, most of which were confidential. GM filed a civil suit that claimed that Lopez had stolen secret data, including data on the future GM Opel vehicle. German officials also started an investigation of Lopez. After the theft of documents was confirmed, VW fired Lopez and settled the suit with General Motors for $100 million and a signed commitment to purchase $1 billion of GM components. Jose Lopez was seriously injured in a European auto accident in 1998, and he moved to Spain, where he resides in semi-retirement.

Rick Wagoner was appointed CEO on May 31, 2000. In Bob Lutz's book, *Icons and Idiots*, Lutz described Wagoner as an excellent "peacetime" CEO. Unfortunately, General Motors was at war. Wagoner inheirited the same problems that Bob Stempel had discovered when he assumed the CEO position. Roger Smith left a real mess for his successors.

Richard (Rick) Wagoner of GM

Wagoner did approve the cancellation of the Oldsmobile brand on April 29, 2004, which was a major step, but the laid-off workers simply moved into the jobs bank and drew 95% of their pay. The loss of market share during the prior thirty years had finally caused the company to eliminate a brand. Oldsmobile was the first GM acquisition in 1908. Founded by Ransom Olds in 1897, the Olds Company was the world's largest producer of automobiles in 1903, and had produced over 35 million vehicles, and Ransom Olds was the first to assemble vehicles on a moving process. Oldsmobile sales had declined from 1.1 million units in 1985 to fewer than 300,000 by 2003. Due to the continuous loss of market share, GM had too many brands for the reduced volume, and Oldsmobile was the first to go. The elimination of the brand was long overdue, but it cost General Motors $2 billion to close the dealer franchises.

In February 2005, it was necessary for GM to purchase a put option at a cost of $2 billion to avoid the acquisition of the Italian carmaker Fiat. A prior agreement with Fiat had included the put option when GM had bought 20% of Fiat. The $2 billion cash payment could not have come at a worse time.

Kirk Kerkorian, the Las Vegas financier, had purchased 9.9% of GM stock, and was the largest single stockholder in the company. Recognizing GM's financial problems, Kerkorian recommended that Renault buy 20% of GM. Carlos Ghosn, the Renault CEO, turned the deal down, and Kerkorian sold his stock.

General Motors had a major study going to merge with Chrysler. The merger would have eliminated considerable overhead, the cost savings would have been enormous, and the merger could have possibly avoided the GM bankruptcy. The topic was discussed at great length, but Wagoner finally rejected the idea. The merger would have taken at least two years to intergrate Chrysler into General Motors, and Wagoner did not have two years. GM was in deep trouble, and the acquisition would have required GM management to spend all their time on the Chrysler merger. Wagoner was confident he could fix GM, but there were simply too many problems.

Instead of the Chrysler acquisition, Wagoner began selling assets to obtain working capital to keep the company alive. In March 2006, GM sold over 90% of its interest in Izuzu for $2.3 billion, and in April of the same year, sold 51% of GMAC for $14 billion. In June 2007, Wagoner sold the Allison Transmission Division for $5.6 billion, and then sold the balance of Izuzu for $300 million. Unfortunately, GM was burning cash faster than Wagoner could sell assets.

The necessity of selling off parts of GM to keep the company open was helping with working capital, but the GM problems were simply too big to fix with the sale of assets. General Motors was near bankruptcy, but Wagoner believed that bankruptcy would put General Motors into receivership, because he thought there was not enough cash available to keep the company going throughout bankruptcy court proceedings. He missed the target on this one because Chapter 11 in 2008, was better than the five-year government takeover that resulted from the 2009 government controlled bankruptcy. Rick Wagoner had followed Bob Stempel as CEO, and both inheirited the dilemma created by Roger Smith. Excess capacity created huge overhead costs, and the approval of the jobs bank prevented correcting the fixed cost problem. The Saturn program added to the fixed cost issue, and Saturn sales were not incremental volume since the sales were taken from other GM brands. Costs were out of control in a company known for its strong finance department, and Roger Smith was from the financial community. There is certainly enough blame to go around for the decline of General Motors, but if there was any one individual responsible for the downturn, it was Roger Bonham Smith. As mentioned earlier, Roger Smith was listed as number five on "Fortune Magazine's" list of the worst auto CEOs in history. Both Bob Stempel and Rick Wagoner had an impossible task.

In addition to trying to fix all the problems in GM, Wagoner had to manage the 2007 UAW contract negotiations. He did a good job, because for the first time, the UAW gave concessions. The contract changes were a help for GM, but not near enough to avoid bankruptcy.

2007 UAW Contract Changes

- Two-tier wage structure
- VEBA (Voluntary Employee Beneficiary Assoiciation) established for retiree health benefits
- Lump sum payments instead of wage increases
- COLA diverted to health care costs

The Big Three obligation to the UAW pension fund was $120 billion, and another $25 billion was owed for health care. For 70 years, the UAW had successfully used the pattern bargaining technique to gain wage and benefit increases. The cost of labor and fringe benefits had reached a level that was no longer attainable, and the auto companies were near bankruptcy. When an analysis was made comparing Toyota to General Motors at a 9-million-vehicle volume level, Toyota's profits were $17.2 billion, and GM lost $38.7 billion – a $4000-per-vehicle penalty.

General Motors was suffering through the worst period in history, and the last thing that Rick Wagoner needed was a downturn in the economy, and a further loss of vehicle sales.

The housing bubble peaked in 2006 but burst in 2007. The legislation that caused the housing bubble and the Great Housing Recession of 2008 began with Jimmy Carter's Community Reinvestment Act of 1977. Bill Clinton's requirements for an increase in mortgage loans for minorities and low-income families in 1993 added to the problem. HUD eliminated mortgage down payments and income verification, created the adjustable rate mortgages, and 95% of the toxic mortgages were ARM. The Federal Reserve lowered interest rates from 5.25% to 0.25% in one year, which poured money into the housing market. The Federal Government interference in the housing market had created a recipe for financial disaster, and resulted in the 2008 recession. The government objective to give home loans to low- income families was admirable, but resulted in the worst economic recession since the Great Depression.

With the relaxed lending rules, mortgage applicants who could not afford to own a home obtained mortgages. Many could not make the payments, and toxic mortgages resulted in foreclosures. Wall Street issued mortgage bonds consisting of the worthless toxic mortgages, and sold the bonds to unsuspecting investors. The rating agencies rated the toxic bonds Triple A without checking the validity of the bonds. Wall Street made record profits and record bonuses, and this was the same group that was bailed out by the government without any Congressional Hearings. By 2006, the housing market was out of control, prices declined, and the housing bubble burst.

The sub-prime mortgage values declined, and when home foreclosures increased in 2006, the subprime mortgage market failed. During 2007, many mortgage companies were closed. Wall Street was also near bankruptcy; the CEOs of Fannie Mae and Freddie Mac were fired, along with the CEOs of Merrill Lynch and Citigroup. Housing prices dropped 40% and homeowners lost their home equity. For the first time in history, the economic recession hit the housing market. In prior recessions, the stock market fell, but home equity remained solid. Consumer confidence fell when homeowners saw their historically "safe" investment in their homes decline. The net worth of households fell by a record amount, declining by $7.1 trillion between mid-2007, and the third quarter of 2008. The government caused Great Housing Recession hit the country hard, and similar to the Great Depression of 1929, politicians refused to accept responsibility.

Bear Stearns was close to bankruptcy in 2007, and in March 2008, the government attempt at a bailout with $30 billion failed, and forced a merger with J.P. Morgan Chase. The financial institutions were beginning to topple.

On September 15, 2008, one day before GM's 100th birthday, Lehman Brothers filed for bankruptcy. The $660 billion bankruptcy was the largest in U.S. history. The Federal Reserve had backed a $135 billion advance to Lehman, so taxpayers paid for the disaster. The stock market dropped 500 points (4.4%), and another 7% by the end of September. On September 17, two days after the Lehman bankruptcy, the Federal Government bailed out AIG with $180 billion of taxpayer money. Why Secretary of the Treasury Paulson failed to bail out Lehman was the big question that has yet to be answered, but he started the housing depression by allowing Lehman to go into bankruptcy.

During this period, GM was running out of cash, but Wagoner still refused to accept bankruptcy. Cost reductions had not worked, and vehicle sales had fallen from 17 million to 10.7 million, and the auto industry was in a depression, not a recession. No company could survive a 40% drop in revenue in such a short period and survive.

Credit tightened, which made it more difficult for customers to buy vehicles, and made it impossible for GM to borrow cash from the banks. The 2008-second quarter loss for General Motors was $15.5 billion, the largest quarterly loss in the 100-year history of the company. The GM stock price had dropped to $11.50, and Wall Street was predicting bankruptcy for the company.

With the financial market in such difficulty, Congress passed the Emergency Economic Stabilization Act on October 3, 2008, creating the Troubled Asset Relief Program (TARP). The TARP fund allocated $700 billion for troubled assets. There was an immediate concern that giving the TARP fund responsibility to Paulson created a conflict-of-interest situation, since Paulson was the former CEO of Goldman Sachs. This turned out to be a valid complaint, since Paulson immediately bailed out Wall Street, but refused to bail out Main Street.

Chrysler and GM had requested a $35 billion loan for working capital from TARP, and Paulson had the authority to aid the car companies, but he refused any bailout funds for automotive. Henry Paulson's rejection of the automotive loan request will go down in history as a biased decision, favoring his friends on Wall Street but refusing to bail out the automobile industry.

Since the banks were near bankruptcy, the government was the only source of cash for Chrysler and General Motors. Ford had obtained a $23.6 billion loan from the banks in 2006 for restructuring, and used the cash for working capital to avoid bankruptcy.

Instead of immediately allocating a portion of the approved troubled asset fund to the automobile industry, Congress began a series of Congressional Hearings in November 2008. The chairman of the hearings was Senator Chris Dodd, one of the instigators of the legislation for affordable housing. During the hearings, the Big Three CEOs and the president of the UAW were seated together like a kangaroo court. Rick Wagoner started the discussion by stating that the recession had caused vehicle sales to decline by 40%, and that was the reason that the auto companies were requesting loans. Congress not only rejected that idea, but openly criticized Wagoner, along with Alan Mulally of Ford and Bob Nardelli of Chrysler. Just as the 1930 politicians refused to accept that the government had caused the Great Depression, the 2008 politicians refused to accept that they had caused the mortgage depression. Senator McConnell of Kentucky said, "Very few of us had anything to do with this dilemma." McConnell conveniently forgot that his Senate voted for the legislation that caused the affordable housing debacle.

A question that received considerable media attention was why the CEOs traveled to Washington in their company planes. This topic received nationwide publicity for months. Obviously, Congress conveniently forgot that some members in Congress had their own government airplanes for travel. Nancy Pelosi had demanded a large jet outfitted with 90 first-class seats for her use. Other members of Congress used government airplanes for their "investigative" junkets to warm resorts in wintertime. The adage "don't do as I do, do as I say," certainly applied to their airplane questions.

The House approved a $14 billion auto loan on December 11, 2008. However, Senate Republicans demanded that the UAW agree to match the Japanese wages and fringes. When the UAW refused, and Democrats supported the union, the Senate rejected the bailout bill by a vote of 52-35 on December 12, 2008. Congress actually voted to allow Chrysler and General Motors to go into bankruptcy – not a bailout, but bankruptcy. Surprisingly, the Senate vote against a bailout has received little or no attention by the media, and the public is unaware of the negative vote.

President Bush was reluctant to allow the car companies to go into bankrupty, and allocated $17.4 billion (2.5% of the TARP money) to keep the two companies solvent until President Obama took office. This turned out to be a big mistake since the new president's objective was to protect the UAW, not the companies.

In President Obama's first meeting with his advisors on automotive, the proposal to allow Chrysler to go into bankruptcy was recommended. The advisors believed that General Motors could be saved, but that Chrysler was too weak to survive. The "advisors" were politicians, not business people, and were evidently unaware that a CEO can fix a company. Lee Iacocca had taken Chrysler from bankruptcy to record profits.

President Obama was concerned about the public's reaction to a Chrysler bankruptcy when the government had bailed out Wall Street. The President wanted to delay a decision on automotive until the furor died down. President Obama formed a task force to further "study" the automotive issue. Another study was certainly not required because GM and Chrysler had submitted complete financial data and restructure plans, and the Treasury and Congress had "studied" the auto business for nearly four months.

The three million people working in the auto industry and affiliated businesses had been waiting patiently for a decision, but there was no help coming out of Washington. Auto people could not understand why the government had immediately bailed out the GSEs, AIG, and Wall Street without any meetings or Congressional Hearings, but after nearly four months of Treasury meetings and hearings, Congress had rejected the bailout of the automotive business, and now President Obama was "studying" the situation again.

The solution to the auto problem was granting TARP funds for working capital to allow Chrysler and General Motors to restructure. The government had given trillions to financial institutions, but rejected the loan request by automotive.

The final decision for a bailout of Chrysler and General Motors was in President Obama's court; however, he refused to make a decision, and started another study. Steven Rattner was appointed the "car czar," and recruited several Wall Street types to join "Team Auto." The Wall Street instant auto experts had never been near an automobile plant, and some did not even own a car.

Rattner was a Wall Street multi-millionaire under investigation by the state of New York for pension fraud. He was forced to resign his task-force job before his work was finished because of the New York lawsuit. Rattner paid a $10 million fine to avoid jail, and was banished from any company pension work for five years.

The Rattner Team Auto began interviewing auto executives at GM and Chrysler in Detroit. After two months of meetings, Rattner met with GM CEO Rick Wagoner. On March 27, 2009, the "car czar" fired Wagoner. The GM board of directors, who alone had the authority to deal with Wagoner, objected, but President Obama supported Rattner, and Wagoner was gone.

General Motors had been headed toward bankruptcy for 20 years due to the rising wage, pension, and health-care costs obtained by the UAW with pattern bargaining. Fixed costs were excessive since GM had not downsized the company to the reduced volume level. Foreign carmakers had taken over 50% of the U.S. market, and the UAW jobs bank prevented cost reductions if plants were closed because the jobs bank benefit paid them for not working. The job bank paid laid-off workers 95% of their wages and 100% of their benefits if laid off, and was costing GM a billion dollars a year. The 11% loss of market share during Smith's tenure as CEO added to the fixed-cost problem.

The wage and fringe benefits gained with pattern bargaining became impossible to pay, and caused a $4000 per-vehicle cost disadvantage with Toyota. General Motors lost $70 billion between 2005 and 2008; an average of $17.5 billion a year, and the company was unable to survive with such losses. The Government-caused housing recession triggered the bankruptcy, but GM was on the way to bankruptcy court before the recession.

Team Auto, led by Mr. Rattner, questioned the Chrysler and GM executives for five months, but did not find a plan to save Chrysler and GM. The delay accomplished the political objective of President Obama, because the five months of task force meetings had taken the public's eye off the automotive problem. However, the five months of meetings and questions cost the nation $60 billion for working capital to keep the two companies alive while Rattner was asking his questions. Working capital was still the problem, and the government decision-making delay of eight months with Treasury meetings, Congressional Hearings, and task-force studies had not solved anything. Rattner forced Chrysler into bankruptcy on April 30, 2009. GM followed Chrysler into bankruptcy court on June 1, 2009.

An item missed by Rattner in his book *Overhaul*, and missed by the media, was the eight months of government delay after the auto companies requested a government loan in October 2008. Chrysler and General Motors were essentially bankrupt, and required an immediate transfusion of cash for working capital. The two companies burned thru $60 billion of working capital while they were waiting on a government decision. This was an unnecessary cost caused by government indecision. The total TARP money allocated to GM and GMAC was $67 billion, and Chrysler, with Chrysler Finance, took $12.2 billion. The combined total was $79.2 billion. The $60 billion of working capital was 75% of the total cost. The country certainly could have done without the Obama-Rattner "study."

The government actually made the decision to reject a bailout of the auto companies when the Treasury refused to allocate TARP funds for automotive in October, and Congress voted against a bailout in December 2008. The Obama-Rattner task force was a political delaying action to get the public's attention off the auto problem. The five-month "study" was started for political reasons because bankruptcy was the only option for Chrysler and General Motors unless the government furnished working capital while the companies restructured. The government furnished trillions to the GSEs, Wall Street, and banks for restructuring, but rejected the auto companies' $35 billion loan request.

The bankruptcy court gave 60.8% of General Motors to the U.S. government, and 11.7% to the Canadian government, hence the nickname "Government Motors." The UAW VEBA received 17.5% and bondholders lost 90% of their $30 billion investment. The UAW kept their wages, pension, and health care. The court ruled that Pontiac, Hummer, Saab, and Goodwrench, be closed. Even though the UAW fought the decision, the court ruled that the infamous jobs bank be eliminated. GM retained Chevrolet, Buick, Cadillac, and GMC.

Rattner had recommended that 2400 GM dealers be eliminated, which was a reduction of 30%, and the court ruled in his favor. Dealer lawsuits reduced this number to 2000. Rattner's lack of knowledge in automotive was demonstrated in this decision. Automotive dealers are private businesses, and their profit or loss have no effect on General Motors. The decision to cut dealers caused over 100,000 dealer workers to lose their jobs. Many of the dealerships eliminated were in outlying locations, and when forced to close, customers were required to choose another dealer. In many cases, the closest dealer was foreign competition. Therefore, Rattner cost General Motors sales with his dealer reduction demand. General Motors did have too many dealers because the GM volume had decreased with the loss of market share. The company had added dealerships during the years as GM acquired over 50% of the U.S. market. As private businesses do when in trouble, dealers revised their business model to increase used-car sales, and increase their service volume to remain profitable. Those dealers unable to change with the times of reduced volume closed their doors, but General Motors did not absorb their losses. The number of dealers should have been reduced by attrition, rather than a wholesale reduction, but concern for people evidently was not Rattner's priority.

The government had fired GM CEOs Rick Wagoner and his successor, Fritz Henderson, and appointed Ed Whitacre as the new CEO, but he lasted only a few months and never moved to Detroit. Whitacre commuted from his home in Texas, evidently thinking the CEO position was a part-time job. Dan Akerson, another non-automotive government appointee, followed Whitacre as CEO. Both Whitacre and Akerson were in charge when the company ignored the GM ignition-switch-airbag recall. The government sold its GM stock in December 2013, and in the first quarter of 2014, the company announced recalls of 31 million vehicles for the ignition switch and other problems. The timing of the recalls was interesting. No announcement of recalls was made when the government experts were in control of GM, but shortly after they left the company, GM announced the recalls. The government was running GM when many of the problem vehicles were produced, but the government CEOs and consultants obviously failed to act on the recall problems during their reign. There were 67 recalls in 2014. This was an astounding number of quality and engineering problems and why the government-appointed experts did not react to the problems remains a mystery. The old adage "do as I say, not as I do" certainly applied to the government management of General Motors. The government officials also did a poor job of repaying the loan. Only $39.3 billion of the $50.7 billion loan had been repaid as of May 2014.

Safety and quality did not receive priority as the government experts were running General Motors, and the safety recall of 17.6 million vehicles for ignition switch problems was a classic example.

The new ignition switch allowed the key to turn to the off position, causing the engine to stop. When the engine stopped, power brakes and power steering failed to work. The driver was unable to steer the vehicle and the airbags would not operate. The switch problem resulted in 54 crashes and 13 fatalities. GM paid a $5 million settlement for a lawsuit on the switch problem, and the large expenditure must have required top-level management approval.

GM finance required that any design change be justified with savings. Most companies use this standard, but if there is a safety issue, the auto company must treat safety as a top priority. GM reported that cultural failings resulted in the failure to recall the problem vehicles for 12 years. Whatever the reasons were, General Motors failed in the safety area with the decisions on the ignition-switch problem. The recalls were front-page news, GM stock price declined, and the number of recalls had a negative effect on the company's quality reputation.

Takata, a Japanese airbag supplier, had an explosion problem with their airbags, and GM stopped production on the Cruze, its top-selling vehicle. The Takata airbag problem has resulted in a recall of 10 million vehicles, primarily Japanese cars.

GM has set aside $2.5 billion to cover the 2014 recall costs, and established reserves of $80 million a year for 10 years for future recalls. In addition to the $2.5 billion cost, the recalls will cost GM a loss of customers due to the loss of their quality reputation.

The government bailout of 1065 financial institutions was driven by the ridiculous *too big to fail* idea. The Treasury included many former Wall Street executives who believed that Wall Streeet and banks were interconnected, and bankruptcy would cause an ecomonic crisis. The Treasury and Federal Reserve used the too big to fail concept to bailout Wall Street, banks and mortgage companies to avoid bankruptcy, but the economic crisis still happened. Obviously, the too big to fail theory failed.

The Treasury, Federal Reserve, and Congress failed to bailout businesses, including GM and Chrysler, while bailing out the financial community. A small credit union in Indiana was more important than Chrysler and General Motors.

Every "expert" in Washington had analyzed the auto issue for four months, so President Obama had sufficient study data to make a decision on the bailout in January 2009. However, as the president had done in previous years when difficult decisions were required, he voted "present," and initiated the Rattner "study" to avoid a decision and delay the auto issue until public opinion died down. The Obama-Rattner task force study required five months, and cost the nation $60 billion for working capital to keep the companies going while the study was taking place. Eight months after the automakers requested a loan, Rattner made a decision and the decision was bankruptcy - not a bailout.

Chrysler and GM suffered through the Treasury meetings, Congressional Hearings, and the Obama-Rattner study in silence, since the government held all the cards. Three million workers associated with the auto industry waited patiently, but the Federal Government failed them.

Despite the 52-35 Senate vote against bailing out Chrysler and General Motors, and President Obama's refusal to allow a bailout, the government still takes credit for a bailout. Evidently, the Washington definition of bankruptcy is bailout. Unfortunately, the media has supported the bailout fallacy. President Obama used the auto bailout theme in his 2012 campaign for reelection, and he won a second term.

The dangerous situation is that the White House and Congress refuse to accept that legislation and executive orders created the housing boom that led to the Great Housing Recession of 2008. The recession caused a decrease in consumer spending, and vehicle sales declined 40%. This created the auto problem. The government caused the crisis, but as usual, blames business.

General Motors management did an outstanding job of running the business for 50 years. The firm overcame the chaos of Billy Durant's twenty-three acquisitions in a rwo-year period to become the largest automobile and truck producer in the entire world. Karl Benz invented the automobile with his *Motorwagen,* and the Daimler and Benz companies were the first to produce automobiles. However, General Motors was successful in outproducing the German carmakers, overcoming the Ford Model T, and taking over 50% of the U.S. market. Alfred Sloan's management controls enabled GM to survice the Great Depression without losing money during the entire depression, and the creation of the brand ladder by Sloan was a stroke of genius.

The failure to react to the market change to small cars in the late 1960s allowed the VW Beetle and other foreign imports to take an increasing share of the market. The focus on profit failed to include market share in the equation, and the failure to recognize the loss of volume in the annual budget process created a huge fixed cost problem.

The UAW pattern bargaining tactic allowed the union to win every contract negotiation, and resulted in excessive labor costs, but the contract requirements of the jobs bank and excessive job classifications were also backbreakers. The UAW did more than its share to cause the bankruptcy of GM. However, the real culprit was our friendly government with its affordable housing legislation that caused the 2008 recession.

The government bailed out Wall Street and banks with trillions immediately after the 2008 recession hit, and GM management assumed that politicians would bailout automotive. The $35 billion loan request by the auto companies was peanuts compared to the bailout funds given to financial institutions. However, management failed to recognize that the negative attitude of Washington politicians toward the auto industry would not allow a bailout. The result was bankruptcy.

The negativism was certainly evident during the 2008 Congressional Hearings, but GM management held out hope that bailout funds would be granted. This was a monmuntal mistake by General Motors management, and resulted in a government controlled bankruptcy, and a takeover by the Federal Government.

The government anti-business attitude was evident when the Treasury refused TARP funds in October 2008, and the Senate voted against a bailout in December 2008. Rick Wagoner was too cautious with his thinking that General Motors could not survive banksurptcy, and should have immediately filed for Chapter 11. The company could have avoided the five-month Obama-Rattner task force study, the government-controlled bankruptcy, and the government takeover.

The government bankruptcy court changed General Motors; GM was no longer a public corporation. The UAW was given 17.5% of the company while bondholders with $30 billion in secured bonds received ten cents on the dollar. General Motors became *Government Motors,* and the government-appointed management ran General Motors from June 2009 until December 2013, a total of four and a half years.

The entire government process in handling the automotive problem was a joke. Congress had created the recession with the government goal of affordable housing for minorities and low-income families. The recession had killed consumer spending resulting in a 40% decline in vehicle sales, and the automakers revenue dropped dramatically resulting in the loss of working capital – the firms could not pay their bills. Instead of helping one of the largest industries in the nation, the government voted against a bailout. The government gift of $14 trillion to the financial community, and the failure to bailout the nation's automobile business was inexcusable.

THREE

FORD

Ford Motor Company Headquarters Dearborn, Michigan

Henry Ford's influence in the auto business was without parallel. Even though he did not invent the automobile, the engine, or any components, he was the pioneer who put America on wheels. There were hundreds of individuals in the automobile business at the turn of the twentieth century, and Ford succeeded while the majority failed. Henry Ford's determination to provide a vehicle for the average person made him successful, wealthy, and one of the most famous people in the world. Ford's mistrust of banks and the government would be justified 115 years later when Wall Street banks and the government caused the 2008 recession.

Henry Ford was born on a farm in Greenfield Township, Michigan, near Detroit, on July 30, 1863. His father came from County Cork, Ireland and his mother was born in Michigan of Belgian immigrants, and was the youngest child in her family. Ford was the oldest of five, with two brothers, and two sisters.

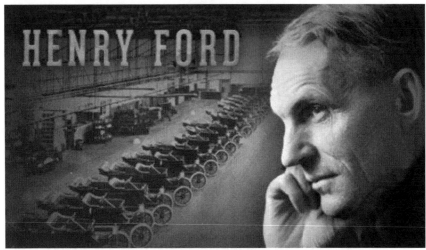

Henry Ford 1863-1947

He left home at age 16 to work as a machinist in a Detroit factory, and his next job was at Westinghouse working on steam engines. Henry Ford married Clara Brant in 1888, and turned to farming to support his new wife. He returned to his engineering career working for Detroit Edison as chief engineer in 1893 at age 30. His only son, Edsel, was born on November 6, 1893.

Karl Benz obtained the first automobile patent in 1886 in Germany, but there were no auto companies in America. Ford's experience as a machinist and an engineer at Edison, led him to start working with a small gasoline engine in his garage. After three years of tinkering with the engine, he mounted it on a platform in 1896, and began planning an auto company.

There were many individuals experimenting with vehicles in the 1890s. The Durea brothers, Charles and Frank, built their first car in 1893, and the vehicle is considered the first gas-engine car built in the nation. The Durea Motor Wagon Company was started in 1895 in Springfield, Massachusetts, and was the first American automobile company. The two brothers had a disagreement on who developed the Durea car, and went their separate ways at the turn of the century. The Dureas had the product, and the timing, to be one of the big auto producers, but gave it up due to a personal disagreement – unbelievable.

Henry Ford's wife Clara worked with her husband in their garage-labrotory, and on June 4, 1896, after almost three years of experiments, Henry Ford mounted his two-cylinder engine on a platform. The new Ford *vehicle* had four bicycle wheels, and he called it the Quadricycle. The Quadricycle was driven with a leather belt and chain, had two forward speeds, but no reverse or brakes. The gearing failed to work, and the speed was limited to 10 mph. The gear problem, lack of a chassis, brakes and reverse, indicated that considerable design work was required before a production vehicle was possible.

The Quadricycle has been publicized as Henry Ford's first car, but it was actually a prototype with a small engine mounted to a wood platform with four bicycle wheels, and looked nothing like an automobile. Amazing that some early books gave credit to Henry Ford for inventing the automobile with the Model T, since the Model T was not introduced until 1908. The Quadricycle was a prototype vehicle; Ford's first production car was the 1903 Model A that was produced in Henry Ford's third company, the Ford Motor Company. Ford's first two companies, the Detroit Automobile Company, and the Henry Ford Company, failed because he did not have an automobile design that was suitable for production. The Henry Ford Company was sold to Henry Leyland, and Leyland produced the first Cadillac in the plant, using Ford's inventory.

The Ford Quadricycle

However, Henry Ford was a salesman as well as an inventor; he was always able to sell his ideas to investors. The launch of a car company required engine knowledge, engineering ability to design a drive train, and assembly expertise to put a vehicle together. Henry Ford had the perseverance to accomplish the tasks, but a production vehicle was required before a car company could be successful. However, the sales ability to convince financial backers to support the company during start-up was also a requirement, and this was Henry Ford's strong suit.

The Quadricycle was too large for the doors of his labrortary-garage, and it was necessary for Ford to knock down part of a wall to get the vehicle outside in 1896. Despite the lack of brakes and proper gearing, he began testing the prototype Quadricycle on the streets in Detroit, but the engine failed on his first attempt.

Henry Ford was able to get three distinguished Detroiters to finance his first company. The Detroit Automobile Company was founded on August 5, 1899, with the Detroit Mayor William Maybery, Senator Thomas Palmer, and lumber baron William Murphy supplying the capital. However, Ford's new vehicle design was not complete, and no automobiles were produced. Under pressure from the financial backers, Ford developed a delivery van and shipped the product. The delivery truck was difficult to assemble, had quality problems, and failed to sell. Ford said later that the vehicle was "rushed into production," but the fact was that Henry Ford had not developed a production vehicle.

Because of the lack of a production product, the Detroit Automobile Company closed fourteen months later. The three financial backers lost $90,000 ($2.5 million today). Ford found new investors two years later, and started his second company, the Henry Ford Company, on November 20, 1901.

Historians have ignored that the first auto company founded by Henry Ford failed, that his second company also failed. The company closed after four months because Ford still had no product. He left the company with $900 ($25,000 today).

Henry Ford was a long way from being the prosperous father of the U.S. automobile industry, but his perseverance allowed him to continue the effort. Most would have given up after two business failures, but not Henry Ford. He continued with his plan to start an automobile company.

The price of the early automobiles was high, with some steam cars costing over $100,000 in today's dollars. Electric cars were popular in the early years, but cost nearly $60,000 in today's dollars. The automobile was a rich person's toy at first, but when the low-cost 1901 Curved Dash Oldsmobile, priced at $650 ($17,500 today), was introduced, the automobile became a mass-market product.

Car racing was a popular sport in the 1900s, and Henry Ford decided to get into racing to advertise the Ford automobile (which was still being designed). He won his first and only race on October 10, 1901. The race was held in Grosse Pointe, Michigan, and his opponent was Alexander Winton. Ford's racecar averaged 43.5 mph, and he won easily since Winton's engine failed. Edsel Ford II stated that the publicity of the race was the beginning of his grandfather's success.

The Detroit Automobile Company, Ford's first company, did not have a product, but it did have a catalog. The catalog presented a cost comparison of owning a horse versus an automobile. The analysis covered a five-year period and included the annual costs of food, shelter, and depreciation for the horse, versus annual maintenance costs for the car. The automobile was obviously the better choice according to the catalog.

The new Henry Ford Company was in business, but Henry Ford was still developing his vehicle, and did not have a product ready for production and shipment. The financial backers demanded that he ship something, but Ford refused to launch a vehicle until the design was complete. Six years after pushing the the Quadricycle out of his garage, Henry Ford still did not have a product design.

The financial backers decided to liquidate the Henry Ford Company, and hired Henry Leyland, an engine-company owner, to value the facilities. He reviewed the facility, tooling, and inventory, and recommended that the company be reorganized, rather than liquidated. The lumber baron, Murphy, and Leyland bought the Henry Ford Company. The new company was named Cadillac, and within four months began shipping vehicles. Leyland used Ford's in-process material, along with a new engine from his engine company, to make the first Cadillac. The Cadillac looked very similar to Henry Ford's Model A produced by his third company, the Ford Motor Company, the following year. In today's legal environment, Ford could have filed suit and would have probably won. However, there were not that many lawyers at that time.

Henry Ford's grit, perseverance, and sales ability allowed him to find another group of financial backers to start his third company, the Ford Motor Company, on June 16, 1903. The race with Winton had been highly publicized, and for the third time, Henry Ford was able to convince investors to finance a new company.

The eleven new shareholders invested $42,000 in cash ($1 million today), which evidently was not enough, because when the first car was shipped, Henry Ford only had $223.65 in his bank account. Malcomson had financed Ford in his earlier company, but did not put any cash into the new company. Henry Ford did not put money into the company either, and was given 25% of the stock for his technology. The investors made a wise decision, because each $1000 invested returned $2.5 million in 1919 when Henry Ford bought out every shareholder. Four of the eleven (Malcomson, Bennett, Fry, and Woodall), sold their shares to Ford in 1906 and 1907, and did not receive the big payoff in 1919. The seven who held their stock became millionaires. The new car business was a financial windfall for investors who put money into successful carmakers. The automotive pioneers also became wealthy, although David Buick died penniless.

Investors in Ford Motor Company

Investor	Shares
Henry Ford	255
Alexander Malcomson	255
John Gray	105
John Anderson	50
Horace Rackham	50
Charles Bennett	50
Vernon Fry	50
Albert Strelow	50
Horace Dodge	50
John Dodge	50
James Couzens	25
Charles Woodall	10
	1000

James Couzens was Malcomson's clerk, and was later Ford's controller. In 1916, Couzens had a disagreement with Henry Ford over Ford's pacifism during World War I, and he resigned from the company. He was later elected a United States Senator. Henry Ford owed the Dodge brothers, Horace and John, $7000 for parts supplied by the Dodges to Ford's prior company. They put in an additional $3000 cash for their 100 shares. The $10,000 would be $250,000 today, so the Dodge brothers were the largest investors in the Ford Motor Company.

Henry Ford had finally completed his production car, and shipped his first automobile, the Model A, in July 1903, barely a month after starting his third company, the Ford Motor Company. The Model A was an open-air two-passenger vehicle, with a two-cylinder, 100-cubic-inch engine mounted under the seat, and a planetary transmission. The steering wheel was on the right-hand side, and the Model A had no doors. Most early automobiles had right-side steering because the wagon drivers steered wagons form the right side. The first Ford car to have a left-hand side steering wheel was the 1908 Model T, and historians conclude that the change was made to allow passengers to enter from the sidewalk.

1903 Ford Model A

The Model A, like all internal-combustion engine vehicles at the time, required a hand-crank to start the engine. The driver had to pick up a hand crank, get out of the car, insert the crank into a hole in the engine, to start the car. The process was dangerous and sometimes time consuming. A hand-crank tool killed Byron Carter (1863-1908), founder of Cartercar, when the engine backfired, and the tool hit him in the face. The 1903 Oldsmobile had a side-crank mechanism that allowed the driver to start the car without getting out of the vehicle. The 1903 Ford Model A sold for $850 ($22,900 today, and cost $5400 more that the Olds in today's dollars.

Henry Ford's determination enabled him to survive two company failures and the disappointing launch of his first vehicle, the delivery truck. The Ford Motor Company was immediately profitable and paid a 10% dividend to the shareholders in November 1903, five months after the company was started. In 1904, Ford paid a 300% dividend, and produced three models in 1904, the B, C, and F.

It is hard to believe that only 210,000 vehicles were produced in 1904, when today's volume approaches 17 million, but the automobile was a new product, there was little advertisement or publicity, there were few paved roadways, and the price of the automobile was high

Henry Ford had finally developed an automobile suitable for production, and his company would grow to be the largest family-owned company in the world. However, similar to the situations in Karl Benz, Gottlieb Daimler, and Ransom Olds's companies, the financial backers demanded that the company produce luxury cars to maximize profits, and the founders wanted to build low-priced vehicles. Henry Ford was determined to build cars that the average person could afford, so he and Malcomson went their separate ways. Ford bought out Malcomson and became a 51% owner of Ford Motor Company in May 1906. Henry Ford was named president of the company.

By 1907, Ford was producing models K thru S, with the model K being a stylish two-seat roadster that was designed to look like a racecar. The Model K was priced at $2800 ($69,000 today), so in addition to low-priced cars, Ford offered luxury vehicles. The Model K was an impressive car with a "mother-in-law" seat but had no windshield or doors. The Model K could reach 60 mph, which must have been dangerous with the road conditions at that time. Ford produced 15,000 vehicles in 1907, 35% of the market, and the company opened sales offices in Paris, and Hamburg, Germany. Also in 1907, Ford started the "Ford and Son" tractor company to produce Fordson tractors. Henry Ford's only son, Edsel, had joined his father in the company right out of high school, but Henry Ford ran the business. The tractor business segment was borderline profitable, and Ford sold the segment to Fiat in 1993.

By 1908, Ford was using a rope and pulley process to pull the vehicles through assembly. Ransom Olds had developed a moving vehicle-assembly process by mounting the chassis on wheeled carts, and pushing the carts from assembly station to assembly station. Both methods were an improvement over the stationary vehicle-assembly process, and reduced the assembly time. Ford would later improve the assembly process by mounting the chassis on a moving conveyor.

The famous Model T was developed in 1908, and C. Harold Wills was the design executive for the Model T. Wills was trained as a toolmaker and had taken night courses in mechanical engineering. He joined Henry Ford's first company, the Detroit Automobile Company, in 1899, and remained with Ford through the early years. When Ford started the Ford Motor Company in 1903, Wills was too poor to buy stock, but Henry Ford gave him 10% of the company's first dividend out of his share. In addition to Wills' design work on the Model T, he also designed the removable cylinder head.

When Henry Ford bought out his shareholders in 1919, Wills thought he should be given some share of the company in payment for his work. Charles Sorensen, one of Ford's production managers, disliked Wills, and demanded that Wills be fired. Henry Ford gave Wills $1.5 million ($20 million today) in severance, and Wills left the company. Wills had been a key player in the design and development of vehicles over the years, and he would be missed.

Catalogs on the new Model T were sent to dealers in March 1908, showing the introduction date as October 1, 1908. The Model T was a four-passenger car that some called the "Tin Lizzie." A windshield and canvas top were extras. The top folded down, but hung over the rear of the car. A four cylinder, 22 hp engine enabled the vehicle to reach 45 mph. There were initially five models with prices starting at $825 for the Runabout ($21,150 today), that had a one-passenger back seat, but no doors. The four passenger Town Car was priced at $1000 ($25,600 today). The Model T was not a stylish vehicle, but it appealed to the public because of its simple function and price.

1908 Ford Model T

By May 1909, orders exceeded production capability, and Ford announced that no new orders would be taken for at least two months. Ford Motor Company produced nearly 18,000 Model T cars in 1909, and with the total industry volume of 124,000, Ford's market share was 14.5%. Manufacturing problems limited production and had an effect on the market share. Production doubled in 1910, and Ford's market share increased to 18%.

Billy Durant had started General Motors in 1908, and acquired 23 companies in two years. In 1909, Durant attempted to buy Ford Motor Company, but Henry Ford demanded $8 million in cash ($200 million today). Durant was unable to come up with a $2 million down payment and the $8 million in cash, and the deal fell through. Henry Ford was stubborn and refused to back down on the demand for $8 million in cash. He only had $223 to his name five years earlier, but he held out for the $8 million.

Ford bought the John R. Keim Company in 1911 for its steel stamping capabilities, and William S. Knudsen was a manager with Keim. Knudsen was an experienced executive and rose through the Ford ranks to be in charge of automobile assembly. He survived the in fighting in the Ford executive offices for 10 years, but he left in 1921, and joined General Motors. Knudsen was later named president of GM, and during World War II was a lieutenant general in the army. Knudsen's son, "Bunkie" Knudsen, was an executive vice president at General Motors, and left GM to become president of Ford in 1968. Henry Ford II fired Bunkie Knudsen sixteen months later.

Ford moved vehicle assembly to the new Albert Kahn designed Highland Park plant in 1911. The Highland Park plant was a multi-story facility where component parts were lowered onto the vehicle during assembly. In 1913, Ford changed the assembly process to a moving conveyor assembly line. The same basic process is still used today in assembly plants around the world. The new process reduced the vehicle assembly time from 12.5

hours to 1.5 hours, an amazing accomplishment that eliminated many bottlenecks in the assembly process. Annual production increased to over 200,000 vehicles by the end of 1913. Most of the Ford Model T models finally had doors in 1913.

In January 1914, Henry Ford doubled his workers' pay to $5 a day, and reduced the workweek from 50 hours to 40. This historic wage increase had never happened prior to 1914, and has never happened again. The hourly wage rate for the 40-hour workweek would be $14.30 per hour today, equal to the hourly rate for new hires. The wage increase was strictly Henry Ford's idea, and his controller did not agree with the increase. This wage increase was given without a union or any government legislation. The UAW was not formed until 1935, eleven years later, and the government was not involved. The $5-a-day wage reduced absenteeism, which had become a major problem.

The new, faster assembly process caused a paint problem. The only paint that would cure properly was "Japan" black. Other paints did not cure with the faster assembly time. Henry Ford fixed that problem by declaring that customers could have a Model T "in any color, so long as it's black." The paint problem was not solved until lacquer paint was developed in 1926, thirteen years later.

Station wagons were not in Ford's lineup, but the company did produce a "Depot Hack" vehicle for hauling passengers and baggage to and from train stations. The body was produced by an outside company, and included wood paneling that was a forerunner of the wood-paneled vehicles, including station wagons, of the late 1940s. Unfortunately, the wood panels were hand built, and replacement parts required hand construction.

By 1915, the Model T was so popular that Ford Motor Company had 56% of the U.S. market, and was the largest auto producer in the world. General Motors was still in disarray with Durant's acquisitions, and no yet a strong competitor.

Henry Ford was a pacifist during World War I, and he participated in a peace trip to Europe in an attempt to stop the war. The effort was unsuccessful and alienated many in the country. Ford was also anti-Semitic, and wrote anti-Jewish articles in his newspaper, the *Dearborn Independent.*

Edsel Ford had the talent and desire to be involved in styling, but his father would not allow his son to be active in the company. While Henry Ford was in Europe in 1913, Edsel built a stylish, prototype Model T. The Model T was a carryover vehicle for years with few styling revisions. When his father returned, he was angry that Edsel had made changes, and destroyed the car.

Ford was expanding, and by 1916, there were 28 assembly plants across the country, with William Knudsen managing the assembly operations. Henry Ford's name was on the first Republican ballot for president, and Ford ran for the U.S. Senate in 1918, but lost by 4337 votes. Henry Ford had come a long way in the 20 years since his Quadricycle. He was running the largest family-owned business in the world, had become wealthy, and had accomplished his dream of producing an automobile for the public. Ford had accumulated $60 million in cash ($1.36 billion today), and he wanted to use the cash to build all-new manufacturing facilities for the Model T. Unfortunately, Ford failed to read the tealeaves. The market was changing.

The Model T was still the number-one seller, but customers wanted more than the basic vehicle. General Motors had Cadillac, Buick, Oldsmobile, and Chevrolet brands, and was making inroads in the market. Ford Motor Company did not cover the entire market with the Model T.

The Ford stockholders objected to Ford using all the cash for expansion, and they demanded that dividends be issued. The Dodge brothers attended Edsel Ford's wedding reception on November 1, 1916, and celebrated with Henry Ford. The next day Henry Ford received the notice that the Dodges had filed a lawsuit against Ford to obtain dividends. The Dodge brothers still owned 10% of Ford Motor Company. The lawsuit went to the Michigan Supreme Court, and the court ruled in 1919 that a company was organized primarily to make a profit for stockholders, and that Henry Ford must declare an extra dividend of $19.3 million ($275 million today).

Henry Ford was livid at the court decision, resigned as president of the company, and threatened to start another company to force the shareholders to sell their stock. Edsel Ford was named president of Ford Motor Company on January 1, 1919, at age 26, and would remain president until his death in 1943 at age 49. The problem for Edsel was that he was president in name only, and everyone knew it. Edsel was more of a diplomat than his father was, and he convinced the stockholders to sell their shares.

In July 1919, Henry Ford was the sole owner of the Ford Motor Company. Sixteen years after going hat-in-hand to Alexander Malcomson to obtain funds to start his third company, and starting out with only 25.5% of the company, Henry Ford was the sole owner of the largest automobile company in the world. He was also a multi-millionaire.

World War I cut domestic auto production in half, and Ford's volume was reduced to slightly over 400,000 vehicles, but the company still held 46% in market share. In 1919, Ford finally introduced the electric starter as an option on the Model T, but it was seven years after General Motors had introduced the starter on the Cadillac in 1912. Henry Leyland of Cadillac had demanded that the Cadillac offer an electric starter after a close friend, Byron Carter, owner of Cartercar, was killed when the engine backfired, and the hand crank hit him in the jaw. He developed gangrene and died a short time later. It was surprising that Ford waited seven years to introduce the electric starter on the car, but was an indicator that Ford was slow to make changes to the Model T. The Model T remained the same basic vehicle until the mid-1920s.

In December 1919, the Federal Reserve started raising interest rates, and continued raising rates through June of 1920. The tight money policy caused the recession of 1920-1921. Unemployment went from 5.2% to 11.7%, GNP declined 6.9%, and automobile sales fell by 60%. Ford's volume was cut in half, and the market share was reduced to 22%, the lowest level in eight years.

Henry Ford's typical reaction to a sales problem was to cut prices, and the company drastically cut prices in 1920. Model T price cuts averaged $148 per model, but sales did not recover. The Highland Park plant was closed from Christmas 1920 until February 1, 1921, the first time this had ever happened. Wall Street experts were forecasting financial problems for the Ford Motor Company. Ford revenue was down due to the sales decrease, and was facing a cash shortage. Ford demanded that dealers pay for vehicles when received to save cash.

Henry Ford cut prices again in 1921, with the lowest-priced Runabout costing $440 ($5500 today), and the market responded. Ford's market share was again over 50%. More price cuts came in 1922 with the Touring Car priced as low at $298 ($3900 today). Ford was cutting prices every year to counter the sales drop caused by the 1920-1921 recession, but if Henry Ford could have read the tealeaves, the sales problem was not only the recession, but also stiffer competition. The Federal Reserve tight-money policy made financing an automobile difficult, which also hurt sales, since 73% of vehicle purchases were with credit. General Motors had formed GMAC as their credit arm and was able to provide credit for vehicle buyers. Henry Ford objected to credit purchases on moral grounds, which gave GM another advantage. Ford Motor Company did not start Ford Credit for financing vehicle purchases until 1959.

Henry Ford made a brilliant move with the purchase of the Lincoln Motor Company in 1922 from Henry Leyland. Leyland had founded Lincoln in 1917 after leaving General Motors following a dispute with Billy Durant. The company was named after Leyland's hero, Abraham Lincoln. The Lincoln brand was a luxury vehicle, but the firm became insolvent in 1922 due to the 1920-1921 recession.

Ford Motor Company was limited to the low end of the automobile market with the Model T, while General Motors covered the entire market with five brands. Ford needed a luxury brand to compete with Cadillac, and mid-market brands to compete with Buick, Oldsmobile, and Pontiac. Henry Ford was stubborn, and refused to accept that the Model T no longer served the entire market, but his son Edsel pushed for the purchase of Lincoln to compete with the Cadillac. Henry Ford agreed to the acquisition, but for an entirely different reason. Ford was still angry with Henry Leyland for "stealing" his design and tooling when he acquired The Henry Ford Company in 1902.

The Lincoln Motor Company had been started by Henry Leyland in 1917 to build the V-12 Liberty engine for the war effort. Leyland was president of Cadillac and had an order for 10,000 Liberty engines from the government. Billy Durant was a pacifist and refused to allow Leyland to build the engines. Leyland left General Motors, took his Liberty engine order, and started the Lincoln Motor Company. After the war, Leyland reorganized the company to build the Lincoln luxury automobile. The company was moderately successful, but the 1920-1921 government-caused recession resulted in a drop in auto sales, particularly luxury vehicles, and caused the company to go into receivership. The Lincoln facilities and tooling were valued at $16 million ($215 million today), and to pay Leyland back, Henry Ford low-balled his offer at $5 million ($67 million today), a difference of almost $150 million (today). Since Henry Ford was the only bidder for Lincoln, the court was forced to consider his offer, but demanded that Ford pay $8 million. Henry Ford was successful in sticking it to Leyland to the tune of nearly $100 million in today's dollars.

Henry Leyland's purchase of the Henry Ford Company had occurred because the company's financial backers wanted to liquidate the company since Henry Ford's new automobile was not ready for production. Leyland used Ford's in-process inventory and installed his Leyland Company engine to produce a new automobile named Cadillac. This was twenty years prior to Ford's purchase of Lincoln Motor Company, but Henry Ford had a memory like an elephant.

Ford's price cuts continued in 1923 and 1924, and the company managed to hold on to 50% of the market. The ten- millionth Model T was shipped in June 1924, and Henry Ford was looking forward to the new manufacturing facilities capable of additional Model T production. Prices were reduced again with the Runabout priced at $265 ($3550 today). A Ford worker could purchase a new Runabout with less than three months' pay. Henry Ford had accomplished his dream of providing an automobile that an average person could afford. Ford was able to maintain market share with continual price cuts, but the brand offerings by General Motors in all segments of the market were an increasing threat. The Model T was only available in black because of the paint problem, and GM offered customers most any color.

The paint-curing problem raises a question about the problem solving at Ford. That it took 13 years to make the paint problem go away is difficult to accept. The new lacquer paint corrected the problem in 1926, but Ford should have been able to fix the problem sooner. Other car companies were able to paint cars in color, and why Ford could not correct the process was a question that has never been answered, but it was probably due to Henry Ford's stubbornness.

Ford Motor Company got into the airplane business in 1925 by purchasing the Stout Airplane Company. The famous Ford Tri-Motor plane evolved from the Stout acquisition, and was known as the "Tin Goose" because of its corrugated metal construction.

Most planes at that time were of fabric construction. Transcontinental Air Transport, the forerunner of TWA, used the Ford Tri-Motor airplane. The Airplane Division was instrumental in building B-24 bombers during World War II, and Ford constructed an airport in Dearborn for testing the airplane. Henry Ford even built the first airport hotel, and the hotel is still operating as the Dearborn Inn.

Ford made several design changes to the Model T in 1925, but the vehicle remained basically the same. That was the last year open-air automobiles were produced, and electric starters were finally standard on the Model T.

Walter Chrysler, the former president of Buick, started the Chrysler Corporation in 1925, and Chrysler acquired the Dodge Motor Company in 1928. Ford, General Motors, and Chrysler, were the largest three auto companies in the nation, and became known as the Big Three.

Model T sales fell 75% in 1927 despite Ford's continual price reductions. The Model T had few styling changes, and Ford had not introduced the annual model change. General Motors offered a range of models in the brand ladder consisting of Chevrolet, Pontiac, Oldsmobile, Buick, and Cadillac, and was taking an increasing share of the market. GM had adopted the annual model change, and the styling of the General Motors automobiles was attractive to the customers. The Model T was becoming obsolete, and GM volume was increasing dramatically.

Henry Ford denied the report that the Model T was being replaced with a new model, and he refused to believe the market had changed. The annual sales of automobiles were approaching the four-million mark, and the new buyers were interested in more than the basic car that Ford offered with the Model T. Edsel Ford was president of the Ford Motor Company but his dad controlled the company. Edsel recognized the Model T market problems, and had started work on a new automobile design. The development work was done in secrecy because of Henry Ford's strong belief that the Model T was still suitable for the market. This was reminiscent of the situation in Karl Benz's company three decades earlier when the elder Benz refused to listen to his sons who wanted to change the design of the Benz cars when they were losing sales to the Daimlers. The difference between the Ford and Benz situations was that Karl Benz was hurt by his sons' actions, and retired to a consulting position in his company. However, Henry Ford remained in control of his company. His stubbornness enabled him to survive the trials in the early years, and survive two failures with his first attempts to start an automobile company, but his failure to adapt to the changing market was costly.

By 1927, the Model T was finished. Ford had produced 15.5 million Model T cars between 1908 and 1927, a record that would be broken by the Model T replacement, the Model A. Cartoons at the time pictured the Model T with wings, flying into heaven.

Henry Ford's stubbornness was to cost the company $250 million ($3.3 billion today). The company was closed completely for six months in 1927 to launch a new automobile, but the company did not have a new model ready for production. Edsel Ford's back-door design department had new styles in the works, but no prototypes had gone through engineering testing. The engineering development work for a new vehicle takes time, and if short cuts are permitted, disasters usually occur. Ford must have taken short cuts because the new Model A, which was a scaled-down Lincoln, and a stylish vehicle, had quality problems. Henry Ford's first vehicle, the delivery truck, had been rushed into production 25 years earlier and had quality problems. Customers were less discerning at that time, and despite the quality problems, the Model A was an immediate success.

The six-month Ford shutdown allowed General Motors to become the largest producer of automobiles in America, and Ford would never again regain that position. In 1926, Ford produced

1.4 million vehicles, 500,000 more than General Motors. In 1927, GM production was four times that of Ford at 1,445,148. However, the Model A increased Ford's volume to 1.5 million in 1929, and was only 11% behind General Motors. The Ford Model A was a great success story, but unfortunately, Edsel Ford received little credit.

1928 Ford Model A

Chrysler also increased volume when Ford shut down to launch the Model A. Chrysler would take over as the second largest producer of vehicles in 1937, and Ford would not move to the number two position until 1950. Henry Ford's refusal to adapt to market changes had cost his company dearly.

Henry Ford's decision to continue with the Model T despite every market indicator telling him to develop a new model vehicle was a disaster for his company. Unlike Alfred Sloan of GM who delegated authority and built an organization, Henry Ford continued to run the company like a dictator.

His plan was to add capacity for Model T production, but the market changed, and the Model A, not the Model T, would be the vehicle produced in the new Rouge manufacturing location. The new manufacturing facilities included steel, and glass plants, a tool-and-die plant, engine plant, stamping plant, and an assembly plant. The complex was the largest self-contained automobile operation in the world. The Rouge complex was near the Detroit and Rouge rivers, and raw materials for steel and glass came by boat. Ford even constructed a private railroad to move material and vehicles within the complex. The Rouge facilities are still in production today, although on a reduced scale. Ford no longer produces steel or glass.

General Motors had adopted the annual model change in their brands, but Ford stayed with the "running change" concept. The growth era of the automobile industry ended in 1929 with the onset of the Great Depression. The Federal Reserve raised interest rates in 1928, creating a tight-money situation, and causing the stock market crash on "Black Thursday," October 24, 1929. The Fed also failed to control the money supply, and this caused the Wall Street crash to continue. Stock prices dropped 70%, and vehicle sales fell 75% between 1929 and 1932.

The Great Depression era of 1929-1941 was the worst economic period in the history of the nation, and was caused by the government. The Federal Reserve was oblivious to the effects of its interest rate increase, and raised the rate again in 1936 to "increase its reserves", and caused the Great Depression to continue until World War II production finally ended the debacle.

Government politicians were at a loss as to how to fix the economy. Most government officials were attorneys, and attorneys simply do not know how to solve problems. Most legislators were educated and trained in the law, and in their law practice, they simply raised their rates when they ran into financial difficulty. When attorneys are elected into the government, they practice the same policy; raise taxes. During the Great Depression, income taxes were raised from 25% to 63% in 1932 and to 79% in 1936; the rate increase did nothing to help the depression.

Engineers are educated and trained to solve problems, and one of the techniques used is to determine "what changed" in problem analysis. If legislators had been trained as engineers, possibly they could have determined that "what changed" to cause the Great Depression was the Federal Reserve raising interest rates.

Ford's production fell to 540,000 in 1931, down from 1.25 million in 1928, a 56% decline, and the company was forced to lay off 75,000 employees. General Motors, with Alfred Sloan's leadership, reduced costs dramatically, and changed its marketing strategy to meet the changing conditions. Ford's fixed costs were extremely high because of the huge investment in the Rouge complex. Henry Ford had never installed a good financial system, and was unable to control costs.

The unemployment rate exceeded 30% in the Detroit area and people were suffering; soup lines and shantytowns were popping up all over the country. Democrats had been voted into office in 1932 and they began calling the shantytowns "Hooverville," in "honor" of Herbert Hoover, the Republican president in 1928.

The city of Detroit formed an unemployment council and started a hunger march on March 7, 1932, and 5000 people joined the march. Most were the unemployed, but many were paid rabble-rousers. The march ended at the Ford Rouge complex, and when police attempted to break up the riot, five people were killed.

In 1933, Ford finally adopted the annual model change. The Ford vehicle rear doors were changed to "suicide doors," with the doors opening into the wind. Also in 1933, the "rumble seat" was popular, and Ransom Olds introduced the first automatic transmission on his REO cars.

Henry Ford received some unwanted publicity in 1934 when gangsters John Dillinger and Clyde Barrow sent letters to Ford praising his Model A as a great getaway car. Henry Ford continued to spend money in spite of the Great Depression. The new Ford test track was constructed in Dearborn in 1935.

The UAW was formed in 1935, and immediately took steps to organize the car companies. In 1936, workers at GM plants began sitting down at their workstations and occupying the plants. The sit-down strikes were effective and stopped production. Within a few months, General Motors agreed to be represented by the union. Chrysler soon followed, but Ford held out until 1941.

The government had been unable to stem the Great Depression for six years and the economic debacle was not getting any better. President Roosevelt's New Deal had not fixed the crisis, and politicians were on the spot to take action. Unfortunately, the government had no solution for the depression, and the usual government step in that case was to find a scapegoat. The government blamed employers for the Great Depression.

The National Labor Relations Act (Wagner Act) was passed in 1935. The language of the Wagner Act blamed employers by stating: "the denial of employers of the right to organize a union…impairs the efficiency of the current economy." Under "Findings and Policies," the Wagner Act stated: "The inequality of bargaining power between employees, who do not possess full freedom of contract, and employers who are organized as a corporation tends to aggravate recurrent business depressions."

The National Labor Relations Act blamed employers for depressions, and recommended unions as the solution. Evidently, Congress failed to recognize that Henry Ford doubled his workers' pay and reduced the workweek to 40 hours.

Ford Motor Company agreed to UAW organization in 1941, the last of the Big Three to do so. The "Battle of the Overpass" in 1937, in which UAW organizers were beaten by Ford security, was a key element in Henry Ford's decision to allow a union. Ford believed that he had, and could, take care of his workers without a union. In addition to his wage increases, and shorter workweek, Henry Ford had loaned money to employees during the depression, and had given plots of land for farming.

The Great Depression continued, unemployment remained at 20%, and the UAW had promised workers a job if they would join the union. The stress of the sit-down strikes and the union-management difficulties were probably the cause of Henry Ford's stroke in 1938 at age 75.

Ford never had products in the mid-market segment but in 1938, Ford introduced the Mercury brand to compete with the GM Buick, Oldsmobile, and Pontiac brands. This was a stiff challenge, and the buying public considered Mercury as a higher-priced Ford with added features. The brand never made it, and many Mercury sales were a takeaway from the Ford model. The Mercury was dropped in 2010, and Ford continued to lack brands in the middle market secttio of the market. The problem continuies today.

Alfred Sloan had created separate divisions for each GM brand, and each division had its own engineering and styling groups that produced unique vehicles. Ford used one engineering and styling studio, resulting in the Ford and Mercury brands appearing similar in styling.

The depression continued and the government still had no solutions for the economy. By 1940, the war effort was beginning, and Ford started building aircraft engines in the Rouge plant. Chevrolet outsold Ford by almost 300,000 vehicles. Ford's Deluxe station wagon had wood side panels, and the rear "suicide" door hinges were eliminated.

The production for the war build-up reduced unemployment, and there was finally light at the end of the depression tunnel. In 1941, Chevrolet again outsold Ford by 300,000 vehicles, with Chevy selling one million vehicles, and Ford just under 700,000.

The Japanese bombed Pearl Harbor on December 7, 1941, and the country entered World War II. Ford stopped all commercial production shortly after Pearl Harbor and changed over to military production. Henry Ford was convinced he could assemble airplanes on an assembly basis similar to the automobile, and built the largest manufacturing plant in the world in Ypsilanti, Michigan, about 30 miles west of Detroit, for airplane assembly. An airfield was constructed next to the assembly plant for testing the completed planes. The Ford Aircraft Division was successful in the production of the B-24 bomber, and assembly reached one plane every hour (actually 55 minutes).

By 1943 Henry Ford was 80 years old, had suffered a stroke in 1938, and had heart problems and dementia, but he was still running the Ford Motor Company. Ford's experience with the UAW organizers led him to believe that he needed additional security, and he gave his security chief, Harry Bennett, a former boxer, additional authority. Edsel Ford attempted to limit Bennett's authority, but his father overruled him.

Edsel Ford died of stomach cancer on May 26, 1943, at age 49. Even though he was enormously wealthy, his father never gave him a chance to be his own person. His experiences in life, and in the Ford Motor Company, were always in the shadow of his father.

Edsel Ford 1893-1943

Even with numerous government military contracts, Ford was losing money. Harry Bennett, Ford's security chief, was running the company. The executives who objected to his Gestapo-style tactics, or had a disagreement with Bennett, were fired or quit the company. Henry Ford's longtime assembly chief, Charles Sorensen, left in March 1944, when the company needed him the most, but he and Bennett were at odds.

It was obvious to the government that the Ford Motor Company was out of control, and the War Department developed a plan to take control of the company if Henry Ford died. The Navy released Henry Ford II from active duty on July 26, 1943, two months after his father died, to permit him to join his grandfather in running the company. However, Harry Bennett was in complete control by that time, and Hank the Deuce had little or no authority. Henry Ford was almost unreachable, and Harry Bennett ran the company like a tyrant.

By 1945, Ford Motor Company was losing $10,000 a month, ($1.6 million annually today), and was in a total state of disorganization. Henry Ford II consulted with his mother and grandmother, and filled them in on the Harry Bennett problem. Clara and Eleanor Ford told Henry Ford that he should turn the company over to his grandson, and if he refused, they would sell their stock, which amounted to 50% of the company.

Henry Ford was shocked, and refused. However, he finally agreed because of his wife Clara, and retired after running Ford Motor Company for 42 years. His big problem was that he never accepted that the Model T was obsolete.

Henry Ford II took over as president on September 21, 1945, and his first act was the firing of Harry Bennett. Hank the Deuce had no experience in running a company, and he obviously needed help. He hired Ernest R. Breech, president of Bendix, as executive vice president. Just as Billy Durant had found Alfred Sloan, Henry Ford II found an outstanding executive with Ernest Brech.

Henry Ford II 1917-1987

Bendix was a $40 million company ($7 billion today) founded by Vincent Bendix in 1907 to build automobiles called the *Bendix Buggies.* The company closed in 1909. Bendix invented the starter drive in 1910, a gear that engaged the engine and made the electric starter work. The starter drive is used in all vehicles today, and oldtimers call the gear the *Bendix.* Bendix started the Bendix Brake Company in 1923 and the firm became the auto industry's largest brake producer.

Henry Ford II had no experience in any area of the business, and had a monumental task ahead of him to reorganize a company that had never been organized. The elder Henry Ford was brilliant in starting the company and developing the Model T, but his management style caused problems with people. His pricing of vehicles to allow the average person to buy a car was a stroke of genius, and he changed the automobile from a rich person's toy, to a middle-class necessity. Ford made mistakes along the way – with people, and with the failure to recognize the market changes.

Henry Ford could have avoided many mistakes by building an organization to function and handle details, but that was just not his personality. His refusal to develop a successor to the Model T was a tragic mistake that drove his company to the edge of bankruptcy. Henry Ford was a true pioneer in the automobile industry, but he was number one on "Fortune Magazine's" list of the worst auto CEOs in history.

Ford's hiring of Ernest Breech from Bendix was the smartest move that Hank the Duece ever made. Breech was an outstanding executive and had learned the Sloan management style, including strict financial management. He installed a financial system into Ford, where one had never existed. Breech turned the company around, but has never received proper credit for his efforts. However, "Automotive News" named Breech "The Napolean who saved the empire." Henry Ford II later forced Breech to retire so he could take over. Breech retired from Ford and assumed the CEO position of TWA.

Hank the Deuce also hired the Whiz Kids in 1946. The Whiz Kids were a group of ten U.S. Army Air Force veterans who had worked together in the department of statistical control under "Tex" Thornton. After the war, Thornton wrote to several corporations offering his services and demanding that all ten (including Thornton) be hired as a group. This was an unheard-of demand, but Henry Ford II needed help, so he hired the ten statistical experts. It was uncertain whether Ernest Breech agreed with the hiring of the Whiz Kids, but he probably did not. Thornton left Ford within two years because of a disagreement with Breech.

According to Lee Iacocca's biography, the group was originally named the "Quiz Kids" because of their habit of asking questions about how the business was run. The group objected to the name and started using the name "Whiz Kids," which stuck. All worked in finance or planning. None worked in the operations side of the business, which turned out to be their weakness. The Whiz Kids moved up in the organization, which is normal when the owner of the company hires you. Robert S. McNamara became president of Ford in 1960 and, shortly after, Secretary of Defense under President John F. Kennedy. J. Edward Lundy became chief financial officer, and Henry Ford II's right hand, Arjay Miller worked in finance and became president in the 1960s. Ben Mills became head of the Lincoln-Mercury Division, and Jack Reith was in charge of the Edsel. The Edsel was the debacle that cost Ford $450 million ($3.3 billion today).

The post-war era at Ford was difficult with a major reorganization, a changeover to commercial automobiles, and a new financial system. However, there was a pent-up demand for vehicles, and the auto companies could sell everything they could make. There were no new vehicles in the oven since the company had completely changed over to military development and production. Ford announced in March 1946 that there would be no new models until 1949. Even though Ford was selling everything they could produce, the company lost $8.1 million ($95 million today). Ford was disorganized and losing money. The firm was close to bankruptcy. Chrysler had taken second place in the market-share race in 1937, and continued to be second in sales until 1950. Ford Motor Company badly needed new models to gain market share, and the 1949 Ford styling was a hit with car buyers. By the June introduction date, the 1949 models were a success, and turned the company around. The new models generated profits of $177 million ($1.76 billion today) and saved Ford. Industry voume of 6.3 million units was an all-time high, and Ford reclaimed second place in the market.

Henry Ford died at home in Dearborn of a cerebral hemorrhage on April 7, 1947, at age 83. A public viewing was held, and 5000 people an hour passed his casket. Ford was buried in the Ford Cemetery in Detroit.

Ford's volume beat Chevrolet by 100,000 vehicles with a production volume of 1.1 million units, but quality was a problem. The fit between sheet metal parts was poor, and many cars had water leaks. Similar to the introduction of the Model A 20 years earlier, customers were less discerning since there was such pent-up demand; no new vehicles had been produced since before World War II. Ford made running changes to correct the quality problems.

The styling of the 1949 Ford vehicles outclassed the General Motors and Chrysler models, but total GM volume was 300,000 units higher than the Ford and Mercury brands. The changes between the 1949 Fords and the Model T, produced only twenty years earlier, were so dramatic that if you put the two vehicles side by side, you would think the Model T was from the Neanderthal era. The 1950 Ford models were carryover; the only sheet metal difference in 1950 was the addition of a cover over the gas cap. Total vehicle volume in 1950 remained at 6.3 million unis.

1949 Ford Convertible

Clara Ford died in September 1950 and was buried in the Ford Cemetery. Mrs. Ford should be credited with saving the Ford Motor Company because she forced Henry Ford to resign, and turn the company over to their grandson, Henry Ford II. If Harry Bennett had stayed in charge much longer, the company would have been taken over by the government to protect the wartime production. When Clara Ford threatened to sell her stock and leave her husband if he refused to retire, he retired, and Henry Ford II was finally able to take over, and fire Harry Bennett.

The 50th anniversary of Ford Motor Company was celebrated on the Ed Sullivan television show in June 1953. The Korean War truce was signed, and commercial vehicle production increased. In its golden anniversary year, Ford was selected to furnish the pace car for the Indianapolis 500 race and William Clay Ford Jr. was the driver of the Ford convertible pace car. The trend toward two car families had begun, and Ford's advertising focused on the two-car family vehicles. Ford was second in total volume; Chrysler had lost sales and market share after their 1949 UAW strike, and would continue to suffer financially with the loss of production volume.

In 1955, Ford launched the two-seat Thunderbird, which outsold the Chevrolet Corvette. Industry volume set another record with sales of 7.2 million vehicles. Ford's volume was 1.4 million units, 20% share of the market, and its profits of $437 million ($3.7 billion today) set an all-time high. It was a great year, but Chevrolet still outsold Ford by 250,000 units.

Ford Motor Company had a big year in 1956, with the company going public, the introduction of the Lincoln Continental Mark II, and the decision to launch the infamous "Edsel." When Ford went public on January 17, 1956, it was the largest IPO in history. The company sold 10.2 million shares, which yielded $660 million ($5.7 billion today). The Ford IPO was different from todays in that thousands of everyday people bought shares. Merrill Lynch indicated that the average number of shares sold by the firm to individuals was ten. It was reported that people stood in line outside stockbrokers' offices to buy Ford stock. This was before the Edsel and the Pinto, and the public was still enamored of Ford. The share price was $64.71, which would be $563 in today's dollars. The stock offering was structured so that the Ford family owned special Class B shares, which gave the family 40% voting rights. Today the Class B shares represent just two percent of the total shares, but the Ford family still controls 40% of the voting rights. Several large shareholders, such as pension funds, have contested the control of the company by the Ford family, but they have not been able to break the 40% control.

Ford offered 17 different models in the 1956 model year, and for the first time it brought out the four-door hardtop design. The Lincoln Continental Mark II was launched with a "Lifeguard" option that included seat belts and crash padding in the instrument panel. Unfortunately, the dog didn't eat the dog food, and few buyers bought the Lifeguard option. The government has complained for 50 years that the Big Three failed to provide safety features, but evidently the legislators did not do their homework.

The tail fin era of the late 1950s introduced automobiles with fins almost as high as the roof of the vehicles, but Ford's designs were less obtrusive. Fortunately, the fin designs were short lived.

The Whiz Kids developed the infamous Edsel after developing a market analysis that showed that the Ford Motor Company did not compete with General Motors in the mid-market range. Customers considered the Mercury a higher-priced Ford and the company needed a brand to compete with Buick. This situation had existed since the 1920s, so a "study" was not necessary.

The name Edsel was proposed, but Henry Ford II objected because he didn't want to see his father's name "rolling around the country on hubcaps." However, Ernie Breech approved the Edsel name. The decision may have been the last straw for Hank the Deuce, because Breech was forced to retire.

The Whiz Kids excelled at cost cutting, and this led to the use of common parts on the Edsel. Many Ford components, even sheet metal, used on the Edsel were common to the Ford and Mercury except for the "horsecollar" grille. The new Edsel Division caused a shake-up in the Ford organization, which had a negative effect on the company for years. The 1187 new dealers would make large investments in real estate and buildings, only to see their world fall apart two years later.

The Edsel was launched on "E-day," September 4, 1957, as a 1958 model. The advertising and promotion of the Edsel were the largest in Ford's history. Sales of the 1958 Edsel were 63,000 units, but many of the sales were a takeaway from other Ford brands. Sales in 1959 fell 25%, and only 3000 1960 model Edsels were sold. Ford Motor Company cancelled the Edsel on November 19, 1959, 26 months after "E-day."

Customers never accepted the Edsel, and many considered it "another Mercury." The Edsel was planned to compete with the mid-market General Motors' brands, but the price was squeezed between the Ford and Mercury brands, with an overlap in some models, and customers were confused about the Edsel position in the market. Robert McNamara, a future president of Ford and a Whiz Kid, was running the Ford Division at the time, and he convinced CFO Ed Lundy to slash the advertising budget for the Edsel. The market had changed and was trending toward small cars, and the Edsel was certainly not a small car. The styling was too similar to the Ford and Mercury brands because of the "common part" focus, and critics called the vehicle "homely." The Edsel made the "Worst Car" list.

The Edsel was a disaster that cost Ford $400 million, nearly $4 billion today. The Edsel missed the target in size, price, and styling, and the car was introduced during the 1957-1958 recession. Ford needed a new brand to compete with the GM mid-market bands, but pundits reported, "The wrong car at the wrong time."

1958 Edsel

The Ford Edsel project and the GM Saturn program had many similarities. Both were well intended from a market standpoint, but the execution was faulty. The creation of complete new and separate organizations and new dealers was unnecessary and costly. Neither vehicle hit the intended market segment.

While Ford was eliminating the new Edsel Division and reorganizing the company, which was a major task, the import threat became a reality. The VW Beetle started the import market penetration in the late 1950s, and by the 1960s, the Beetle had become a serious competitor. The U.S. car companies had been riding high in the post-war era but forgot to look in the rear-view mirror to see what was creeping up on them. Being able to sell practically anything they could make made Big Three management overconfident. The Beetle would exceed the Ford Model T's record 15.5 million-vehicle production record, and continued to be a factor in the U.S. market until 2003.

In an attempt to meet the small-car competition, Ford launched the 1960 Falcon. The initial Falcon sales were over 400,000 vehicles, but many of the sales were taken from the Ford brand, and were not incremental volume. The *Falcon* brand name originated in 1905 when Edsel Ford used the name for a new car he designed. The Falcon was produced between 1960 and 1970.

Robert S. McNamara, the Whiz Kid, was named president of Ford Motor Company on November 9, 1960, but he had the shortest term in the history of the company. President John F. Kennedy selected McNamara to be U.S. Secretary of Defense on January 21, 1961. He served until February 29, 1968, becoming the longest serving defense secretary in the nation's history. McNamara had little effect on Ford during his time as president. John Dykstra succeeded McNamara as president.

Lee Iacocca was named vice president of the Ford Division in 1960. He had a B.S. in industrial engineering from Lehigh University, and masters in mechanical engineering from Princeton. Iacocca started his career at Ford in engineering, but soon went into sales. He moved up rapidly and was credited with the "56 in 56" sales promotion, in which a customer could buy a Ford product with 20% down and pay $56 a month in 1956. Iacocca was given credit for the 1964-1/2 Mustang, although some Ford insiders claimed that the credit should have gone to others.

The Mustang was a highly successful "pony" car that built Iacocca's reputation. The Mustang was chosen as the Indianapolis pace car in 1964. It was changed to a two-seat model, was priced at $2368 ($17,300 today), and was selling well above the budgeted volume. The Thunderbird was decling and sold fewer than 10,000 units, despite a price of $4500 ($32,850 today). Industry sales set another record at 9.3 million vehicles, and Ford's market share was 23.6%.

Arjay Miller, another Whiz Kid, succeeded John Dykstra as president of Ford in 1963. Miller had spent his career in finance, and was a non-descript executive. Miller was replaced by Bunkie Knudson five years later.

Henry Ford II attempted to buy Ferrari in the early 1960s and was unsuccessful, but Ford entered the racing business. In 1965, Jim Clark won the Indianapolis 500 in a Lotus-Ford. In 1966, Ford outsold Chevrolet and produced 2.2 million vehicles. Ford endured a 68-day strike in 1967, and agreed to pay high- seniority workers during a layoff. The jobs-bank benefit gained by the UAW in the 1984 contract negotiations would expand the layoff benefit to all workers and become a huge cost problem for the Big Three.

In 1968, Henry Ford II brought in a new president to the company. On February 6, 1968, Bunkie Knudsen, son of the former Ford executive and executive vice president and board member of General Motors, joined Ford as president. Knudsen thought he was in line to be president of GM, but Ed Cole got the job. After being passed over for the GM presidency, he was easy pickings for Ford.

Knudsen was an experienced car guy with a strong resume of accomplishments at General Motors. The hiring of an outsider was a surprise to Ford executives, particularly to Lee Iacocca who thought he was in line for the job. Iacocca would do all in his power to discredit Knudsen.

When Knudsen joined Ford, he assumed that he could take the top job and the vice presidents would accept the move and support him; but Ford was different from General Motors. GM was a more stable organization with management executives backing up each position. Ford had less strength in management, and as a family-owned company, top executives would attempt to gain Hank the Duece's ear on issues, many times behind their immediate boss's back. Knudsen was blind to this situation since GM did not operate that way. Bunkie Knudsen should have brought executives with him to Ford who would protect his back.

Sixteen months after leaving a secure job at General Motors Bunkie Knudsen was fired. According to some Ford insiders, Iacocca met with Henry Ford II in 1969, and demanded that Ford fire Knudsen or he would leave, and take a number of key executives with him. For whatever reason, Ford fired Knudsen in September 1969.

Knudsen became CEO of White Motor Company, a heavy-truck manufacturer, and he turned the company around. He retired from White in 1980, still shocked at being fired from Ford Motor Company. Lee Iacocca was named president in 1970.

The Ford Pinto was introduced on September 11, 1970. The Pinto was a subcompact that was to compete with the Japanese imports and the VW Beetle. American Motors brought out the Gremlin, and GM launched the new Vega in the same period, all to compete with the subcompact imports. Evidently, Ford had learned a lesson when the Falcon failed to compete with the Beetle because of its size, six-cylinder engine, and six-passenger body style. The first Pinto was a two-door sedan with a four-cylinder engine and priced at $1850 ($10,800 today), which undercut the Vega, and the size was competitive with the Japanese imports.

The Pinto was a success for the first few years, but in 1977, the company was accused of faulty design when a number of vehicle fires were reported. The Pinto fuel tank was located behind the rear axle, and critics claimed this to be a design fault. A 1972 accident in California resulted in a lawsuit in which Ford was required to pay $2.5 million in compensatory damages and $3.5 million in punitive damages. In 1977, the National Highway Traffic Safety Administration (NHTSA) demanded that Ford recall the Pintos. Some engineering studies showed that the Pinto design was safe, and no different from many imports and American designs. However, the negative media publicity killed the Pinto and it made *Forbes* list of the "worst cars of all time" in 2004.

The 1973 OPEC oil crisis changed the U.S. automotive business. The gasoline shortage and steep rise in gas prices had a major effect in the marketplace. Customers began rushing to buy small, fuel-efficient cars and trucks. Shortly before the OPEC crisis, a customer had to wait 12 weeks for the delivery of a Lincoln Town Car. During the oil crisis, dealers could hardly sell the vehicle, and inventories of large cars increased at dealerships.

The OPEC crisis forever changed the U.S. car market. Small cars began to take an increasing share of the market in the late 1960s, but the oil crisis caused gasoline prices to double, and vehicle fuel economy became the driver for new car sales. The small foreign imports had better gas mileage than the large U.S. vehicles, and car buyers began to go to import vehicles. The small car market increased dramatically and eventually became over 40% of the total U.S. market.

The government should have immediately loosened the regulations on U.S. oil production to make the country independent of OPEC. The country had an excess of oil reserves, and could have handled the OPEC control of worldwide oil prices. However, bowing to the environmental lobby, legislators decided to give the responsibility for oil independence to the auto industry.

The 1975 Energy Conservation Act was the first government legislation on automobile fuel economy. Instead of doing their job and establishing a strong energy policy, the politicians picked an easy target, the automobile industry, to "conserve energy." The corporate average fuel economy (CAFÉ) standards were established, which set minimum fuel economy targets for the car companies. The first CAFE standard was 18 mpg by 1978 and 27.5 mpg by 1985. Since then the law has increased the fuel economy requirement to 54.5 mpg by 2025, three times the 1978 requirement. The fuel economy in vehicles had improved 114%, but the consumption of foreign oil increased from 35% to 52%, so the government action, as usual, failed its objective. Evidently, the politicians failed to recognize that the number of vehicles on the roads increases every year, and people were driving more miles every year.

The development of the SUV (Sport Utility Vehicle) has completely changed the vehicle market; the new vehicles currently hold 28% of the total vehicle market. Harold Sperlich, one of Iacocca's lieutenants, was vice president of product development at Ford, and some insiders gave Sperlich credit for the Mustang, instead of Iacocca. Sperlich developed a new vehicle based on a market research study, and presented the new product to Henry Ford II, and his CFO, Edward Lundy. The market research showed that women drivers preferred to sit high in the vehicle, and a sliding door would be great for getting kids in-and-out of the vehicle. The new vehicle was called the minivan, and would eventually replace the station wagon. Lundy said the company did not have the capital to launch the program, and Ford rejected the minivan. The rejection of the new minivan by the bean counters would turn out to be a mistake for Ford and a rescue for Chrysler. Ford fired Sperlich shortly after the meeting, and Sperlich joined Chrysler as vice president of product planning, and took his minivan ideas with him. In 1978, Lee Iacocca was fired by Hank the Deuce; Ford reported that "he just didn't like him". Iacocca joined Chrysler a few months later as president.

Henry Ford II, like his grandfather, fired people for no apparent reason. Sperlich was recognized as one of the top product planners in the industry. Lee Iacocca was selected by Ford to replace Knudsen, and was known as the father of the Mustang. Ford fired both for "personal reasons." Ernest Breech, Bunkie Knudsen, Arjay Miller, and Lee Iacocca were replaced by Hank the Deuce, and all were presidents of the company. Miller, Knudsen, and Iacocca left in a ten-year period. Iacocca would outperform Henry Ford II during his Chrysler tenure.

Phillip Caldwell followed Lee Iacocca as president of Ford Motor Company in 1978. Caldwell was a Harvard MBA, and joined Ford in 1953. He headed Philco, Truck Operations, and Ford International. Caldwell was a dour individual, and known to attend meetings with several notebooks of financial data. After reviewing mountains of data, he still had difficulty making a decision, and often would send executives back for more study. He was famous for not making decisions.

However, Hank the Deuce seemed to like him, because he made Caldwell CEO when he retired on October 1, 1979, and chairman, when Ford resigned that position. Caldwell retired in 1985.

Donald Petersen replaced Caldwell as president in 1980. Extremely smart, and an excellent manager of people, Petersen was a mechanical engineer with an MBA from Stanford. He started at Ford in 1949 and progressed up the management ladder. He became a group vice president, then president in 1980, and succeeded Caldwell as CEO when he retired in 1985. Peterson took over at a difficult time. Ford lost $1.5 billion in 1980, and Chevrolet sales were double that of Ford. The poor performance continued in 1981 with a loss of $1.1 billion, and production fell below one million units for the first time since 1958.

The new front-wheel-drive subcompact Escort was launched in 1981, but the Thunderbird no longer looked like a T-Bird, and sales declined to less than 90,000 units. Henry Ford II retired in the middle of the mess. Thunderbird sales fell below 50,000 in 1982, and auto experts were predicting the end for the T-Bird, but it was restyled, sales increased to over 120,000 units, and were nearly three times the 1982 volume. However, General Motors sales were double Ford's volume. The GM mid-market brands dominated the market and Buick volume was equal to the Ford brand. The Mercury sales were 50% of each of the GM mid-market brands, and failed to penetrate the market.

Harold "Red" Poling was named president of the company when Petersen moved up to the CEO position after Caldwell retired. Poling had taken over Ford North America operations in 1980, after serving as CEO of Ford of Europe. He was known as a cost cutter and reduced Ford's costs $2.5 billion by 1982. Even though Poling was from finance, he was also a businessman. Poling approved a $3 billion product program in the middle of the 1980-1982 recession, launching the Ford Taurus brand that became the best-selling car in America. Along with Petersen, Poling led

Ford to record profits of $2.9 billion in 1984. Poling was also a believer in product quality, and he directed Bill Scollard, the vice president of manufacturing, to benchmark competitors in quality. Scollard visited Toyota and other manufacturers and changed quality efforts in Ford. Another key Ford executive, Jim Bakken, was appointed vice president of quality, and brought in Edwards Deming, the quality guru, to improve Ford's quality.

In addition to being an outstanding executive, Poling was a 7-handicap golfer, which meant he would normally shoot in the 70s. He belonged to Washtenaw Country Club in Ypsilanti, Michigan for several years, and later joined Bloomfield Hills. Poling was in Europe for several years, first as vice president of finance, then president, and finally CEO of Ford of Europe. Red was a serious golfer and rarely spoke on the golf course. He would address the ball, take one practice swing, hit the ball, pick up his tee, and start walking down the fairway, without saying a word to anyone in the foursome. His partner would then drive the cart.

Red Poling assumed the CEO position when the Ford family forced Don Petersen out of the company in 1990. Poling retired at age 69 in 1994, after spending 43 years at Ford. Ford gained 4.3% in market share during his time as president and CEO, and posted a $2.5 billion profit in his final year. Profit and market share are the two key elements of a CEO's report card, so Red Poling did an outstanding job. Harold Authur Poling died at age 86 in Pacific Grove, California, on May 12, 2012.

The UAW negotiated the infamous jobs bank in the 1984 contract negotiations, which paid laid-off worker 95% of their pay and 100% of their benefits while on layoff, and moved direct labor from variable cost to fixed cost. Even if plants were closed due to excess capacity, the company was required to continue to pay the labor costs. This change had a major effect on how management ran the business. Ford was affected less than General Motors because of size and the number of UAW workers, but the jobs bank was a factor in all manufacturing decisions, such as, where to assemble vehicles. The UAW jobs bank benefit eventually cost the Big Three over a billion a year.

Henry Ford II died of pneumonia on September 29, 1987, at Henry Ford Hospital in Detroit. He was 70 and had been having heart problems for several years. Ford was president of the Ford Motor company from 1945 – 1960, CEO for nineteen years, and chairman for a short time after that. He ran the company for nearly 35 years, not quite as long as his grandfather, who ran the business for 42 years. Hank the Deuce was married three times and was reported to be quite a playboy. On one occasion, the police in San Diego stopped him for drunk driving, and Kathleen DuRoss, who later became his third wife, was in the car. The episode received considerable media attention, particularly after he was quoted as saying, "never explain, and never complain."

At the annual SAE (Society of Automotive Engineers) dinner at Cobo Hall in Detroit, he received a standing ovation when his name was announced. It was interesting because the protocol for the introductions was for the audience to hold their applause until all executives were introduced. The annual dinner was a must for automobile executives. The CEOs of the Big Three were there, along with executives from car companies and supplier companies, all dressed in formal attire. There were four long tables, one against each wall, and the CEOs of the Big Three were seated in the middle of three tables, with the center seat of the fourth occupied normally by a local politician, or sometimes by the CEO of a foreign company. CEOs of supplier companies, or vice presidents of the car companies – a very distinguished group, took the remaining seats.

As the announcer began introducing each executive, moving down each row, the audience remained silent until Hank the Deuce was introduced. The attendees began to stand up and applaud, and before long, the entire audience was giving Henry Ford II a standing ovation. It might not have been the right thing to do, but it was humorous. The event received considerable publicity in the Detroit area.

Henry Ford and his grandson ran the Ford Motor Company from its inception in 1903 until 1980 – 77 years, an amazing accomplishment, which will never be seen again. They were successful in keeping the company going, but both had people problems. Henry Ford was dictatorial, and forced several key people out of the company. His big error was refusing to accept that the Model T was obsolete. Henry Ford II, although not dictatorial, made sudden, often angry, personnel decisions, and fired people like Knudsen, Sperlich, and Iacocca. He also forced Ernest Breech and Arjay Miller to retire. The cancellation of the new minivan product was one of his major errors. The Chrysler minivan has been the number-one seller since Ford fired Sperlich and Iacocca, and they took the minivan concept to Chrysler. Ford could have launched the new product, instead of Chrysler, if Hank the Deuce had shown his leadership and overruled the bean counters.

After the death of Henry Ford II in 1987, there was no Ford family member at the top of Ford Motor Company. The Ford family demanded that William Clay Ford Jr. and Edsel Ford II be appointed to the board of directors. Don Petersen did not think either was qualified to be on the board, and objected to the family recommendation. Since the Ford family ran the company, Petersen was out. He was named a "Most Valuable Person" by "USA Today" in 1988, "CEO of the Year" in 1989 by "Chief Executive Magazine," and "CEO of the Year" by "Motor Trend." These awards, and his outstanding performance with record profits, carried little weight with the Ford family. Red Poling took over as CEO in 1990. Peterson was treated better than Iacocca. He was given a nice office in a Ford office building near World headquarters, along with an executive assistant. Iacocca was given a much smaller office away from world headquarters after being fired, and was completely ignored by the company. Peterson was elected to the boards of Boeing, Dow-Jones, and Hewlett-Packard after leaving Ford.

The Ford family had again interfered in the company and this continued the Ford people problem. Edsel Ford II was executive head of corporate marketing, and William Clay Ford Jr. was responsible for business strategy for the Ford automotive group, but neither had ever been a key part of management.

Ford had excellent quality procedures, and a warranty system that included a monthly warranty report that included data on vehicle repairs and cost of each repair at Ford dealers. This warranty report was reviewed monthly at the vice president level. The warranty data included one-month-in-service repair data for each component in the vehicle, and the repair data was reported throughout the 12 months of the model year – amazing detail. Each division general manager reviewed the warranty report monthly with his plant managers and engineers. There is probably no other business in the world with better quality data. However, the key to quality is management, and Ford's performance metrics for management were all financial. There were no quality objectives in bonus metrics. Ford announced in 2014 that employee performance measurements would include quality, which was a step in the right direction. GM did the same.

The buying public has grown to expect superior quality in all products from smart phones to automobiles. It is no longer acceptable to expect car buyers to install plastic seat covers over seats, or repair small defects. Seats must last without cracks or stains for the life of the vehicle. There are some exceptions such as the kitchen sink supplier that advertised a lifetime "drip-free" faucet that had design flaws that not only made the faucet drip, but leak continuously. When customers called to complain, the company sent a new manifold with design corrections for the customer to install. There were no recalls, bad publicity, or even repairs made by the company as would have been required of the car companies. Automobile buyers now expect a quality vehicle and complain if any of the vehicle's 30,000 parts fail.

Car companies consider quality and reliability extremely important, but fail to manage their businesses accordingly. However, mistakes occur. The 2014 General Motors recall of 29 million vehicles for quality problems is a good example of mistakes. With the Federal Government running GM when many of the vehicles involved in the recalls were produced, the poor quality vehicles were shipped to customers, and in some cases caused fatalities. The government appointed CEOs and consultants completely missed the quality problems. The government is now holding Congressional Hearings on the recalls, and threatening GM executives with criminal charges. However, it is doubtful if any former government CEOs, or government appointed executives will be called before Congress to testify.

The Japanese vehicles have gained an outstanding quality reputation, but even the Japanese have quality problems, with the 2013 Toyota accelerator recall being a classic. Customer complaints, and in some cases fatalities, brought the accelerator problem to Toyota's attention. Toyota management delays and refusal to recall vehicles caused even more fatalities. Toyota finally recalled the vehicles after years of denial.

Customers and dealers report the problems, and it is up to management to act on the problems. Quality recalls are costly; the cost of postage alone can cost millions of dollars, and this does not include the cost of fixing the problem or the loss of customer loyalty. However, management has the responsibility to act immediately when safety issues are involved. The focus on profits was the prime objective of Big Three management, and quality was never included in performance objectives.

Unfortunately, Big Three management considered quality to be the responsibility of the quality departments, which was precisely wrong. Quality engineers do not design, test, or manufacture the products; they only sort the good ones from the bad ones. The quality department's responsibilities are comparable to that of the finance department; both measure performance, but are not responsible for performance. Nobody blames the controller for losses, but they surely blame the quality department for quality problems.

This was the situation at Ford for many years. Ford management now claims to have corrected this problem, but it is difficult to change old habits, so it remains to be seen if the change in management attention to quality is permanent.

Vehicle quality and reliability depend entirely on management. A company can have the best quality system and procedures in the world, but management must be totally dedicated to supporting the quality effort. The lack of total support by Big Three management is the reason that the companies are perceived by customers to be second to the Japanese in quality. The ultimate test for a plant manager is to make a decision to stop production when quality problems are found. All performance metrics are based on production counts. If a plant manager stops production for quality problems, it could mean his job because the entire company could be affected. In prior years, the decision would be to continue production, and have the quality department sort for defects. Inspection and sorting are never 100% effective, and result in defects being shipped to customers. This practice was in effect for years, resulting in quality problems and recalls that gave the car companies a bad reputation in quality.

Ford, General Motors, and Chrysler management denied for years that they had quality problems until companies outside the industry, such as J.D. Power, started reporting quality comparisons of automobiles. The Japanese cars were far superior to the Big

Three vehicles in the J.D. Power reports, and management was forced to back down on their denials. Reports show improvement for the Big Three in quality, but it will take continuous quality improvement to regain customer perception of quality products.

Alex Trotman succeeded Poling as CEO, and he served in that position until he retired in December 1998. Trotman was a career Ford executive, starting in purchasing in Ford of Britain in 1955. He moved to Ford North America in 1969 and worked in product planning. Trotman was made vice president of truck operations in 1979, was CEO of Ford of Europe in 1988, and executive vice president of Ford North America by 1989. Trotman was a capable executive with experience in Europe as president and CEO of Ford of Europe, in Asia, as president of Ford Asia-Pacific, and he had run Ford's North American operations. However, he ran into the same problem that Don Petersen had experienced – the Ford family. After Henry Ford II died, and his younger brother, William Clay Ford retired as vice chairman, there was no Ford family member in the executive level of Ford Motor Company, and the Ford family was determined to have a family member running the business. The Ford family recommended to the board that William Clay Ford Jr. be appointed chairman. In September 1998, the board elected 41-year-old Bill Ford chairman of the board, and he took office January 1, 1999. Bill Ford is the great-grandson of Henry Ford.

Even though Alex Trotman was not due to retire for over a year, the board appointed Jacques Nasser CEO. Bill Ford had pulled off a "palace coup," and the Ford family had done it again. Alex Trotman's final year resulted in record profits of $6.9 billion, which paid employees a record profit sharing check of $6000. Not bad for a CEO who was kicked out of the company. After spending 43 years at Ford Motor Company, Trotman congratulated Bill Ford with the sharp comment, "Prince William, your kingdom awaits you."

Bill Ford had joined the company in 1979 in product development, and later attended the MIT Sloan School of Management, graduating in 1984. He served in several positions, few of which were in the operations side of the business. He was managing director of Ford of Switzerland for a short time. The only time anyone had heard of Ford of Switzerland was when someone asked about Bill Ford's prior experience.

Jacques Nasser was a Lebanese born Australian known as "Jac the Knife" for his cost cutting with suppliers. Nasser had his own plans for the Ford Motor Company, and Bill Ford went along with major changes to the organization, which included changing the culture of the company from automobile production to a diversified corporation. Nasser acquired several companies like a chain of repair shops, and a junkyard business to recycle vehicles. His personnel moves were even more severe, changing the long accepted method of salary performance reviews and the rating system for employees. He changed people down to the manager level, and brought in consultants to teach employees to think like business people rather than automotive people. Bill Ford was focusing on long-term strategy and environmental issues, and allowed Nasser to take control of the Ford Motor Company.

In 1999, Ford acquired Volvo, the Swedish auto manufacturer, for $6.45 billion, and created the Premier Auto Group, which included Lincoln, Volvo, and Aston-Martin. Ford also purchased Land Rover from BMW. The company created Visteon as an independent organization for the plants supplying automotive components. The Electrical and Electronics, Plastics, Fuel Systems, and Climate Control divisions were separated from the parent company, and called Visteon.

The Firestone tire disaster of 2000 caused a split between Bill Ford and Nasser. Henry Ford and Harvey Firestone were close friends, and Firestone had been the primary tire supplier to Ford Motor Company for almost a hundred years. Bridgestone, the

Japanese tire company, had acquired Firestone in 1988, but the family ties between the Fords and Firestones were still strong. Harvey Firestone Jr. was Bill Ford's grandfather on his mother's side.

The tire problem was caused by the edges of the steel-belted radial tires breaking down, which resulted in the rollovers of the Ford SUVs. The tire treads would separate at high speeds, and there were over 100 deaths attributed to the tire problem. Nasser blamed Firestone for the problem, and Firestone blamed Ford. Congress called for Congressional Hearings, and both Ford and Firestone were criticized for the problem. Ford's recall of 20 million vehicles for the tire problem cost the company $3 billion.

Ford not only lost money, the company's quality reputation fell dramatically. In addition to the tire problem, the new subcompact car, the Focus, was recalled six times in the first year of production, and the Ford Escape was recalled five times. Another tire problem resulted from Ford UAW workers in the Louisville, Kentucky assembly plant slashing tires on the Explorer SUV, which caused another recall. The J.D. Power annual quality report rated Ford Motor Company last in quality. Nasser's regime was falling apart.

On October 30, 2001, Bill Ford fired Nasser, and assumed the role of CEO. Jac Nasser made "Fortune Magazine's" list of the "worst ever auto chiefs." Bill Ford and Nasser's first three years were a disaster, going from record profits under Alex Trotman, to a disorganized, mismanaged company losing money, with serious quality problems, and little or no experience at the top of the company. Ford lost $5.5 billion in 2001, $1 billion in 2002, and the market share was dropping. By 2003, the market share had dropped to 19.1%, down from nearly 25% in Red Poling's final year. This six-percent decrease in market share was an utter disaster, causing billions in lost profit, and would be almost impossible to regain. Bill Ford had copied Roger Smith's failure mode.

The Bill Ford era had turned out to be a disaster, going from record profits to record losses, and going from quality improvement under Red Poling, to last place in the J.D. Power annual quality ratings. Ford acquired Saab and Land Rover, which were later sold at a huge loss. The culture change from its core automotive business, to a diversified business approach, caused employees to focus on outside interests, and the stringent performance review system created serious morale problems. As they say, other than that, everything was OK.

By 2006, the market share had declined to 18.5%, and Ford posted the largest loss in the history of the company, $12.6 billion. Ford's corporate bonds were rated as "junk" for the first time in history. During Bill Ford's eight years as chairman, he had accomplished several firsts, but they were all bad. The firsts were; first time to recall 20 million vehicles in a single year for quality problems; first time Ford's bonds were rated as junk; first time to lose market share every year, and first time to lose $12.6 billion. The performance was less than stellar, but Bill Ford remains as the top Ford family member at Ford Motor Company. Prince William still runs the kingdom.

Nicholas "Nick" Scheele of Ford of Europe was named president of Ford following Nasser's ouster and remained in the position until 2004. Jim Padilla, former president of Ford's North and South American operations, followed Scheele, and retired at age 59 in 2006. Padilla was an experienced manufacturing executive, and Ford had few VPs with any operating experience. Bill Ford needed Jim Padilla, but he was unaware of the need because of his inexperience in operations. Bill Ford created an executive committee to run the company. With an executive committee running the business, there was no leadership in the firm, with each member of the "committee" doing his own thing. A committee has been defined as a group that "keeps minutes, but wastes hours."

With the market share loss, Ford's volume had dropped below their break-even point, and the company was in deep trouble. Vehicle production was cut by 20% for the fourth quarter. Don Leclair, the chief financial officer, had prepared a bankruptcy plan, but Bill Ford refused to accept that bankruptcy was possible. The board of directors finally went into action, and demanded that Bill Ford prepare for bankruptcy.

Ford Motor Company had been close to bankruptcy in 1945 when Henry Ford was in his final years, and Ernest Breech, an outsider and former General Motors executive, had turned the company around. Possibly another outsider was required to turn the company around again.

The Ford family, who had caused the problem, was upset since the Ford share price had gone from $16 a share in 1998, when they demanded that Bill Ford take over the company, to less than $7. They were obviously concerned by the loss of market share and the record losses, but the drop in the share price hit each Ford family member in the pocketbook. In a family meeting, some family members declared that they were considering selling their shares, and both Bill and Edsel Ford pleaded with the others not to sell. The family had hired an outside consulting firm to advise them on alternatives, but Bill Ford was able to quiet the meeting by declaring that he would step down, and start a search for a new CEO. Since it was necessary for Ford to search outside for a new CEO, it was obvious that the company had not done its job in developing people. The problem was the Ford family interference in demanding that family members be selected for top management jobs, and because of this, the infighting between executives continued. Ford's best years had been when Petersen, Poling, and Trotman were running the company, but the Ford family had forced both Petersen and Trotman out of the company. The other executives could read the tealeaves, and continued to attach themselves to Edsel and Bill Ford in an attempt to be next in line.

William Clay Ford Jr.

The search for a new CEO was started, and Joe Laymon, Ford's vice president of human resources, called Carlos Ghosn, CEO of Nissan and Renault, who would have been an excellent choice. Ghosn and was an experienced CEO, but he refused to listen to the offer because of the Ford family control. Dieter Zetsche of Daimler Benz also turned Ford down.

While Ford searched for a new CEO, its executive team was in disarray. Mark Fields, president of Ford North America, and Don Leclair, the CFO, were at each other's throats on a daily basis, and Ford executives did not know who was running the company.

Alan Mulally, a Boeing aircraft executive, was suggested as a possible candidate. Mulally had turned around Boeing's commercial airplane business and was recognized to be an outstanding executive. One problem faced by the search committee was what to do with Bill Ford. The new CEO would demand to be in charge, and would object to having Bill Ford and the Ford family looking over his or her shoulder. Two cooks in the kitchen at Ford would be a problem.

Mulally had heard of the Ford family problem, and that Ghosn and Zetsche had refused to be interviewed because of the family influence. When Mulally asked Bill Ford about the family interference, Ford committed that Mulally would be the boss. Bill Ford offered the CEO position to Mulally and he accepted.

When Mulally met with the CEO of Boeing to tell him he was leaving, the discussion turned Mulally around and he decided to remain with Boeing. He then told Laymon that he had changed his mind, and both he and Bill Ford were shocked. Laymon flew to Seattle determined to stay as long as necessary to convince Mulally to join Ford. After long talks, Mulally agreed to Ford's offer, and on September 1, 2006, he accepted the CEO position. Bill Ford would remain chairman of the board, but Mulally would run the Ford Motor Company as CEO. The "outsider" had a big job ahead, and the executive committee had been working directly for Bill Ford, and would probably have a problem with an outsider.

Alan Mulally

Don Leclair had been working on Ford's cash shortages for months, and recommended that Ford Motor Company borrow over $20 billion to provide working capital to finance the restructuring of the company. For the first time in history, Ford mortgaged every asset, including the Blue Oval, and borrowed $23.6 billion. The loan allowed Ford to handle the immediate cash problem, and provided sufficient working capital to live through the government caused housing recession of 2008 that was just around the corner. Don Leclair did an outstanding job in steering Ford Motor Company thru the losses of 2006, and did an even better job in executing the $23.6 billion loan. It was unfortunate that Leclair was not able to patch up the problem with Mark Fields. Mulally had to pick between the two executives and Fields won out.

Donald Leclair was the forgotten man in the Ford restructure, but deserved credit for recognizing the financial disaster early and recommending the bank loans. If Ford had not borrowed the cash the company would have certainly gone into bankruptcy during the 2008 recession, and the stock price would have fallen to the junk level. A key point that has received no media coverage was that the Ford family would have lost their control of the company if Ford had gone into bankruptcy court. Don Leclair actually saved the company for the Ford family but they failed to recognize and appreciate his role in saving the firm.

Mulally took over the reins at Ford and found a company in complete disarray. The company was much like the Titanic situation that existed at Ford in 1945, when Henry Ford II took over the company from the elder Henry Ford. In both cases, it was necessary to go outside the company to recruit a new executive to run the company. In 1946, Ernest Breech was brought in to run the business, and 60 years later, Alan Mulally was brought in as CEO to rescue Ford Motor Company. Henry Ford had driven the company into near bankruptcy, and William Clay Ford Jr. had done the same.

Mulally's first task was to convince the Ford vice presidents that he was the boss. Most of the executives sized up Mulally as a cheerleader, and not tough enough to fix Ford. Evidently, they thought that if Bill Ford, who had his name on the building, couldn't fix it, an airplane guy certainly couldn't.

Mulally's first change was to hold weekly management meetings with all key executives to review their part of the business, and to develop a plan to solve any problems they had. These meetings have been well publicized by the media, and based on how the Ford Motor Company had been managed in the past, it was not surprising that the executives were not happy with Mulally's meetings. They were not used to the CEO being involved in the day-to-day business dealings in their organizations, and some went behind Mulally's back to complain to Bill Ford. This move was normal in a family-owned business, because most of the top people were always trying to gain favor with the owner of the company. However, Bill Ford kept his commitment to Mulally and supported him.

After Henry Ford retired, the CEO had never been involved in the day-to-day problems of the company, and vice presidents normally did not hold weekly meetings with their division managers. The management system involved quarterly business review meetings with executive vice presidents and their general managers. The division general managers held monthly meetings with their direct reports, and plant managers held weekly meetings with plant people. The president and CEO of the company were not involved in the weekly, monthly, or quarterly meetings. The Mulally approach to running the business was a big change.

In the automobile business, there are new model changes every year. New vehicles are introduced in some years, but even when there are no major model changes, there are still styling changes every year. Front and rear lamps and grilles change, and interior components also change. For every change, there is a job one date. The Ford commercials that mention job one are often misunderstood, and the public does not understand that *job one* is the date that the vehicle is fully tested and ready for shipment. The job one date at Ford was sacred, set in stone, and nobody missed a job one date if they wanted to keep their job. If you can envision each division and manufacturing plant in the company making independent decisions on the job one date, you can imagine the program timing required to launch a vehicle. If a component division were to miss its job one date, the probability was the vehicle introduction would be delayed. The launch of products is reviewed daily in management meetings throughout the company to assure that the job one date is met.

    The emphasis of meeting the job one date led management to close one eye to problems and ship the products to meet the job one date. The problems could be late engineering changes due to test failures, supplier problems, quality problems, machine, or tooling problems. The timing is all-important to coordinate the launch of new vehicles, but the emphasis on meeting the job one date sometimes-allowed quality problems to be shipped to customers.

    Prior to Mulally's weekly meetings the job one date was never missed; problems would not be reported, because the messenger would be shot. Mulally required that problems be reported and solutions developed before products were shipped. Finally, the job one barrier to sensible decisions was broken. Ford management would have never made this change

    Always meeting the sacred job one date without developing solutions allowed problems to be shipped to customers just to meet the date. The problems that were overlooked led to customer dissatisfaction and costly recalls. Mulally was an executive who demanded quality products, and even though he was an *outsider,* his decision to ship only fully tested products was a major change in the corporation.

Mulally's weekly meetings and his hands-on, day-to-day management style completely changed the way the Ford Motor Company was managed. He changed the company from one that was close to bankruptcy, into the best-managed company of the Big Three. Both Chrysler and General Motors were going through organizational changes and were close to bankruptcy. Mulally changed the culture of Ford, but his management style of teamwork was a problem for some executives. The culture change was difficult for the executive committee and many others in the corporation. Mulally found it necessary to get rid of some top-level executives who preferred the old system, and could not adapt to Mulally's team methods. These causalities are often necessary when a new CEO is brought in, and people have different agendas. Ford Motor Company is still managed by the Ford family.

While Alan Mulally was completely changing the way Ford Motor Company was managed, and the results were showing progress, the Ford family was upset. The dividend reduction had hit them in the pocketbook, and some family members were even thinking of selling their stock. Bill Ford was not doing the job of communicating the improvements to his family. Possibly one reason that he failed to discuss the Mulally improvements with the Ford family was that he did not fully understand what Mulally was doing. Bill Ford's experience was in the staff side of the business; he had never been involved in operations or launch meetings. Because of this, he was unable to understand the effects of the job one date allowing engineering and quality problems being shipped to customers. The change that Mullay made on "job one" was a company-changing event that improved quality ratings, but Bill Ford did not understand the significance of the change because of his lack of experience.

Ford's stock price had not risen, and the family called for a meeting with Mulally and Bill Ford. The Ford family was obviously unaware that the bank borrowing had saved the

Ford Motor Company from bankruptcy, saved the stock price from junk levels, and that bankruptcy probably would have cost the family control of the company.

Mulally had no choice but to agree to the family meeting, and he was successful in convincing them that he knew what he was doing, and the company was making progress. He had turned around Boeing's commercial-airplane business, and he was doing the same with Ford Motor Company. The Ford stock price reflected the Wall Street disaster in the housing market, the drop in vehicle sales, and the near bankruptcy of Chrysler and General Motors, and was not an indicator of how Ford was doing.

Mulally knew that the UAW controlled the fate of the Ford Motor Company. The UAW contract gave the union the right to disapprove the closure of a plant, and if a plant were closed due to over-capacity, the UAW workers would go into the jobs bank, which required the company to continue to pay them for not working. Mulally decided to meet with UAW president Ron Gettlefinger, and discuss ways to work together and save Ford Motor Company. When the subject of the jobs bank came up, Gettlefinger refused to talk about it.

When Mulally started to discuss Ford losses, Gettlefinger cut him off and demanded to see the Ford financials. Mulally agreed, and gave the financial data to the UAW financial experts. After reviewing the data, Gettlefinger was told by the UAW auditors that Ford was in more trouble than the UAW had estimated. The next subject was the hourly retiree health-care obligation, which was $23 billion. The UAW had agreed to take over the Caterpillar retiree health-care obligation in their 1998 contract negotiations, but this had never been offered to Ford. Gettlefinger at first had no comment on the Caterpillar agreement, probably because the 2007 Big Three contract negotiations were only days away. Mulally had successfully negotiated with unions while at Boeing, and his experience was helpful in changing several UAW problems.

The UAW selected General Motors as the strike target for the 2007 negotiations, and called a strike before the talks began. The strike lasted two days, and then GM and the UAW went to work on the 2007 contract. The UAW agreed to take over the retiree health care obligation. The agreement required GM to pay $35 billion, into VEBA over a three-year period. The contract also reduced wages for new hires, and even changed the infamous jobs bank; however, the changes to the jobs bank were minor. Employees in the jobs bank could reject a job offer at another location only one time, and after that, they were kicked out of the jobs bank. Prior to this change, the workers could continually reject job offers, and remain in the bank until retirement – a ridiculous situation.

After General Motors settled, Mulally and the UAW started on the Ford contract. The UAW agreed to assume the retiree healthcare obligation in VEBA, if Ford would pay $17 billion into the VEBA trust fund. The $17 billion would be 75% of the $23.6 billion that Ford had borrowed for restructuring, and was not feasible. The 2008 housing recession was approaching at that time, and the UAW agreed to a $7 billion cash payment (30% of the $23.6 billion loan).

On September 15, 2008, Lehman Brothers filed for bankruptcy because of the toxic mortgages on their books, and the Dow dropped 500 points. The government caused Great Housing Recession had begun.

CEOs balance many balls in the air at the same time. While holding the weekly Ford management meetings, handling the Ford family, reviewing the financial numbers with Don Leclair daily, developing a plan for the recession, and negotiating with the UAW, Mulally had decided that a new sales and marketing vice president was needed. Mulally selected Jim Farley, Toyota's chief of Lexus, and Farley agreed to join Ford on October 11, 2007. Farley was concerned about the infighting at Ford, and the Ford family control, but Mulally committed to cover his back.

The sale of Jaguar and Land Rover began to get considerable attention in the weekly business reviews, and Mulally made the decision to sell both brands. The decision was a good one, and in truth, neither brand should have been purchased. On June 8, 2008, Ford sold Jaguar and Land Rover to Tata Motors of India.

Ford made $750 million in the second quarter of 2008, but the recession was driving vehicle sales down, and the upcoming two years would be disastrous.

The Great Housing Recession was the worst economic period since the Great Depression, and the Federal Government had worked years to make it happen. Unemployment doubled, the banks were near bankruptcy, housing prices had declined 50%, and the economy was sinking fast. Automotive stock prices had dropped, and Ford was down to less than $6 a share.

Kirk Kerkorian started buying Ford stock. Kerkorian had attempted to buy Chrysler, but lacked financing, and had also bought 10% of GM stock, but later sold. He was now after Ford, and had his automotive guru, Jerry York, study the possibility of buying the Ford family stock. Bill Ford was afraid of Kerkorian, and convinced the family members not to listen to Jerry York's sales pitch. Kerkorian bought another 20 million shares of Ford to bring his total to 6.5%. However, the housing market recession was causing vehicle sales to drop dramatically, and the outlook was not good for automotive with the tight money market, and Kerkorian sold his Ford stock.

With the drop in sales and continuing losses, CFO Don Leclair demanded deeper cost cuts, including the delay of new product spending. Mulally refused, and took the stand that new product spending was not to be cut, because new products were the future of the company. In prior years, when CFO Ed Lundy had demanded cancellation of new product spending, Henry Ford II had agreed. When competitor's new products were introduced and Ford had nothing to offer, sales went down and the company lost market share. Lundy never did understand the sales and profit effect of his cost control decisions, and this was typical of a bean counter. Don Leclair was more than a bean counter, but Mulally was a businessman, understood the need for new products, and overruled Leclair.

Gasoline prices were approaching $4 a gallon, which caused additional reductions in light truck and SUV sales, the big profit product lines, and Ford's working capitql was dangerously low. Don Leclair was still preparing for bankruptcy. Chrysler and General Motors were also running short of working capital, and were in deep trouble. Both Bob Nardelli of Chrysler and Rick Wagoner of General Motors met with Mulally to discuss joining with Ford to form stronger companies. GM wanted to take over Ford, and Chrysler wanted to merge with Ford. Mulally turned them both down.

The housing bubble that had begun in 2001, burst in 2006, and when Lehman brothers filed for bankruptcy on September 15, 2008, the Great Housing Recession hit. The Wall Street subprime mortgage fiasco also burst, and the financial community was in bankruptcy. For several years, Wall Street posted huge profits, and the executives raked in huge bonuses. Wall Street firms like Lehman Brothers and Bear Stearns borrowed to the hilt to buy toxic securities. When the mortgages started failing because of foreclosures, the toxic bonds were worthless, and Wall Street had billions on their balance sheets. The government attempted to bailout Bear Stearns with $30 billion of taxpayer money, but Bear was too far-gone. With the government *too big to fail* concept, it was surprising that politicians did not bailout Lehman Brothers.

Treasury Secretary Paulson refused to bail out Lehman despite his *too big to fail* ideas, and the firm went into bankruptcy. The stock market dropped, and the financial institutions holding the toxic mortgages were near bankruptcy. Credit tightened during the 2007-2008 period, and the housing recession was in full force.

Congressional legislation had created the worst economic crisis since the Federal Reserve caused the Great Depression of 1929–1941. By February 2008, the economy declined 8.9%, a disastrous reduction, and there were six straight quarters of negative growth beginning with the first quarter of 2008. Fannie Mae and Freddie Mac, the government morgage agencies, went into bankruptcy, and were bailed out with $400 billion.

With the steep decline in the economy in 2008, vehicle sales fell more than 40%, and the Big Three were burning cash to pay their bills. Chrysler and General Motors were in worse shape than Ford, since Ford was using the $23.6 billion loan of 2006 for working capital. Unemployment rose to 10%, banks failed, mortgage companies closed, and most investment houses on Wall Street were near bankruptcy. Henry Paulson, the infamous Secretary of the Treasury and former Wall Street CEO, was concerned that a financial collapse could cause another depression, and petitioned Congress for help.

When Congress passed the Emergency Economic Stabilization Act in October 2008, the $700 billion TARP fund became available. The Big Three were the largest troubled assets, but Paulson refused any TARP funds for automotive. The auto CEOs believed the government would provide bailout funds for working capital to survive the recession, but Paulson refused to allow the $35 billion loan request even though he had bailed out Wall Street. Paulson's position was that TARP was only for Wall Street, and he passed the auto problem to Congress. Congress saw an opportunity to be on television, and called the automotive CEOs and UAW president Ron Gettlefinger to Washington for Congressional Hearings. The hearings were similar to a kangaroo court with negative questions by legislators. The House passed a bill for a $14 billion loan for automotive, but Republicans in the Senate demanded that the UAW reduce wages and benefits to the Japanese level. The UAW refused, and Senate Democrats supported the union. The result was the Senate refused to accept the House bill, and voted 52-35 against bailing out the auto industry. The Senate voted to allow the bankruptcy of GM and Chrysler – not a bailout – bankruptcy.

President Bush was supportive of a bailout and approved a $17.4 billion loan to automakers to keep the companies alive until President Obama assumed office – big mistake since the new president was obligated to the UAW, and not the auto business.

Instead of using the available TARP fund to bail out the car companies, President Obama formed a task force to "study" the auto issue. When executives are unable to make a decision, they send the troops back for more study, and President Obama used the same tactic. The government had been studying the auto problem for nearly four months, and another study was certainly not required. The Rattner task force study was a political ploy to delay a decision until the public furor over financial bailouts died.

Ford continued to run their business in spite of the GM and Chrysler situation, and introduced the new Taurus product line at the Detroit Auto Show in January 2009. The Taurus was an immediate success. The celebration was short lived, however, because Ford announced a loss of $14.6 billion for 2008, the largest loss in history.

The Chrysler and General Motors problem had not been resolved. The $17.4 billion TARP cash infusion was a temporary Band-Aid, and the companies required more help if they were to survive the recession. Both companies were burning cash for working capital while the politicians were wasting time. Congress had made a decision with their negative vote on an auto bailout, but President Obama was avoiding a decision with his Rattner task force. An additional $21.6 billion was required for working capital in February to keep the two car companies open while the Obama-Rattner task force was going on. A total of $39 billion had been used for working capital since the Senate vote in December.

The task force was getting costly. GM and Chrysler had submitted complete financial data to Paulson and Congress, but they ignored it, and preferred to talk about the executives using their company airplanes to attend the kangaroo court hearings. Instead of analyzing the firms' financial reports, Rattner began a study of the automobile business. He k new nothing about the business, and his cohorts knew even less. The Obama-Rattner task force study was a political move to delay a decision on the auto companies until public opinion died down. The decision was being delayed with the task force study, but at the end of the study, there was only bankruptcy for Chrysler and General Motors, certainly no bailout. Mulally and his team continued to run Ford Motor Company, and fortunately they did not have to put up with Rattner's "Quiz Kids" questions.

Joe Hinrichs, Ford's vice president of manufacturing and labor relations, suggested to Mulally that the company should approach Ron Gettlefinger and attempt to gain some concessions before GM and Chrysler went into bankruptcy. After daily meetings in secret locations, Ford obtained concessions from the UAW in early March, 2009. As usual, Gettlefinger demanded that Mulally and his executives take a cut in pay.

Rattner, the "car czar," was not invited to the Ford-UAW negotiations, and he was livid, because he didn't get any credit. The one automobile company that did not need his "study help" had beaten him to the punch, and had accomplished something that Rattner was unable to do.

Steven Rattner gave priority to helping the union since the UAW had donated over $400 million to President Obama's campaign against John McCain. Rattner did not demand that the UAW take a pay or benefit cut. Rattner stated, "We did not ask any UAW member to take a cut in their pay." Evidently, Rattner was poor with mathematics because he was unable to read the numbers to determine that labor cost was a huge problem.

The Obama-Rattner task force ran out of questions, and obviously had no solutions. The infamous *study* of the automobile business failed. Rattner forced Chrysler into bankruptcy court on April 30, 2009. General Motors followed Chrysler into bankruptcy on June 1.

The government controlled the bankruptcy court, and the resulting rulings showed the favoritism to the union. The U.S. government was given 60.8% of GM, the Canadian government 11.7%, for 72.5% government ownership. The UAW VEBA was given 17.5%, and bondholders received 10% of their $30 billion secured bonds. The UAW was given 55% of Chrysler but fondholders lost 100% of their $9 billion in bonds.

An underpublicized result of the Chrysler bankruptcy was that a foreign company, Fiat, was literally "given" 20% of Chrysler. Fiat was known as "Fix it Again Tony" for its quality problems. A near bankrupt Italian carmaker that had never been successful in the U.S. market happily accepted the Chrysler gift, and proceeded to purchase controlling interest with Chrysler profits. Fiat later moved the Chrysler headquarters to London, so the U.S. government will lose the taxes on Chrysler profits.

Why the media have not reported on the gift of an American car company to a foreign, near bankrupt, Italian company is unexplainable. Fiat now owns over 50% of Chrysler, with most of the money used to purchase the additional 30% coming from Chrysler profits. Fiat lost $1.4 billion in 2012, and was bailed out with Chrysler's $1.7 billion in profits. The only car company bailed out by the Obama-Rattner task force was Fiat.

The media attention has been on the "bailout" of the auto industry despite the bankruptcies of Chrysler and General Motors. A poll of university students showed that they knew of the auto bailout, but knew nothing of the bailout of financial institutions. The trillions given to Wall Street, AIG, 888 banks, and 172 mortgage firms, Fannie Mae, and Freddie Mac, has been masked.

Another area that has escaped media attention is the eight-month government delay in making a decision. GM and Chrysler had presented financial data to Paulson and Congress in September 2008 showing that unless the government provided working capital, both companies would go into bankruptcy. Paulson and Congress rejected the bailout of the auto companies, but the decisions required three months of meetings and Congressional Hearings. President Obama then started another study, and Rattner took five months to drive Chrysler and General Motors into bankruptcy. Three million people associated with the auto business waited patiently, hoping that the government would help their companies as it had helped Wall Street, but the politicians refused to bailout the auto industry and 200,000 small businesses.

Our government failed – again. The Japanese Imperial Government would have immediately aided their car companies without any "hearings." That is one of the reasons that Japan out produces the U.S. in auto production. Interesting that the government takes credit for "bailing out" the automobile industry. Bailout is defined as *providing help*, and bankruptcy is defined as *complete failure*. The government, after eight months of hearings and task-force "studies," drove Chrysler and General Motors into bankruptcy – "total failure." There was no bailout.

Ford Motor Company avoided bankruptcy and survived the Great Housing Recession without any "help" from the government because the company had sufficient working capital from the 2006 loans. Ford did take advantage of Obama's dream for electric vehicles by borrowing $5.9 billion from the government's Advanced Technology Vehicle Manufacturing program in June 2009 for development of hybrid and electric vehicles. This was not bailout money, but advanced technology money. Nissan and other auto manufacturers also used these funds. The public lumps Ford into their assumption that the government bailed out the auto industry, but Ford made it without any political interference.

Alan Mulally reorganized the Ford Motor Company, and for the first time since the Henry Ford days, the CEO was running the company. It was necessary for Ford to bring in an outsider to make the management changes that were required. Ford was operating without direction before Mulally, and even though his experience was in the airplane business, he was an outstanding executive. He was a hands-on manager who paid attention to the details of the business. The weekly management meetings in which all areas of the company were reviewed in detail, and solutions for problems developed, proved to be a successful tool for Ford management. The elimination of the sacred adherence to the job one date was a company changing event that allowed executives to make the right decisions.

The hands-on management style was a major change in the way Ford Motor Company was managed. Prior to Mulally the company was run by a "committee" of vice presidents, and each ran the divisions without any input from the CEO. Each group vice president knew the job one date was sacred and never missed the date. In the weekly executive meetings Mulally changed the job one philosophy from a practice of accepting problems to meet the job one date, to one of correcting problems before vehicles were shipped. This was a major change and eliminated the risk of shipping vehicles before they were fully tested. This would have never happened without Mulally's involvement in the day-to-day operations. The Ford executives would have never made the change because job one was in cement. It required an auto outsider to make the change, and it is amazing that the auto experts and media have ignored the change.

On April 22, 2014, it was announced that Alan Mulally would retire from Ford in July, and Mark Fields would be the new CEO. Unfortunately, Don Leclair, the "forgotten" CFO, had been forced to retire, and did not survive to see the results of his efforts. Leclair was the individual who had the foresight to see the need for the loan that enabled Ford to avoid bankruptcy. Without the $23 billion loan Ford would have joined Chrysler and General Motors in the Rattner task force fiasco that led to bankruptcy. The bankruptcy court would have eliminated the Ford family voting rights and changed the company completely. Neither Bill Ford nor Mark Fields supported the loan request, and the Ford family failed to recognize Leclair's outstanding performance. The Ford family fired Fields in late May 2017; the Ford family had done it again.

Ford had 15.3% of the market in 2014, GM had 17.1%, and only 1.6% separated the two. However, Ford has never been a major player in the mid-market segment, and the cancellation of the Mercury brand in 2010 was another nail in the coffin. Henry Ford's refusal to recognize the brand ladder of GM, and the need for additional models to cover all segments of the market set the stage for GM dominance.

The last time Ford was the market leader was 90 years ago before the company lost out to General Motors because Henry Ford refused to accept that the Model T was obsolete. The production of the Model T continued too long and caused Ford Motor Company to close for six months in 1927 because Henry Ford refused refused to develop a replacement. His son Edsel had developed rough drafts for a new model but the design and testing had not been completed. The Model A was the successor to the Model T in 1927 and was a stylish automobile. The Model A was a success in the marketplace but the company lost six months of production and sales.

With the quality and reorganization problems at GM, and the control of Chrysler by Fiat, Ford might be able to again lead the nation in auto production. If Ford Motor Company can form a strong management team the firm will prosper; however, the brand offerings of Ford still do not cover the entire market. The Mercury and Edsel brands did not make it and Ford Motor Company desperately needs a brand in the mid-market segment.

The problem of providing vehicles in all segments of the market has plagued Ford since the Model T days over a hundred years ago, and the problem still exists. Ford Motor Company has only two basic brands, the Ford and Lincoln. The Ford brand is a strong competitor in its segment, but Lincoln sales lag competition in the luxury vehicle market.

Ford introduced the Mercury brand in 1938, but the Mercury styling was too much like the Ford, and the sales volume was one-third the GM mid-market brands, and was dropped in 2010. The Edsel was launched in 1958 to compete in the mid-market segment, but again the styling was too similar to the Ford. The Edsel was cancelled after two years.

General Motors mid-brands included Pontiac, Oldsmobile, and Buick before dropping Oldsmobile in 2004. The Pontiac was discontinued after the General Motors bankruptcy in 2009, leaving Buick as the only brand in the middle market. Ford needs a product to compete with Buick.

When Alfred Sloan developed the brand ladder in the 1920s, the General Motors vehicles covered the entire market. Sloan was the first to create customer loyalty and many customers progressed up the ladder as their income increased. The GM customer loyalty continues to this day and is one reason that General Motors has continued to be the largest seller of automobiles in the nation. The General Motors volume allowed separate styling departments and resulted in unique vehicles that were popular with customers.

Ford has one styling area because of cost, and Ford volume has been approximately half the GM volume since 1927. To increase sales, Ford must develop a competitive vehicle for the middle market, and this may require a separate design studio.

FOUR

CHRYSLER

Now Fiat Chrysler (FCA) of London

Walter Percy Chrysler was a former railroad mechanic who started Chrysler Corporation on June 6, 1925. He would have been devastated to learn that the government would give his company to the UAW and Fiat 85 years later.

Walter Percy Chrysler 1875-1940

Walter Chrysler was born in Wamego, Kansas, on April 2, 1875. His father was a railroad engineer, and the younger Chrysler started working as a janitor for the Union Pacific Railroad. After apprentice training, he became a machinist, and worked his way up; first as a foreman, then superintendent, and finally as a works manager. He worked for several railroad companies in the western states, and moved to Pittsburg as the works manager for the American Locomotive Company. Chrysler took an interest in automobiles after attending the 1908 auto show in Chicago.

In 1911, at age 36, Chrysler took the opportunity to become the production manager of Buick Motor Company in Flint, Michigan. Charles Nash was president of Buick at that time. Billy Durant had acquired Buick in 1908 as the first automobile company in GM. Walter Chrysler became president of Buick in 1916 when Nash was named president of General Motors.

When Billy Durant took control of General Motors for the second time in 1916, he fired Nash, and Chrysler submitted his resignation. Durant wanted Chrysler to remain at Buick and offered him a three-year contract at $10,000 a month, with an annual bonus of $500,000, or stock in General Motors equal to the $500,000. Chrysler could not believe it, and asked Durant to repeat the offer. He did, and Chrysler accepted. The $10,000 a month would be $225,000 today, or $2.7 million a year. The $500,000 bonus would be $11.2 million today. Chrysler's income amounted to $14 million a year, guaranteed by contract. Walter Chrysler, the 41-year-old ex-railroad mechanic, had struck it rich.

Walter Chrysler, like many others, did not get along with Billy Durant, and in 1919, at the end of his three-year contract, Chrysler resigned as president of the Buick Motor Company. He was paid $10 million for his General Motors stock ($141 million today). Walter Chrysler, the former railroad mechanic, started at Buick in 1911 making $6000 a year ($144,000 today), and left eight years later as one of the richest people in the country.

Willys-Overland Car Company was in trouble, and the bankers hired Chrysler to fix the company. Chrysler obtained a two-year contract at $1 million a year, and the size of the contract must have caused the bankers to squeeze their toes up in their shoes. Chrysler worked his contractual two years and made improvements at Willys, but when he attempted to buy the company, he was unsuccessful.

Walter Chrysler's next venture was to take control of the Maxwell Motor Company, which was in financial difficulty. He stopped the Maxwell production and started producing the Chrysler automobile in 1924. Chrysler had taken some of the features of a Willys-Overland prototype vehicle, incorporated them into his new Chrysler, and formed Chrysler Corporation in 1925.

Chrysler added the Plymouth and De Soto brands, and Plymouth would become a key competitor to Ford and Chevrolet. In 1928, Chrysler bought the Dodge Motor Company from the Dodge widows. Both Dodge brothers, Horace and John, had died in 1920. Dodge Motor Company was larger than Chrysler was, and Walter Chrysler had a major task to integrate Dodge into the Chrysler Corporation.

The Dodge brothers were pioneers in the automobile business, and had owned a profitable bicycle business in Windsor, Ontario before starting their auto supplier business. The Dodges began supplying component parts to Oldsmobile and Henry Ford at the turn of the century, and they supplied most of Ford's parts. Henry Ford was unable to pay for the parts and owed the Dodges $7000. When Henry Ford started the Ford Motor Compan in 1903, he gave the Dodge brothers credit for $7000 in unpaid bills, and the Dodges supplied $3000 in cash for 10% of the new Ford Motor Company. The $10,000 ($250,000 today) would soon be repaid with Ford's dividends. The Dodge brothers became wealthy and started the Dodge Motor Company in 1914, designing and building their own automobiles.

John (left) and Horace Dodge

Chrysler Corporation was successful and became the third member of the Big Three in 1928. Chrysler took second place in the U.S. market in 1937 and maintained its second-place position behind General Motors until 1950. The company fell into third place in sales due to the 104-day UAW strike in 1949. The UAW pattern bargaining tactic caused the strike that resulted in a major loss of market share. The strike by the UAW changed Chrysler from a viable company to the weakest of the Big Three.

Walter Chrysler was named "Time" magazine "Man of the Year" in 1928, the same year that he began construction of the Chrysler Building in New York City. The Art Deco Chrysler Building was completed in 1930.

The Great Depression began in 1929, and put an end to the Roaring Twenties and the great economy of the 1920s. Unfortunately, the Federal Reserve had not learned from its mistake in 1919 in raising interest rates and creating a tight money policy that caused the recession (or according to some economists, a depression) of 1920-1921. The Federal Reserve raised interest rates again in 1928, causing the Great Depression. Not only did the Federal Reserve cause the depression, the agency again raised rates in 1936, causing the economic debacle to last eleven years.

When the depression hit, Walter Chrysler immediately took action. He called his executives together and demanded a 30% reduction in the workforce. When they objected, he asked the personnel director to bring him a list of employees, drew a line at the 30% level, and said any name below his line was to be laid off.

Chrysler also cut vehicle prices, particularly on the high-priced models, and reduced purchased-part costs by working with automotive suppliers. Chrysler gained volume and market share during the Great Depression. The market share increased from 8% to 27%, an amazing jump, and as a result, Chrysler Corporation remained profitable in every year except one during the Great Depression. Most of the gain in volume was at the expense of Ford, which lost 12% of the market.

The Plymouth brand increased sales during the depression, which could be expected as customers moved to the low end of the market because of the financial crisis. The other Chrysler brands lost sales, but Walter Chrysler reduced costs, increased productivity, and the company became the low-cost producer of automobiles. His earlier experience as a foreman and superintendent in the railroad business aided him in cost cutting. Walter Chrysler had gained a reputation as a strong manager and a cost cutter while in his railroad jobs.

Walter Chrysler's strong management style saved the Chrysler Corporation from bankruptcy during the Great Depression. The company had acquired the Dodge Motor Company in 1928, and was integrating the two companies when the depression hit in 1929. It normally takes years to fully integrate an acquired company, but Chrysler was able to organize the two companies and survive the depression. The job he did was astounding.

Walter Chrysler had purchased a large waterfront estate on Long Island, New York in the early 1920s, and moved to New York when he retired in 1936. He suffered a stroke in 1938, and died in 1940 at the age of 65. Chrysler was buried in Sleepy Hollow, New York.

The UAW was founded in 1935, and after the sit-down strikes in 1937, Chrysler followed General Motors in accepting the union, but Ford held out until 1941. Walter Reuther was named president of the UAW in 1936, and remained in the office until he and his wife were killed in a plane crash in 1970.

Walter Reuther 1907-1970

During World War II Chrysler turned all its facilities to wartime production. The company produced military vehicles, including tanks, and was instrumental in developing radar. The post-war Chrysler products were restyled pre-war vehicles, but due to the pent-up demand for automobiles, the company could sell everything they could produce. Because of the war, steel was in short supply, and Chrysler used wood side panels on many models.

Thje new Chrysler models introduced in 1949 were impressive, but Ford's models were even more impressive. Ford took over second place in the market. Touche Ross was the Chrysler accounting firm, and many of their executives were recruited to Chrysler. The cost-conscious accountants reduced the new vehicle launch costs, but similar to the GM situation in the early 1980s, the demand for the use of common parts on all vehicles resulted in all brands looking alike. The Touche Ross common-part cost control failed in the styling area.

Chrysler management refused to agree with the contract signed by Ford in the 1949 UAW contract negotiations when Ford had agreed to provide company-paid pensions. The pattern bargaining tactic used by the UAW demanded that all auto contracts be similar, and the union demanded that Chrysler agree to Ford's concessions. When Chrysler management refused to accept the Ford contract, the UAW called a strike that lasted 104 days. Chrysler finally had to agree to the Ford concessions because the company was near bankruptcy because of the strike. The 104-day strike resulted in huge financial losses and a major loss of market share. The market share loss pushed Chrysler into third place in sales, and the volume dropped to a level near its break-even point. When later recessions caused a drop in vehicle sales, Chrysler lost money. The lower volume caused Chrysler profits to decline, and the firm began losing money.money. The financial losses reduced cash, and Chrysler was unable to fund sufficient styling changes to meet the competition in the annual model-change race.

The result of the volume loss was that Chrysler became the weakest of the Big Three and was always near bankruptcy during recessions. The 1980 near-bankruptcy situation in which the company obtained a government loan was a direct result of the volume loss. The 104-day strike in 1949 changed the company from a viable business to a weak company struggling to survive. The UAW pattern-bargaining tactic forever changed the company.

Chrysler established a missile division in the 1950s to work with the government space center in Huntsville, Alabama. The German rocket scientist Wernher von Braun had been relocated to Huntsville, and was developing the first U.S. spacecraft. The Chrysler Missile Division became the Chrysler Space Division, and was the prime contractor to the government on the Redstone spacecraft. The Redstone was based on the World War II German V-2 rocket used against England during the war. Chrysler Space Division and Wernher von Braun's scientists upgraded the V-2, and in 1961 launched Alan Sheppard and Gus Grissom on three suborbital flights.

Both Chrysler and Ford had holes in their brand ladder when attempting to compete with General Motors. GM had Chevrolet at the foot of the ladder, Cadillac at the top, and Pontiac, Oldsmobile, and Buick as steps in between. Chrysler had Plymouth at the foot, the Chrysler brand at the top of their ladder, with Dodge and De Soto in the middle range. However, General Motors had decentralized the company, and each of its brands was a completely separate business unit. For example, Chevrolet had its own styling, engineering, manufacturing, and sales organizations, and the same was true for the other brands. This allowed uniquely styled vehicles. Both Chrysler and Ford brands shared styling and engineering which resulted in commonality in their vehicles, and many brands looked alike. Chrysler attempted to expand the brand ladder in 1955 with the launch of the Imperial. The Imperial was to be at the top of the brand ladder, and the Valiant brand was introduced in 1960 as a new low end of the ladder.

Chrysler's size limited the capital that could be spent on the various brands, resulting in an overlap between brands, and little difference in styling. Customers considered the Valiant and Plymouth one brand, Dodge an upgrade of the Plymouth, Chrysler and Imperial one brand, and De Soto somewhere in between. The brand ladder required different styling.

The automotive industry was, and still is, a capital-intensive business, and size was all-important. General Motors could afford to have separate brand divisions with their own styling and engineering, but Chrysler and Ford could not. The De Soto brand was discontinued after the 1961 model year.

In the early 1960s, Chrysler was the first of the Big Three to use unibody construction in its vehicles, instead of the body on frame design. The unibody design is used on most vehicles today. Chrysler was also the first to use the alternator in its electrical system instead of the generator. Alternators are standard on all vehicles today. The Plymouth Barracuda was launched in April 1964, the same time as the Ford Mustang. The Barracuda was one of the first "pony" cars, but was outsold by Ford's Mustang by a 10-1 margin.

When the government passed the first smog-control legislation in the mid-1960s, General Motors was the leader in emission technology, but Ford and Chrysler engine engineers were working around the clock to catch up. In the late 1960s the Big Three petitioned the government to allow their engineers to work together to solve the technical issues for emission controls. There was very little scientific data on smog or emissions at that time, and the first emission law was incomplete because of lack of complete data on smog. Unlike the Japanese, the U.S. government objected to Big Three joint efforts, and threatened jail time under the anti-trust law if companies shared data. In Japan, the government encouraged the Japanese automakers to work together to meet the new emission requirements. The government anti-trust ruling caused a duplication of engineering and development work in the Big Three that added months to the development time, and cost millions.

The VW Beetle imports started taking an increasing share of the U.S. market in the 1960s, and Chrysler attempted to meet the small car market demand with the Plymouth Valiant and Dodge Dart, but both vehicles were much larger than the Beetle and did not seriously attack Beetle sales. The Japanese imports began to take an even larger share of the market, and when the OPEC oil embargo created the 1973 oil crisis; customers began flocking to small, more fuel-efficient vehicles. Chrysler, Ford, and General Motors had failed to develop a small car to compete with the Beetle and the Japanese imports. This problem will go down in history as the main reason for the loss of U.S. market share by the Big Three. The product planners failed to develop small cars because finance demanded added content for profits. Evidently, the bean counters failed to include market share in their profit formula.

The vehicles that Chrysler, Ford, and GM developed were the "American" small cars, six-passenger vehicles, with six-cylinder engines, and all the extras. Profit was the target, rather than the competition. The Big Three had made money on large vehicles, including light trucks for years, and could not force themselves to recognize the small-car threat.

Chrysler made another effort to combat the imports with the launch of the Plymouth Volare and Dodge Aspen in 1976, but both vehicles had quality and engineering problems that seriously damaged Chrysler's quality and engineering reputation. Both models failed to compete with the imports.

The Chrysler European operations, always a minor player in the European market, suffered with the sales drop in Europe in 1977, and the unit was sold to Peugeot in 1978. The U.S. recession was beginning and Chrysler, being the smallest of the Big Three, needed the cash.

The years 1977 and 1978 were important for the Chrysler Corporation because Harold Sperlich and Lee Iacocca were both fired by Henry Ford II and later joined Chrysler. Sperlich, vice president of product development at Ford, was well recognized in product planning and development, and was instrumental in the development of the Ford Mustang, although Lee Iacocca received all the credit. Sperlich had done market research on a new product, the minivan, and made a presentation to Henry Ford II and Ed Lundy, the chief financial officer, with a recommendation that Ford develop the minivan. Lundy, the bean counter, responded that the company did not have the capital to launch such a vehicle, and Hank the Deuce agreed, which was a major mistake. A short time later Sperlich was fired. Sperlich joined Chrysler as head of product development and took his ideas for the minivan with him. An interesting caveat was that the Chrysler design office had started developing a minivan to accompany the Dodge and Chrysler van products that held 45% of the market. The concept was that the minivan would replace the station wagon. When the design office presented the minivan to Lynn Townsend, the Chrysler CEO and a former Touche Ross executive, Townsend rejected the minivan because neither GM nor Ford had the product. This reasoning was certainly faulty, since that was exactly the reason that Chrysler should have launched the new product. Townsend and Henry Ford II both made a huge error in refusing the development of the minivan.

Lee Iacocca was next to be fired by Ford. Henry Ford II fired Iacocca in 1978, because "he just didn't like him." Iacocca was named president of Chrysler a few months after the firing. When Sperlich presented the minivan product, the Chrysler treasurer said the company did not have the money; Iacocca responded: *Go find the money!* Iacocca approved the minivan program, and the treasurer soon left the company.

Chrysler was in deep financial trouble in 1979 and the company was near bankruptcy. John "Rick" Riccardo had succeeded Lynn Townsend as CEO of Chrysler. The OPEC problems of 1973 and 1979 drove the U.S. market to small, fuel-efficient vehicles and hit Chrysler the hardest because of the company's size and lack of product. Chrysler was running out of working capital.

Chrysler appealed to the government for help to prevent bankruptcy. Congress, called for Congressional Hearings, and Riccardo attempted to answer the politicians' questions, which were, at best, very negative. Rick turned the podium over to Iacocca, and not only did Iacocca answer the questions, he gave more than he took. Iacocca knew the business, and he was not about to let politicians beat him to the punch. Iacocca later told an audience in one of his speeches, that he had to put up with Senator "Abscam" Kelly from Florida, and one of the government experts in the Congressional Hearings. Later, Kelly was one of the politicians convicted of accepting bribes in an FBI sting.

Most of Congress was against loaning Chrysler any money, even though it was not taxpayer money. Chrysler was requesting a government guaranteed loan from the banks, and Congress was demanding all of Chrysler's assets as security, so there was no risk to the government. If Chrysler failed, the government would be first in line to receive funds from the sale of Chrysler's assets.

Congress passed the Chrysler Corporation Loan Guarantee Act on December 20, 1979, which guaranteed $1.5 billion in bank loans. The government demanded that Chrysler cut costs by $2 billion, and develop a three-year business plan. One reason for the loan was that 360,000 Chrysler workers would be laid off if the company failed, and another 350,000 jobs would be lost in supplier, dealer, and other companies tied to Chrysler.

In 1980, Tom Stallkamp, the future Chrysler president, left Ford and joined Chrysler purchasing. He moved up the ladder rapidly, becoming vice president of purchasing and later a group executive. He was appointed president of Chrysler Corporation in January 1988, one week before the Daimler Chrysler negotiations.

Lee Iacocca succeeded Rick Riccardo as CEO of the Chrysler Corporation, and began his work in the product area. Iacocca immediately directed engineers to reduce the complexity of vehicles by using common parts in areas not visible to customers.

The use of different components increased inventories and costs. The customer would immediately notice common exterior sheet-metal parts, so Iacocca focused on non-visible parts.

Chrysler launched the K-cars in 1981 to replace the Aspen and Volare product lines. The Plymouth Reliant, Dodge Aires, and Chrysler LeBaron, were successful, selling an average of 300,000 cars a year between 1981 and 1988. The K-cars were profitable and helped Chrysler in the turnaround. The minivan also helped the turnaround. Launched in 1983, the minivan was the product rejected by Ford finance. The Chrysler minivan led the industry in sales from its introduction in 1983 until today – an amazing success for the product rejected by Henry Ford II and Lynn Townsend.

Chrysler reduced losses to $500 million in 1981, and reported a small profit in the second quarter of 1982. The 1983 full-year profit was $500 million, and Chrysler was able to pay the loan back four years ahead of the deadline. The Federal Government earned $500 million on the stock certificates granted by Chrysler at the time of the loan guarantee. This was an amazing return for a low-risk loan guarantee. The media reported all the negative possibilities of a Chrysler bailout in the 1979-1983 period, but failed to accurately report the $500 million government profit. The negative attitude toward the auto industry by the media and government officials was clearly demonstrated during the Chrysler loan episode.

Iacocca brought several Ford vice presidents and executives into Chrysler. Gerald Greenwald became vice chairman, Bennett Bidwell became executive vice president of sales, Hans Mathias joined as a quality executive, and Bob Lutz left Ford in 1986 to join Iacocca as a vice president, and later became president. Lutz had worked for several auto companies, starting his career with General Motors Europe. He became vice president of sales for Opel, and then moved to BMW in Germany for three years. Lutz joined Ford of Germany, and was promoted to the Ford of Europe headquarters near London. Lutz was later made CEO of Ford of Europe. He then took over as executive vice president of Ford International, ran into a problem with the top people at Ford, was cut back to vice president of truck operations, and soon left Ford for Chrysler.

Harold Sperlich was named president of Chrysler in 1987, and he and Bob Lutz worked closely together improving the K-cars and minivans. Lutz was promoted to president of Chrysler when Sperlich retired in 1988. Another big year for Chrysler was 1987, when they acquired American Motors (AMC). American Motors had the Jeep brand, which Iacocca wanted.

Automotive volume increased in the mid-to-late 1980s, and Chrysler profits were high. However, Iacocca violated one of the cardinal rules and started a non-automotive acquisition binge. He bought Gulfstream Aviation because he liked fancy private planes. Iacocca had outfitted the Ford Boeing 727 with gold bathroom fixtures without Henry Ford II's approval. Hank the Deuce objected, and sold the plane to the Shah of Iran.

The Japanese imports continued to take an increasing share of the U.S. market, and Iacocca was often critical of the Japanese government controlling the yen to make the imports cheaper in the U.S. market. His favorite topic was that "an uneven playing field" existed, and that the U.S. government must correct it. The Japanese car companies sold cars in the U.S. for prices lower than they were priced in Japan. This was difficult to accept because of duty and freight.

The Big Three CEOs asked President George Bush to help, and Bush agreed to travel to Japan with the Big Three CEOs on a trade mission. The trade mission accomplished nothing because the Japanese were determined to take over the U.S. market, and they threw up their usual "yakamashi" response. Another reason the Japanese government refused to listen to Bush's request was that they simply did not understand why the President of the United States was suddenly interested in the automobile business when the American government had done nothing to help its car companies during the prior 30 years, and openly criticized the auto executives and companies in the media.

The Japanese are consistent in their trade policies, and since the 1960s, Japan had taken advantage of America's lack of ability in stopping Japanese imports. For the U.S. president to fly to Japan on a trade mission without any preliminary meetings with the lower-level Japanese trade groups was something they simply could not understand, so they just threw up their normal barriers. Iacocca was relatively quiet in the meetings, leaving the heavy lifting to President Bush who did a good job, but was unable to overcome the Federal Government's public criticism of the U.S. auto manufacturers in prior years. The Japanese paid attention to the Chrysler Congressional Hearings a few years earlier when Congress was openly critical of Chrysler. The company was asking for a $1.5 billion loan guarantee, which to the Japanese was chicken feed. The Japanese could not understand how the U.S. government would contest a loan to its auto industry.

The Japanese government supports Japanese industries both financially and politically, resulting in Japan being one of the largest producer of automobiles in the world. Japan carmakers had less than 3% of the world market in 1960, and increased their production to reach 28% by 1980, an amazing achievement. The Japanese have taken over 30% of the U.S market with the aid of the government and the Japanese unions. Their government support system has worked. The system has also worked in other industries, with cameras, television, computers, and even heavy equipment like earthmovers. For some unexplainable reason, the U.S. government is against business, while the Japanese government supports its manufacturing businesses. The results speak for themselves.

Lido Anthony "Lee" Iacocca

Iacocca did an outstanding job managing Chrysler through the 1979 government hearings, reorganizing company management, and developing the minivan. Chrysler became profitable again, was the low-cost producer, and the company was in good shape.

Unfortunately, Iacocca began to spend less time running the business. He ran the Statue of Liberty refurbishing program, wrote books, made non-automotive acquisitions, and became a celebrity, all at the expense of Chrysler. Chrysler lost $0.8 billion in 1981, and some members of the board decided it was time for Lee Iacocca to retire. However, retirement was the last thing on Iacocca's mind, and in an attempt to stay on, he told the board that Bob Lutz, his obvious successor, was not capable of taking over as CEO. This was a dirty thing to do, but that was how badly he wanted to stay on as CEO. He liked the good life.

The board of directors formed a search committee and found Bob Eaton, who was president of General Motors Europe. Eaton was an engineer who had been promoted through GM's engineering ranks, before taking over GM Europe in 1988. When the search committee approached him, he told them, "I am no Lee Iacocca," and he wasn't. Bob Eaton was named vice chairman and CEO of the Chrysler Corporation in 1992, and took over as chairman and CEO when Lee Iacocca retired nine months later. Instead of coming to Chrysler in the near-bankruptcy situation that Iacocca inherited, Eaton came to a profitable company in good shape. Bob Lutz was running the company while Eaton was finding his way. With Lutz at the controls, Chrysler set sales records in 1994 and 1995, and Chrysler employees hardly knew Eaton was there. He had the practice of staying in his office, and not using Lutz's "walking around" management style. He certainly was not a Lee Iacocca. In 1994, Chrysler reported a profit of $3.7 billion, with production of 2.8 million vehicles and a market share of 15%. Iacocca had turned Chrysler around, and the company was in the best shape in many years.

Robert J. Eaton

Kirk Kerkorian had Jerry York, the former Chrysler CFO, and Lee Iacocca, the former CEO, on his payroll, and owned 10% of the Chrysler stock. In 1995, Kerkorian developed an IPO plan to take Chrysler private. Chrysler stock was selling at $40 a share and the company was generating cash.

Bob Eaton was in New York for an investor meeting when Kerkorian called and asked to meet. Bob Eaton was inexperienced in dealing with leveraged buyouts, but Kerkorian was an expert in takeovers. Kerkorian told Eaton that he had the financing (which he didn't), and wanted to take Chrysler private. On April 12, 1995, Kerkorian announced that he was going to buy Chrysler. The announcement also said that Lee Iacocca was part of the Tricenda IPO team.

Eaton was shocked at the announcement, but he shouldn't have been, since Kerkorian had met with him, told him of Tricenda's plan, and requested his support. Eaton had no experience in acquisitions, and this had caused a serious problem. On April 24, 1995, Chrysler's board announced that Chrysler was not for sale, and would fight the Tricenda takeover. The Kerkorian friendly takeover had received a negative response from Chrysler, and he didn't understand it. His team had told him that Eaton would agree to the takeover, and Eaton had not objected to his proposal in his meeting. Eaton's weakness in the Kerkorian meeting had created a situation in which Tricenda and Chrysler were fighting, and it was too late to stop the bleeding.

The Tricenda takeover announcement had caused a rush to buy Chrysler stock; the stock price went up 25% to $50 a share, and Kerkorian's 10% had earned him $300 million. Bob Eaton was incensed at Iacocca for attempting to take over Chrysler, and he took action to take away Iacocca's stock options, which were worth $50 million. The board approved the cancellation of the options on the basis that Iacocca had violated his contract, but Kerkorian paid the $50 million to Iacocca.

Daimler-Benz approached Bob Eaton with the offer to aid Chrysler in the fight against Tricenda. Bob Lutz, with his German experience, was fluent in German, and joined Eaton in a meeting with Daimler-Benz. Both were surprised that Daimler was interested in helping in the Tricenda issue. Lutz understood the German thinking and was convinced that Daimler-Benz would take control of Chrysler in any "joint venture," and Bob Lutz immediately turned Daimler down. Eaton, in his naïve thinking, was less suspicious of Daimler, but he would soon learn that Lutz was right. Eaton's inexperience in dealing with a leveraged buyout had caused the problem with Tricenda, and would later lead to the takeover of Chrysler by Daimler-Benz. Bob Eaton was a good engineer but an inexperienced CEO, and a poor negotiator. His background at General Motors had not required any negotiating abilities in takeovers, and he failed to ask investment firms for assistance in evaluating the Daimler situation.

Kerkorian was unable to obtain the financing for the $22 billion takeover, and the deal fell through. Lee Iacocca had been the media darling for decades, but the attempted takeover of Chrysler damaged his reputation. With the failure of the Kerkorian IPO, Chrysler management thought the Daimler discussions were behind them. However, Daimler had studied Chrysler for some time, and the German company needed help to improve its 2% share of the U.S. market. Daimler saw the acquisition of Chrysler as an avenue to the U.S. market. Juergen Schrempp, the CEO of Daimler, approached Eaton with the idea of discussing alternatives. Eaton was surprised at the proposal, but agreed to meet, not suspecting the only alternative that Daimler was interested in was a takeover of Chrysler. Chrysler's dealer network and sales would be just the thing Daimler needed to increase Mercedes sales in the U.S. market. Daimler-Benz was not a player in the van market, and Schrempp saw the opportunity to take advantage of Chrysler's strong market position in the minivan and van market.

Even though Bob Eaton had no experience with mergers and acquisitions, he should have been aware of the risk of "going it alone" when meeting with a competitor like Daimler-Benz. Lutz, with his German experience, had warned Eaton about the intentions of Daimler management, but Eaton evidently had an ego and thought he could handle the situation.

The puzzling part of Eaton's thought process was his thinking that Chrysler needed an immediate partner, or a joint venture to survive. A larger footprint in Europe was certainly desirable, but if Eaton thought that Daimler would help Chrysler enter the European market, he was badly mistaken. Daimler's main interest was increasing the Mercedes share of the U.S. market; Daimler did not have a competitive product in the minivan market, and this was another attraction.

Merger discussions require extensive planning and analysis, and Eaton had not done his homework before meeting with Schrempp. Schrempp had a definite plan, and Eaton was uncertain of what to do – he had no plan. Schrempp's strategy was to acquire Chrysler and use the company's dealers and sales force to gain market share in the U.S. market. Daimler-Benz historically had been a small player in the U.S. market, and Juergen Schrempp saw an opportunity for Daimler to increase its market share with the acquisition of Chrysler. Eaton failed to recognize the Daimler-Benz objective, and his thinking was that Chrysler needed a partner to survive. Bob Eaton overlooked the Daimler plan, and blindly agreed to discussions with the foreign automaker. A professional CEO would have asked for opinions from an outside firm to develop a plan, and Eaton should have used Bob Lutz as his right-hand man in all meetings with Daimler. Lutz's knowledge of the German thinking was invaluable. The Daimler and Chrysler discussions and meetings would eventually lead to the acquisition of Chrysler by Daimler-Benz. The supposed "merger of equals" was make-believe.

A joint venture certainly required more planning than a phone call from Daimler. Bob Eaton never should have agreed to a meeting to discuss alternatives with Juergen Schrempp without doing his homework. Eaton kept Lutz out of the negotiations, and his negotiation team consisted of Tom Stallkamp, the new president, Gary Valade, the CFO, Bill O'Brien, the general counsel, and Tom Capo, the treasurer, none of whom knew much about Daimler-Benz.

Daimler had earlier approached Ford Motor Company suggesting a "merger," but Ford turned it down because the Ford family wanted their name on the buildings. Daimler-Benz had already decided that the name of the company would be Daimler Chrysler, but allowed Eaton to continue to negotiate for the Chrysler Daimler name. Eaton should have directed his team to analyze a joint venture to determine the pluses and minuses and decide whether a merger made any sense for Chrysler. Evidently, Eaton had his mind made up before the game started.

The lengthy negotiations with Chrysler took place without Schrempp telling the Daimler-Benz supervisory board of the plan. German companies have two boards; an executive board managed by the CEO, and a supervisory board. Each member of the executive board has a contract with the supervisory board. For example, the vice president of engineering has a contract with the supervisory board to run engineering, and the CEO of the executive board is unable to fire the vice president of engineering without supervisory board approval. This means the CEO position in a German company is not as strong as that of an American company. The CEO of Daimler-Benz must use a matrix-management method to run the business. Of course, there are exceptions to any rule, and Juergen Schrempp was certainly an exception. Schrempp managed with complete authority, and he instinctively knew that he could sell the Chrysler merger to the supervisory board, but he also knew the board would never accept the Daimler name being second to the Chrysler name. The supervisory board of German companies contains six management, and six union members, with the chairman of the board being a management person and able to break any tie vote by the board.

Bob Lutz and Tom Stallkamp were certain that the new company name would be Daimler Chrysler even though Eaton was still holding out for Chrysler Daimler. After the final negotiations, Eaton walked out of a private meeting with Schremp and told the Chrysler negotiating team that Daimler had demanded that the company name be Daimler Chrysler, and that he had agreed. Lutz and Stallkamp looked at each other and laughed, because once again Eaton had been out-negotiated.

Finally, after weeks of discussions about the name, Schrempp told Eaton that the name had to be Daimler Chrysler. On May 5, 1998, Bob Eaton presented the Daimler Chrysler merger proposal to the Chrysler board of directors, but he demanded that Bob Lutz report that the Daimler name be first in the name game. Eaton was embarrassed to recommend the Daimler Chrysler name. The Chrysler board members no longer had a job, and probably wished they had never heard of Bob Eaton.

On May 7, 1998, a joint press release was issued stating that Chrysler and Daimler-Benz were joining in a merger of equals, and that the name of the new company would be Daimler Chrysler. Eaton also told the media that he would be leaving in three years, which shocked the public. The Chrysler employees had no warning that a merger was in process, and were devastated. The chairman of Chrysler's board called Eaton, and asked why he would immediately tell the world that he was leaving because the Chrysler employees would know that Daimler-Benz was taking over Chrysler. When Eaton didn't have an answer, the chairman called Eaton an idiot. Obviously, Bob Eaton was looking out for Bob Eaton, not Chrysler, because Eaton received over $100 million when he left Chrysler.

Bob Lutz had been moved to the vice chairman position at the beginning of the Daimler Chrysler talks to prevent Lutz from ruining the Eaton sell-out to Daimler, and Tom Stallkamp took over as president. Once the Daimler Chrysler "merger" was approved, it was Stallkamp's job to make it work, because Bob Eaton reverted to his "sitting in the office" routine. Stallkamp was smart enough to recognize Lutz's value in dealing with the new partner, but Eaton refused to allow Lutz to take part in the reorganization effort. Eaton then asked Lutz to retire, which he did on July 1, 1998. Lutz received $27 million from the merger, so he could afford to continue his lavish lifestyle.

Daimler-Benz essentially took over Chrysler. It was fortunate that Bob Lutz had retired because he never could have put up with the Germans taking over. Schrempp gave Eaton a new Mercedes as a reward for helping out in the merger. In addition to the $70 million Eaton received in the merger, Schrempp added another $24 million in a golden parachute. Eaton also received a $30,000 a month increase in his pension if he left before the three-year contract period – quite an incentive to leave.

Bob Eaton was recruited from General Motors, and Chrysler had to buy out his years at GM, including his pension, pay him a huge salary and bonus for five years, and pay him another $100 million when he retired. His severance agreement added $360,000 a year to his Chrysler pension, which probably put the total annual pension at over $700,000. A solid management team was in place when Eaton joined Chrysler, the company was making record profits, increasing market share, and was the low cost producer in the Big Three. Bob Lutz and his team were doing an excellent job running the company. In hindsight, the Chrysler board probably wished that they had promoted Lutz, because the character they selected to be the new CEO cost the board members their jobs when Eaton sold out to Daimler. Again, hindsight is always 20-20, but accurate in this case.

Lee Iacocca and his team had rescued Chrysler from bankruptcy and made it a viable company. A strong CEO can fix a company. Bob Eaton was weak, and gave Chrysler to Daimler, and the company had little management from 1992 when Eaton took over, until the bankruptcy in 2009. The board made a serious mistake when they hired Bob Eaton.

The Daimler executives often traveled first-class to the Chrysler headquarters in Auburn Hills, a suburb of Detroit, staying in expensive hotel suites and running up large tabs, all of which were charged to Chrysler. Stallkamp objected to the unnecessary expenses because at Ford the bean counters watched expense accounts like a hawk. However, Schrempp refused to intervene. Ths was probably the first problem that Tom Stallkamp had with Schrempp. Daimler management expected first class travel and expensive hotel suites since they considered Chrysler a subsidiary. Schrempp objected to the nitpicking by the president of a subsidiary, and advised Stallkamp to forget it.

After leaving Chrysler in July 1998, Bob Lutz took over as CEO of Exide Corporation, a large battery maker, in December of that year. After missing the Chrysler CEO job, Lutz finally assumed the top position in a company. GM CEO Rick Wagoner recruited Lutz to be vice chairman of GM in 2001, and he was put in charge of product development. Lutz had started at GM Europe in 1963, was executive-vice president of Ford International, president of Chrysler, and 38 years later, he was back with GM as vice chairman. He flew his helicopter from his home in Ann Arbor, Michigan to GM headquarters in Detroit until he crashed one day. He was not injured and continued to fly His two jet planes. He has a Russian L-39 single jet engine plane, and an Alpha. The Alpha is a twin-engine jet aircraft made by the French company Dassault-Breguet. "Maximun" Bob was a pilot in the Marine Corps from 1955 until 1959, and served in the Marine Reserves, rising to the rank of captain.

Robert Anthony "Maximum Bob" Lutz

Jim Holden received a job offer from AutoNation. Holden had recognized that his future with Daimler Chrysler was a dead-end and had been searching for a new job. Bob Eaton was still around and was surprised at Holden's decision to leave Chrysler, but that was how far away Eaton was from understanding the Daimler impact on Chrysler employees. To keep Holden, Eaton asked Tom Stallkamp to retire at age 53, and promoted Holden to be president of the Chrysler Division of Daimler Chrysler in 1999.

Schrempp reorganized Daimler Chrysler into three divisions; the Chrysler division, with Stallkamp as president; the Mercedes-Benz division, with Juergen Hubbert as president; and the commercial vehicle division, with Dieter Zetsche as president. The reorganization continued, with more Germans coming to Chrysler in key positions, which was normal for a German company that had taken over another business. Bob Eaton certainly didn't expect to see this when he agreed to the "merger of equals," but it was destined to happen.

Tom Stallkamp had lasted nineteen years at Chrysler and moved up in the management ranks rapidly. He was named president of Chrysler Corporation in 1998, shortly before Bob Eaton began negotiations with Daimler-Benz. Stallkamp was a capable executive and worked well with other members of management. Eaton had undercut Stallkamp when Holden had threatened to leave, and gave his job to Holden. Tom was too young to retire and knew he could find another job, so he left on friendly terms. The friendly terms also included $25 million from the merger - almost as good as Walter Chrysler's payday when he left General Motors in 1919.

Holden didn't last long as president of the Chrysler division, which was expected by those who recognized the German culture. Daimler was reorganizing Chrysler, and the new bosses came from Stuttgart. The launch of the new minivan in 2000 was late, and Schrempp blamed it on Holden. Sales had dropped, and Schrempp blamed Holden - his days were numbered. In November 2000, Schrempp fired Holden, and replaced him with Dieter Zetsche.

In less than two years, the entire Chrysler team of executives that had led the company to record profits before the Eaton giveaway to Daimler-Benz, had left the company. Eaton had fired Lutz and Stallkamp, and Schrempp had fired Holden. Dennis Pawley, executive vice president of manufacturing, Tom Gale, vice president of design, and executive vice president of engineering, Francois Castaing, had retired early. Chris Theodore, vice president of engineering, and Shamel Rushwin, vice president of manufacturing, left to join Ford. Sales chief Ted Cunningham, and communications executives Tony Cervone and Kathleen Oswald, also left the company. For eleven top executives (including Eaton) to leave a company in a two-year period, when the company was making record profits, was undoubtedly an industry first. When eleven executives leave, a major shuffle in management occurs, and Chrysler's management ranks were not that strong.

Daimler-Benz had decimated Chrysler management in the first two years of the "merger of equals." Eaton had his $100 million and a pension of $750,000 a year, so he was well off, but the Chrysler hourly and salaried work force suffered the most. The Daimler-Benz takeover created organization changes and morale problems. When the top eleven executives leave a company, the people changes reverberate throughout the organization, and with German management assuming command, the workforce didn't know what was coming next.

Bob Eaton had taken a company with record profits and stylish vehicles to a joint venture company with little organization and huge losses. He was a poor manager of people, and a CEO with little or no knowledge of leveraged buyouts or mergers. He was over his head as CEO. Bob Eaton drove the company to near bankruptcy during his eight-year tenure. Eaton retired in 2000, and it was not surprising that the media completely ignored Eaton after he retired. Bob Eaton is number seven on "Fortune" magazine's list of the worst ever auto chiefs.

After years of profitability, Chrysler reported a $1.2 billion loss in 2000. The German critics of the Chrysler acquisition started their criticism of Juergen Schrempp. The Chrysler losses continued thru 2003, and Schrempp was in trouble with the board of supervisors in Germany. In addition to the cost to Chrysler of the German management people in America, Mercedes took advantage of Chrysler by overcharging engineering and administrative costs to its American subsidary. This tactic normally occurs, and of course added to the Chrysler losses.

Daimler Chrysler began to report profits in 2004, but the European market was down, and Mercedes was losing money. The supervisory board asked Schrempp to retire in 2005, even though he had two years remaining on his contract. Dieter Zetsche replaced Schrempp as CEO of Daimler-Benz, and Zetsche made Tom Lasorda president of the Daimler Chrysler group.

Chrysler lost money in 2006, and Zetche began to look for alternatives for Daimler Chrysler because of the retiree pension and health-care costs. The parent German company was unfamiliar with the UAW pension and health-care-cost problems, but Zetche had learned of the problems while at Auburn Hills. On April 4, 2007, Daimler-Benz announced that it was negotiating the sale of Daimler Chrysler. On April 5, Kirk Kerkorian made an offer of $4.5 billion for Daimler Chrysler, and on April 12, Magna International of Canada announced that an offer would be made.

On May 14, 2007, Daimler-Benz announced that it would sell 80.1% of Daimler Chrysler to Cerberus Capital Management for $7.4 billion. The name of the new company was to be Chrysler LLC. Robert Nardelli, the former GE executive and Home Depot CEO, was named chairman and CEO. Cerberus Capital Management is a private equity firm headquartered in New York. Cerberus was unknown in Detroit, and pundits questioned the Cererus acquisition. The name Cerberus comes from the mythical three-headed dog that guards the gates of hell. The 2009 Chrysler bankruptcy destroyed the value of the $7.4 billion Cerberus investment. Steven Feinberg, the founder of Cerberus, must have thought the three-headed dog was asleep at the gate.

The Cerberus business plan was to split Chrysler into two segments; sell the auto manufacturing division, and keep Chrysler financial. Cerberus wanted to make a short-term profit with a leveraged buyout of the Chrysler automotive division, and with Kerkorian and Magna bidding for Chrysler; this appeared to be a realistic plan. The Great Housing Recession a year later would shoot down their plans.

In planning the purchase of Daimler Chrysler, Cerberus evidently failed to read the tealeaves of the toxic-mortgage debacle. Banks were beginning to write down their investments in toxic-mortgage bonds in 2007, and Wall Street was faltering. In 2007, many mortgage companies closed because of the toxic subprime mortgage problem, so the signs of an upcoming disaster in the economy were there. Cerberus management was overly optimistic about the Chrysler opportunity, and ignored the signals that the economy was about to tank.

The Bear Stearns bailout would occur in March 2008, and when Lehman Brothers filed for bankruptcy on September 15, 2008, the Great Housing Recession killed the economy, and vehicle sales dropped dramatically. The initial signs of the upcoming housing debacle were apparent in mid-2007, but it would have required a crystal ball to forecast the depth of the recession. However, there were enough signals that the economy was in trouble that Cerberus should have recognized a potential problem.

The Dow dropped 500 points in September 2007, and the Great Housing Recession was a year away. Ben Bernanke said that September and October of 2008 was "the worst financial crisis in history including the Great Depression." The stock market decline occurred just four months after the Cerberus acquisition.

In 2008, both Ford and General Motors reported record losses. Chrysler, being a private corporation, did not report losses. Sixteen months after Cerberus bought Chrysler, the automobile industry was heading toward bankruptcy. Chrysler sales declined, and the company laid off 5000 salaried employees in October 2008. Daimler-Benz announced that the remaining 20% of Chrysler had a book value of zero, and wrote off Chrysler. The Cerberus purchase of Chrysler was the worst investment the company had ever made.

Wall Street investment banks were facing bankruptcy with their balance sheets containing billions of toxic mortgages that were worthless, and banks were failing. The legislation to give affordable housing to minorities had created a recession, and the Wall Street subprime mortgage mess had caused the financial community to go into bankruptcy. Treasury Secretary Henry Paulson petitioned Congress for legislation to aid the economy.

However, Congress had caused the recession with legislation to increase homw ownership for low-income families, but denied any responsibility. One senator even said, "none of us had anything to do with the problem." The Housing and Community Development Act of 1992 required that over 50% of mortgages be given to low income families, so Congress was the guilty party. Congressional interference in the housing market, and President Clinton's national homeownership strategy eliminated historical mortgage requirements for down payments and income verification, which allowed low-income mortgage applicants to obtain home loans with a signature.

The Federal Reserve also got in the act by lowering interest rates from 5.25% to 0.25%, which flooded the housing market with funds for mortgages. The legislation and the readily available mortgage money created the housing boom of 2001-2006. Wall Street took advantage of the housing drive by creating mortgage bonds that included the toxic mortgages, and selling the bonds to unsuspecting investors. The housing boom ended in 2006 and Wall Street was stuck with toxic mortgage bonds on their balance sheets. The economy declined for five quarters, with the second quarter of 2008 shrinking 8.9%. Between the summer of 2007 and the fall of 2008, homeowners lost 50% of their net worth in their home equity. The housing recession was the worst economic downturn since the Great Depression.

Congress passed the Emergency Economic Stabilization Act on October 3, 2008. The legislation provided a $700 billion TARP fund for *troubled assets.* The Treasury gave Wall Street nearly $300 billion within two weeks, but rejected the Big Three request for a $35 billion loan. Wall Street had caused the subprime mortgage disaster, but were bailed out by the Treasury with taxpayer money. The auto industry was the victim of the government legislation that caused the recession and a 40% decline in vehicle sales. The automakers were the largest *troubled assets,* but were refused any bailout funds by the Treasury.

Since the banks were near bankruptcy, Chrysler and General Motors were unable to obtain bank loans for working capital, and the government was the only source of cash. Ford had mortgaged its entire company in 2006 to obtain bank loans for restructuring, and was using the loans for working capital to avoid bankruptcy.

    Congress called for Congressional Hearings, demanding that the Big Three CEOs, along with UAW president Ron Gettlefinger, come to Washington for the televised hearings. Washington politicians demonstrated their hostility toward the auto industry with their negative behavior in the hearings. Legislators asked the Big Three CEOs why they had "given away the store" to the UAW. The politicians failed to understand that the UAW had gained the benefits with pattern bargaining.

    The hearings continued with each "business expert" legislator criticizing the executives. Most of the legislators knew little about the auto business, but wanted publicity in the televised hearings. Fortunately, Christmas was near, and Congress never allows anything to interfere with Christmas vacation. After nearly two months of ridiculous hearings, the Senate voted 52-35 against a bailout on December 12, 2008.

    The negative vote received little media attention. How the government can claim a bailout of the automobile industry after refusing the $35 billion loan request and voting against a bailout is anybody's guess, but is a Washington spin on bankruptcy.

    President Bush loaned Chrysler and GM $17.4 billion to pay their bills until President Obama assumed office. The first problem the new president faced was the auto issue. Regrettably, President Obama failed to bailout Chrysler and GM, and started another *study*. The government had been studying the auto problem for nearly four months, so another study was certainly not required. The solution to the auto problem was obvious; the two companies needed cash to pay their bills. The recession had killed vehicle sales, and the firms were out of working capital.

Steven Rattner was appointed the *car czar* and began to recruit people for his task force. Instead of recruiting engineers and management people who knew the auto business, Rattner selected Wall Street types who had never seen an auto plant and many did not even own a car. The nation ended up with an auto task force consisting of Wall Street "instant auto experts" who knew nothing of manufacturing. To think that this group could develop a plan to turnaround Chrysler and General Motors was ridiculous.

This second-generation group of "Quiz Kids" began their study by trying to find their way to Detroit. After three months of meetings with automobile executives, Rattner fired Rick Wagoner, the CEO of General Motors. Rattner had no authority to fire anybody, much less the CEO of the largest automobile company in the country, but President Obama supported Rattner. Nardelli, the CEO of Chrysler, was not fired, but Chrysler was.

After five months of meetings with the Chrysler and GM executives, Rattner finally gave up and pushed Chrysler into bankruptcy on April 30, 2009. Nardelli, who had received a $210 million severance from Home Depot in January 2007, announced that he would retire after the bankruptcy. Tom Lasorda retired as president of Chrysler. Nardelli's tenure as an auto company CEO was short, and added to his loser's resume. Nardelli was later named one of the worst CEOs in history. General Motors followed Chrysler into bankruptcy court on June 1, 2009.

The government studies required eight months. Paulson's meetings and the Congressional Hearings had taken three months, and the Obama-Rattner study had taken five months. The government had bailed out Wall Street in two weeks without any studies. The comparison certainly shows the favoritism to Wall Street, and the negative opinion of the auto industry.

It was necessary for the government to loan cash for working capital to Chrysler and General Motors during the eight months of studies; the firms were bankrupt in October 2008. A total of $60 billion was required to pay the workers and suppliers during the eight-month studies, and amounted to 75% of the $79 billion of the "bailout" funds. The media missed the working capital problem, and the eight-month delay. Evidently, the politicians did not know enough about business to recognize that every company needs working capital to pay their people and keep the doors open.

Chrysler exited bankruptcy court on June 10, 2009. The court gave 55% of Chrysler to the union, 20% to the government, and 20% to Fiat, and zero to bondholders who owned $7 billion in secured debt, and $2 billion in unsecured debt. The union claims were unsecured. Bankruptcy law states that secured debt be paid first, and the court violated the law by favoring the union. President Obama bailed out the UAW and Fiat, not Chrysler.

Rattner made many mistakes as the "car czar," and one of them was the elimination of 25% of the Chrysler dealers on short notice. Automobile dealers are private and public businesses, and do not affect the profit of the Big Three. In some cases, a family's total net worth is tied up in the business. Dealer lawsuits reduced the number of dealer closures, but Rattner's dealer reduction program added over a hundred thousand to the unemployment rolls. The Chrysler dealers that were closed by the government received only a two-week notice.

Dealers are small businesses that the government claimed they were helping; the *help* resulted in 200,000 bankruptcies. Rattner, who missed the "auto business 101" course, added thousands to the unemployment rolls, gave Chrysler to a foreign company, fired the CEO of GM, paid off the union, and then wrote a book about his *accomplishments.* There is something wrong with that picture.

Rattner closed Chrysler dealers that had contributed to the Republican Party. Of the 789 Chrysler dealers closed, 788 had donated to Republican candidates, an amazing coincidence. Chrysler and GM had too many dealers, but a less painful method would have been to allow the dealers to close by attrition.

The government required eight months of Treasury meetings, Congressional Hearings, and the Obama-Rattner task-force study, before finally forcing Chrysler into bankruptcy – not a bailout, but bankruptcy. During this period, Chrysler required cash to pay its workers and suppliers. The government and the media failed to recognize that Chrysler and General Motors were out of the working capital that was required to keep production going and avoid closing their doors.

Chrysler was beyond repair when vehicle sales fell 40% during the government-caused Great Housing Recession. The company was forced to request government loans since the banks were bankrupt. The request was reasonable since the government had given trillions to Fannie Mae, Freddie Mac, AIG, Wall Street, and banks. However, the Treasury and Congress rejected the loan request. Chrysler management still hoped that President Obama would help. However, by April 2009 the Obama-Rattner team had decided that Chrysler was beyond saving, and forced the company into bankruptcy. The public remembers the supposed bailout, but is not aware of the bankruptcy. Only politicians can spin bankruptcy into a bailout.

In hindsight, Chrysler management should have prepared for bankruptcy when Congress voted against a bailout of automotive in late December 2008. The handwriting was on the wall for bankruptcy. Chrysler evidently thought that since the government had bailed out Wall Street, 888 banks, and 172 mortgage firms that a bailout of automotive would follow. Unfortunately, they were dead wrong.

In a normal bankruptcy, the company would have been able to renegotiate the UAW labor contract and become more competitive with foreign competition, and the bondholders would have been the first to receive payment. However, the Obama bankruptcy favored the union; the lawful renegotiation of labor contracts was not allowed, and the bondholders received absolutely nothing.

The number of financial institutions that received bailout money totaled 1065, five Wall Street firms, 888 banks, and 172 mortgage firms. This meant that 99% of all companies receiving bailout money were Wall Street, banks, and mortgage firms. These are amazing statistics considering that the media only talks about the "bailout" of automotive. The term "bankruptcy" is never used.

Fiat has announced that Chrysler headquarters will be moved to London, England. The third largest American auto company now has its head office in England. Fiat management will take over the London office, and more organization changes for Chrysler will occur. The Obama-Rattner team not only gave Chrysler to a foreign company, but Fiat moved Chrysler out of the country, and the nation lost the taxes.

There was little media attention to the Chrysler move to London. The media affinity for President Obama has been well known, and was again demonstrated when the prime media outlets failed to even mention the move. The "Detroit News" did cover the Chrysler move with a one-column article on page 7 of the May 10, 2014 issue, but the "Wall Street Journal" failed to mention the move. The media failed to cover the move of the third largest U.S. auto firm out of the country and the public does not seem to care; even in Motor City, the topic is rarely mentioned. Normally a move of this magnitude would have been front-page news, and the public wou have been outraged. If the "Fox News" roving reporter were to ask people where Chrysler is located, it is doubtful that anyone would reply London. Evidently, the public cares little about the manufacturing capability of the automobile industry.

Daimler-Benz was Chrysler's *partner* in the merger of equals, and the partnership had turned out to be a disaster. Chrysler was a strong and profitable company before the Daimler partnership, but the excessive overhead with German management added to Chrysler management, Chrysler had huge losses.

Daimler is a strong, worldwide auto firm, but Fiat is certainly not a leading carmaker. Fiat dropped out of the U.S. market in the 1980s because the Fiat cars did not sell. Fiat lost $15 billion between 2000 and 2005, and was near bankruptcy. General Motors saved Fiat from bankruptcy in 2005 with a $2 billion payout required if GM backed out on the 2000 agreement to purchase Fiat. Fiat paid absolutely nothing for 20% of a company that was worth $7.4 billion two years earlier. The Obama-Rattner plan to supply a partner for Chrysler was a huge error, and resulted in the loss of the third-largest U.S. automaker to a foreign firm.

The gift to Fiat bailed out Fiat, not Chrysler, and the Big Three became the Big Two and a Half. It is truly amazing that the public, and particularly Detroit, has not objected to the government giving the third largest U.S. automaker to a foreign firm. Walter Chrysler and other automobile pioneers must have rolled over in their graves.

The handling of the auto industry during the 2008 recesion was an utter disaster. Refusal to bailout one of the largest manufacturing industries in the world was bad enough, but taking eight months to make a decision was even worse. The government *too big to fail* idea threw trillions to financial institutiions, and the rejection of a $35 billion loan to automotive was deplorable. Instead of giving Chrysler to Fiat, appopinting a strong CEO like Lee Iacocca would have been a better avenue. Iacocca had rescued Chrysler from bankruptcy in 1980, and turned the company into the low-cost producer with new products. A strong CEO can fix a company, but a partnership often fails.

The future of Chrysler will depend on Fiat. The Italian automaker has been near bankruptcy for years, and there appears to be little opportunity for improvement. The market in Europe does not appear to be getting any better. The outlook for Fiat is not good. Rattner should have ignored Fiat as a partner.

FIVE
UAW

UAW WON EVERY NEGOTIATION

UAW Headquarters in Detroit

The United Auto Workers union was formed in 1935, in the middle of the Great Depression, and became one of the most powerful unions in the country. The International Union, United Automobile, Aerospace, and Agricultural Implement Workers of America, or the UAW, is an American labor union, with members in industries as different as autos and casinos. The UAW was started 40 years after the beginning of the auto industry, and the pattern bargaining tactic enabled the UAW to win every contract negotiation.

In 1935, the country was deep into the worst economic depression in history. Workers could not find work, and unemployment was over 25%. The automobile industry suffered a 75% drop in vehicle sales, and 90% of the auto companies closed their doors. The good old days of prosperity and the growth era of the automobile business ended. Soup lines and shantytowns were prevalent, and hungry workers were selling apples on street corners all over America. On Wall Street, investors were jumping from hotel windows.

You would think an earthquake or tsunami would be required to cause such a disaster, but the U.S. government filled in for the natural disasters by raising interest rates in 1928, causing the Great Depression of 1929. On Black Thursday, October 24, 1929, nearly 13 million shares of stock were sold, causing a run on the stock market. Stock prices fell to 75% of their prior level over the next few days. The Great Depression would last until World War II.

The Federal Reserve interest-rate increase had caused a tight money condition, and the Fed did nothing to correct money supply, which caused the Great Depression. The economic debacle continued through the 1930s. Unemployment was still high, but by 1936, the unemployment rate had declined to 16%. However, the Federal Reserve raised interest rates again in 1936, causing a 33% increase in unemployment, and a decrease of 30% in industrial production. The reason given by the Federal Reserve for the increase was "to increase reserves." The Fed met their accounting standard, but the rate increase created a second depression in 1937.

Franklin Roosevelt was elected president in 1932, and his New Deal of 1933 was intended to stem the depression. Roosevelt created 42 new government agencies, but few had any effect on reducing the economic disaster. Despite the media reporting that the New Deal fixed the depression, many economists claim the program failed to correct the economic disaster. The government had no solution for the depression.

In an attempt to find a scapegoat, Congress picked employers as the cause of the depression. The opening lines of the National Labor Relations Act of 1935 (Wagner Act) state its purpose was to "encourage collective bargaining as the solution for management practices that harm the general welfare of the economy." Later, the "findings" state; "the denial by employers of the right to organize a union causes a diminution of employment and wages." In the case of the automobile industry, the above statements were not factual. Henry Ford had doubled workers' pay to $5 a day and reduced the workweek to 40 hours. This would be $14.30 an hour today, nearly twice the current minimum wage, and equal to the starting wage of new autoworkers. The workweek was 60 hours in some industries at that time. Congress ignored these facts.

The Wagner Act blamed employers for the Great Depression, and recommended unions as the solution for the economic problems. After the National Labor Relations Act was passed, the number of unions increased five times, and labor strikes increased across the country.

The UAW took advantage of the Wagner Act and began its drive to organize the Big Three. The depression had caused the 25% unemployment rate and the layoff of thousands of autoworkers because of the drop in car sales. Union organizers promised workers jobs, even though there were no jobs, if the workers would join the UAW. The workers listened, and signed up, because their children were hungry. Labor strikes date back to 1677 when the first recorded strike occurred, but the UAW developed a new tactic called the sit-down strike. Instead of walking a picket line with placards, the workers stopped working, sat down at their workstations, and occupied the plant.

The first sit-down strike took place at a General Motors plant in Atlanta, Georgia in 1936, but the most famous was at a GM plant in Flint, Michigan. The Flint strike started December 29, 1936 – there were no two-week Christmas vacations in 1936 – and lasted until February 1937, when the Michigan governor acted as a mediator. During the strike, the company cut off heat, lights, and water, but the workers' families brought food and water (and probably other liquid refreshments), and passed these through the windows of the plant. It gets cold in Michigan at that time of year, and workers built fires inside the plant to keep warm. You can imagine what the plant looked like when the strike ended. Police attempted to break up the strike, but workers repelled the police by throwing auto parts from the windows. This was called the "running of the bulls" in union halls across the country.

General Motors agreed to the UAW union on February 11, 1937. After the signed labor agreement, the workers called a large number of "wildcat" strikes across the country. The wildcat strike is called by a local UAW union, and not authorized by the international office, but the strikes still stopped production.

The UAW attacked Chrysler next with sit-down strikes, and Chrysler agreed to a union in March 1937; Ford held out until 1941. Henry Ford was known as the "worker's friend" because of his paternal ways of dealing with employees; he had doubled his workers' wages and reduced the workweek to 40 hours. He was criticized at the time by both the government and other industry officials for "excessive wages." Ford had also helped his workers during the depression with loans to families, and gifts of plots of land to raise crops during the difficult times. However, this had no effect with the UAW, and the union organizers continued to harass Ford Motor Company.

On May 26, 1937, union organizers started a demonstration at the Ford Rouge complex, and Ford security and Dearborn police attempted to break it up. During the melee, several union officials were roughed up, including Walter Reuther, the future president of the UAW. Newspaper reporters and photographers were there and reported on the incident for weeks. Ford finally agreed to a union in 1941. The UAW had organized the Big Three auto companies.

The U.S. automobile industry started in 1896, struggled for the next ten years, took hold with the Model T, expanded through the growth era (1910-1929), and became the largest single industry in the country. All of this was accomplished without any help from the UAW or the government. The auto business had provided jobs for thousands of workers and had created new industries such as dealers, auto suppliers, and auto repair shops. The number of jobs in the associated industries matched the number of jobs in the auto plants. The automobile had become a necessity for travel instead of a rich person's toy. Now that the UAW and the government were involved in the business, the troubles for the industry were just beginning.

Labor-management relations were relatively amicable during the first 40 years of the industry, and the automobile business grew. When the government favored the unions in the National Labor Relations Act, the game changed. With the entrance of the UAW into the game, the situation would change dramatically. UAW leadership took an adversarial role with the Big Three almost immediately, and has continued in this mode for the past 80 years. The UAW leaders and committee members established an anti-management attitude with workers.

In contrast, the Japanese unions work with management in Japan. When the Japanese unions declare a strike, the workers wear armbands, showing they are unhappy with management and are on strike, but they continue to work. In U.S. auto plants, strikes often include violence. Even when workers are not on strike, there is sometimes sabotage to conveyors, and workers slash tires on vehicles. The anti-management attitude is encouraged by UAW headquarters and local union representatives. The UAW worker only hears of the cynical and distrustful management actions, and hears nothing good about management. The UAW workers are told of management supposed abuses in union meetings, and union committees recommend retribution.

The tunnel vision of the UAW leadership causes the anti-management attitude, and few UAW vice presidents or presidents have attempted to change the adversarial behavior. The real enemy of the UAW is foreign competition, not Big Three management. Union workers made up nearly 25% of the U.S. workforce in the late 1970s, but only 11% today. This evidence does not appear to sway UAW management. Other unions preach the anti-management behavior, and have suffered the same fate.

The first 40 years of the U.S. automobile industry were ones of inventions, development, and growth, without labor strife or government interference. The last 80 years have involved UAW strikes and government intervention. The Japanese unions and government work together with the automakers, and Japan has passed the U.S. in annual vehicle production.

The government demanded that unions prohibit strikes during the war years of 1941-1945, and the UAW upheld its part of the agreement. However, three months after V-J Day, the UAW called a 113-day strike against General Motors. The UAW had built up power during the 1937-1945 period, and began to exercise that strength in the 1945 negotiations. In addition to the demands for wage and benefit increases, the UAW also demanded lower prices for vehicles, and demanded to be part of management decision-making on automobile prices. This was an unheard of demand, and if General Motors had agreed to the UAW demands, the union would have controlled the company, and the auto business. GM agreed to wage increases, but held its ground against the demands by the UAW to control vehicle prices and to be part of managing the business.

Walter Reuther was elected president of the UAW in 1946, and he continued in that role until his death in an airplane crash in 1970. The UAW plane was taking Reuther and his wife to a union resort in northern Michigan when the private plane went down in flames.

After World War II, there were a large number of union strikes across the country, and the public became alarmed at the power of the unions. Congress reacted to the public outcry and passed the Taft-Hartley Act in 1947. The Taft-Hartley Act made minor changes to the National Labor Relations Act of 1935, which was the most radical labor-management legislation in history, favoring unions. The number of labor unions had increased by five times after the Wagner Act was passed, and labor strikes became common. The Taft-Hartley Act outlawed several union unfair labor practices, but failed to eliminate the negotiating tactic of pattern bargaining.

The UAW developed the unique bargaining tactic called "pattern bargaining." The union demanded that all contracts in the same business be the identical. The companies in the automobile industry were not the "same." General Motors was three times the size of Chrysler, and twice the size of Ford. As a result, GM's cash resources were far larger than their competitor's, which gave them a huge advantage in funding styling and model-year changes. GM's size permitted separate engineering and styling departments for each brand, but Ford and Chrysler were required to share engineering and styling for all brands because of cost. This difference put both Ford and Chrysler at a disadvantage since styling had become the main feature in sales. For the first forty years, car buyers were primarily interested in a car that worked, rather than the styling and appearance of the vehicle. By the mid-1920s, most auto manufacturers had developed their vehicles to work properly, and styling began to be the main sales driver.

Pattern bargaining includes the tactic of negotiating with one company at a time, instead of the normal method of negotiating with all of the Big Three companies at the same time. Since the union demands that all contracts be similar in pattern bargaining, the contract negotiations should have occurred concurrently. The UAW selects one of the Big Three companies for the contract negotiations, and presents the union demands for the new contract period, which is normally three years. Negotiating with one company at a time is the critical issue. The UAW selects a strike target to begin negotiations, and bargains with only one company instead of negotiating with all the Big Three during the contract period. The tool used by the UAW in negotiations is the strike. A long strike cripples a company, causing huge financial losses, and the loss of market share. The loss of market share is all-important because it reduces volume. Regaining market share after a strike is extremely difficult.

The UAW builds up a strike fund between contracts that provides a "piggy bank" to draw from in case of a long strike. The strike fund is taken from union dues. The UAW deducts union dues from their workers' pay each week, and a portion of the dues go into the strike fund. Over the three-year contract period, the strike fund includes input from all the companies. By negotiating with one company, the strike fund is sufficient to pay workers enough so they can to put food on the table and pay the rent during a strike. If the UAW negotiated with all companies at the same time, the strike fund would not support a long strike, and the negotiation playing field would be level.

Pattern bargaining gives the UAW a definite advantage in negotiations, but the leverage has been ignored by the government and the media. The UAW can afford a long strike, but the companies cannot. As a result, the company negotiators are at a disadvantage. Because of pattern bargaining, the UAW has won every contract negotiation and obtained non-competitive wages and benefits.

The hourly wage in 1914, after Henry Ford doubled the pay, was equal to $14.30 in today's dollars, and there were few fringes in 1914. The current hourly rate is $28 an hour, double the 1914 rate, but fringes increase the rate to $78 an hour. Fringe benefits include four weeks of vacation, company-paid health care that includes dental and eye care, and company-paid pensions. Many workers retire at 50 with the 30-and-out pension benefit. Retiree benrfit cost became a huge cost problem for the Big Three. The UAW also negotiated the infamous jobs bank in 1984 that paid laid-off workers 95% of their wages and 100% of their benefits. Many retired from the jobs bank after spending years not working. Labor became fixed costs with the jobs bank and prevented the companies from closing obsolete manufacturing facilities because the workers would simply move into the jobs bank, and continue being paid. This became a monumental problem when foreign competition took over 50% of the U.S. market, and 30% of the manufacturing and assembly plants became unnecessary facilities. The combination of high wages and benefits, retiree costs, and the excessive fixed costs, caused the U.S. car companies to be non-competitive in cost, and would later lead to bankruptcy.

Pattern bargaining also completely changed the industry. Chrysler was second in market share between 1937 and 1950 and was a viable company. When Chrysler management refused to accept company-paid pensions granted by Ford in the 1949 contract negotiations, the UAW called a strike, and the company closed for 104 days. Chrysler was forced to accept the Ford concessions in order to stop the strike, but the company suffered a financial loss, and a loss of market share. The loss of market share pushed Chrysler into third place in market sales, and the company volume was lowered to a point near its break-even level. When sales fell during recessions, Chrysler lost money, and the company cash position was too low to support the costs of the annual model change. The inability to meet the competition in styling changes caused further market-share losses, and Chrysler became the weakest of the Big Three with the lower volume. The volume change caused the company to be borderline profitable and resulted in the near bankruptcy situation when the 1979 recession caused a shaprp decline in vehicle sales.

Chrysler was required to obtain a government loan to avoid bankruptcy. The $1.5 billion loan allowed Chrysler to restructure, and regain profitability. Lee Iacocca turned the company around in the 1980s, and Chrysler recovered. However, the low volume problem continued and was a major factor in the 2009 bankruptcy. The 104-day strike was an industry-changing event, and eventually drove Chrysler into bankruptcy.

It is surprising that historians and business media have ignored the effects of the UAW 104-day strike in 1949. They have also missed the importance of pattern bargaining. Pattern bargaining is not well understood, but it is the most important factor in UAW labor negotiations. Big Three management took the approach that all contracts would be the same, and each company would suffer the same penalties. Evidently, they failed to realize that the costs would become unbearable. However, there was little management could do since the government supported the unions. During the 2008 Congressional Hearings, politicians asked why auto management had "given away the store" to the UAW during contract negotiations indicating that the legislators were ignorant of pattern bargaining. Neither legislators nor the public were aware of pattern bargaining and its effect on contract negotiations.

The wages and benefits gained by the UAW over the past 70 years with this unique bargaining technique created costs for the Big Three that drove the U.S. auto companies into bankruptcy. Unfortunately, Pattern bargaining remains in effect, and labor costs will continue to escalate.

In the 1949 UAW contract negotiations, the unin gained company-paid pensions, cost of living (COLA), and a 3% annual improvement factor in wages. In addition to the pension and COLA benefits, the annual improvement was a major reason for price increases in vehicles. The annual improvement factor of 3% was included in the cost of every component in the vehicle every year, to pay for the UAW benefit, and vehicle prices increased.

Leonard Woodcock was named president of the UAW after Walter Reuther was killed in the 1970 plane crash. Woodcock was later named Ambassador to China. After retiring from the government, Woodcock taught political science at the University of Michigan in Ann Arbor. Leonard Woodcock died in 1971 at age 89.

The year 1973 was a bad year for the Big Three. The OPEC oil crisis caused buyers to rush to purchase small, fuel-efficient vehicles, and unfortunately, the Big Three had failed to develop competitive small cars. The Japanese sold even more vehicles, increasing their market share at the expense of the U.S. carmakers. Dental benefits were added in 1973, along with more holidays, and the 25-and-out pension was given to foundry workers. Vision and hearing were added in 1976, along with more holidays. The infamous 30-and-out pension benefit was added in 1979, and the number of paid holidays was increased to 26. The 30-and-out benefit added huge costs to the retiree pension cost problem.

Paid holidays increased with every contract. In the 1960s, the number was at a reasonable level, and workers had to work a half day on the days before Christmas and New Year's Day. Today the Christmas vacation is two weeks. The European autoworkers get a month-long vacation in the summer and this had always appeared to be excessive, but the UAW contracts are approaching the European vacation benefits.

The OPEC oil crisis of 1973 was followed by the Iranian oil embargo of 1979, which also raised gas prices and caused long lines at gas stations. These two events resulted in a dramatic increase in foreign imports, particularly Japanese imports. The market share of the Big Three continued to fall, and the number of UAW workers declined. The Federal Government had a perfect opportunity to create an energy policy to make the country independent of foreign oil. The U.S. has adequate oil reserves to make the nation independent of OPEC, but the environmental lobby won the battle, and instead of passing legislation to allow more drilling, Congress passed responsibility for energy control to the automobile industry by passing laws to increase fuel-economy in vehicles.

Congress passed the Corporate Average Fuel Economy Act (CAFE) in 1975, which required an increase in vehicle fuel economy. The legislation was intended to eliminate the U.S. dependence on foreign oil imports, but failed miserably. With the number of automobiles and drivers increasing every year, the gasoline usage increased despite the increase in fuel economy in vehicles. Foreign oil imports increased 15% despite the increase in vehicle fuel economy.

Profit sharing was added in the 1982 contract, along with a moratorium on the outsourcing of products. The 1984 contract gave the union the infamous jobs bank that paid UAW members not to work. The jobs bank benefit was clever move by the UAW because workers remained in the UAW even though they had no job, and were laid off. They continued to pay union dues even though their manufacturing plant was closed.

The loss of market to the imports caused an excess capacity problem with the Big Three. The jobs bank caused labor costs to be fixed rather than variable, and prevented the auto companies from reducing costs when plants were shut down. Many UAW workers remained in the jobs bank for years, drawing their pay and benefits for not working, and some even retired from the jobs bank.

The jobs bank was a ridiculous and costly benefit. The UAW negotiated the benefit to avoid losing jobs when plants were closed. With the jobs bank UAW workers kept their jobs and paid union dues even on layoff. Workers were required to report to a company location daily and sign in, indicating they were available for work. Of course, there was no work available since their plant had been closed. The "workers" would sit around reading magazines all day. Some even left the auto company facility during the day, and worked in other jobs while drawing their jobs bank pay. The so-called workers in the jobs bank were called "bankers."

By 1984, the Big Three market share had declined to 77% and many assembly and manufacturing plants were no longer required. Plant closures would have resulted in huge losses of UAW members. To prevent loss of membership, the UAW used the jobs bank. "Bankers" continued to be UAW members even though their jobs were eliminated, and were no longer working. Pattern bargaining had allowed this fatal benefit. As foreign auto manufacturers continued to gain market share, the Big Three attempted to close plants, but continued to pay workers in the jobs bank. The jobs bank cost the auto companies $4.2 billion between 2005 and 2008. The Big Three attempted to eliminate the jobs bank during conract negotiations, but the UAW refused to agree. Pattern bargaining won again.

To give a comparison as to the value of a billion dollars in the auto business, Honda built a new plant in Ohio for $500 million. When the UAW was asked to eliminate the jobs bank during the 2008 Congressional Hearings, UAW president Ron Gettlefinger refused, and continued to refuse until he retired shortly before the bankruptcy. The bankruptcy court finally put an end to the jobs bank.

The jobs bank is one example of how pattern bargaining in automotive labor negotiations allowed the union to obtain unreasonable benefits. Pattern bargaining, with the tactic of negotiating with one company at a time, was a windfall for the UAW. The government and the media have criticized Big Three management for giving away the store, but both lacked an understanding of pattern bargaining. Neither has studied the industry in enough detail to understand how the negotiations work. The ridiculous jobs bank was a disaster.

In the 1999 contract negotiations, the UAW won the agreement that no plant would be closed during the contract period. The Big Three had 30% excess capacity and many manufacturing and assembly plants should have been closed. The foreign carmakers were increasing market share every year, and many had started engine and assembly plants in the U.S. The union contract agreement that prohibited the closure of plants demonstrated that the UAW was in total control.

It is surprising that Big Three management did not file an unfair labor practice against pattern bargaining. Caterpillar attempted to eliminate pattern bargaining in their 1992 contract negotiations, but the UAW caused a long strike and refused to give up pattern bargaining. Caterpillar finally gave up because of a long strike, and pattern bargaining remained in effect. The bankruptcy court should have eliminated pattern bargaining, but the union support by Democrats prevented the action.

Another area that has received little if any media attention is job classification. The Japanese have two job classifications, and the UAW contract has several pages of job classifications and job descriptions. Union officials use job classifications for featherbedding. By demanding that certain job classifications work on certain jobs, extra workers are required to get the job completed. When changing tooling, often six or seven skilled trades workers sit around drinking coffee while waiting for the correct job classification to complete his/her work. In Japan, the skilled trade's people work together, and attempt to complete the job as fast as they can – big difference.

The effect of the job classification issue was shown in an automotive-supplier company with a UAW contract. The supplier produced brake assemblies for the Big Three, and one of the components of an assembly was a stamping that was manufactured on a seven-station transfer die. When a die changeover was required, the UAW skilled trades group required 24 hours for the changeover. The reason for the 24 hours was that only one job classification worked on the die at any given time. When the first worker started, the other workers sat around drinking coffee until the working operator completed his/her job. The next worker would then start to work, etc. Management had attempted to correct this situation, but the UAW filed grievances, and won, because of the job classifications in the contract.

The supplier had given a license to a Japanese company to make the identical assembly. In Japan, there were only three skilled trade's people involved. When making a changeover, the three worked together to complete the job. The time required for the changeover was 90 minutes. The Japanese had a chart on the wall of the pressroom that showed the changeover time in graphical form. At the completion of every changeover, one of the operators posted the time on the graph. The operators were attempting to improve the changeover time with each occurrence.

Ron Gettlefinger was elected president of the UAW in 2002. During the Congressional Hearings of 2008, legislators were critical of the Big Three for the jobs bank that paid workers not to work, but their criticism was aimed at the CEOs rather than the UAW. The Big Three CEOs stated that this was required by contract, and Congress then asked Gettlefinger to make the jobs bank go away, and he refused. Fortunately, the bankruptcy court later eliminated the jobs bank. Gettlefinger announced his retirement on March 19, 2009, shortly before the bankruptcies. Bob King, who was known for his militant, anti-management behavior, followed Gettlefinger. Dennis Williams replaced King.

The UAW hourly wage rate of $28 increases to $78 when fringe benefits (pensions, health care, vacations, etc.) are included. Newly hired workers make $14 an hour, which jumps to $60 when fringes are added. Retiree benefits are the main cause of the jump from $28 to $78. The wage rate for Japanese companies in the U.S. is $48 an hour, including fringes, a difference of $25 per hour.

The health-care benefits were such a problem that the UAW agreed to move retiree health care costs into a trust fund managed by the union. Unfortunately, it was too little and too late. The union adversarial relationship with the Big Three caused cost and productivity problems, prevented the partnership that existed in Japanese companies, and eventually led to the bankruptcy of Chrysler and General Motors. UAW membership declined from 1.5 million to less than 400,000, a drop of 75%. The adversarial approach has not worked, but continues.

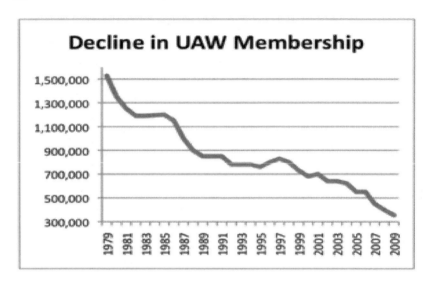

The ship could have been righted if UAW management had attempted to work with the Big Three instead of maintaining its anti-management behavior. The UAW has continued the strike policy, lost jobs, and as a result, they have aided their chief enemy, the foreign carmakers. The result has been a loss of UAW jobs. UAW membership declined from 1.5 million to 300,000 between 1979 and 2009, despite the jobs bank, job classification issue, and the 1999 contract agreement preventing plant closures.

SIX

GOVERNMENT

Dysfunctional

The founding fathers of our country had no intention of controlling business or housing, but for the past 100 years the Federal Government has taken complete control. The government attempts to control the economy have also failed, and the results have been disastrous. The Federal Reserve caused the 1929 depression, and Congress caused 2008 housing recession. The government has also caused 50% of the recessions since World War II - a less than stellar performance.

The government began the control effort in 1913 with the Federal income tax. The Supreme Court ruled the income tax unconstitutional in 1895, but the Sixteenth Amendment, ratified in 1913, removed the Supreme Court objections. The top tax rate was initially 25% but was increased in the middle of the Great Depression to 63% in 1932 and to 79% in 1936. The Great Depression was so bad that it is doubtful that many paid the top rate during the depression, but the steep rise in taxes is indicative of the government's disregard for economic conditions. In 1945, the top tax rate increased to 91% and would remain at least 88% until 1963, when it was lowered to 70%. The Internal Revenue Service became so powerful that by 2009, the IRS targeted political groups with extra audits and harassment, and was even given the responsibility of policing the Affordable Care Act.

The automobile industry had not only changed the world of transportation, but had become one of the largest industries in the country. The average person would think the government would support and protect the auto business, but government politicians took the opposite path. The Japanese government supports not only its auto industry, but other industries as well. It is not surprising that Japan took the lead in worldwide vehicle production and in the production of television, cameras, robots, machine tools, and off-road equipment production. Instead of helping these industries, the U.S. government legislated controls that stifled growth. The negative attitude of the government toward the auto industry was demonstrated during the 2008 Congressional Hearings. Most questions to the automobile CEOs were negative, and some were downright nasty. After nearly two months of kangaroo court hearings, the Senate voted 52-35 against a bailout of the auto industry. Congress voted to allow Chrysler and General Motors to go into bankruptcy.

The present government is dysfunctional Congress was unable to pass a budget for four years, and the The White House issues executive orders that are sometimes illegal, and choke businesses. Politicians in Washington are only interested in reelection, and fail to do their jobs as directed by the U.S. Constitution.

The government did not interfere in the auto business in the first 40 years, and the business prospered. In the last 80 years, the Federal Government has taken control of the industry with legislation and regulations that have suppressed growth. The management of the economy has also been dismal. The Federal Reserve and Treasury have caused recessions with their attempts to control the economy, and many economists have recommended the abolishment of the Fed. The economy was booming during the Roaring Twenties, but the Federal Reserve put an end to the good times by raising interest rates in 1928. The increase in interest rates caused the stock market crash in 1929.

Great Depression

The economy was growing in 1928 with unemployment at 3% and vehicle production at an all-time high, but the Federal Reserve interfered with the economy by raising interest rates. The interest-rate increase created a tight money condition that ended the prosperity of the Roaring Twenties. On Black Thursday, October 24, 1929, the sale of 13 million shares started the stock-market decline. Within a few days, stock prices fell 70%. On Tuesday, October 29, over 16 million shares were sold, and $30 billion ($400 billion today) was lost in one month.

Banks began to fail due to the tight money conditions, and when people withdrew their savings, the bank closure problem worsened; one third of the banks closed. The Federal Reserve failed to stem the bank closures, which was its prime responsibility. Unemployment rose from 3.2% to 25%, and wages were reduced 42% for those still working. More than 50% of families were living below the minimum subsistence level. Families lost their homes, farmers lost their farms, and their children went hungry. The Gross National Product fell 9.4% in

1930, another 8.5% in 1931, and an astounding, record-breaking 13.4% in 1932. Automotive sales fell 75% between 1929 and 1932, and 90% of the auto companies closed their doors. The luxury-car market was decimated because the market turned to low-priced vehicles. Famous brands like Cord, Duesenberg, Pierce-Arrow, and Stutz went out of business. Every statistic was negative. The Great Depression was the worst economic-disaster period in the country's history, and our government caused it.

The Federal Reserve had caused the 1920 and 1929 depressions, but evidently did not recognize the effect of the interest-rate changes, because the politicians were blaming the depression on everybody except the Federal Reserve. The Federal Reserve raised interest rates again in 1936. Unemployment had decreased from 25% to 16% by 1936, but the interest-rate increase caused a further decline in the economy, and unemployment rose above 20%. President Roosevelt blamed "business monopolies" for the increase in unemployment in his radio speeches. The Federal Reserve reported that the 1936 interest-rate increase was required to increase its reserves. The government met its accounting standards but put thousands out of work.

The government obviously had no idea of what caused the Great Depression. Congress passed the Smoot-Hawley Tariff Act in 1930 with the stated purpose of "protecting American workers, provide revenue, and to regulate commerce with foreign countries." The Tariff Act failed to accomplish any of these objectives. Foreign countries retaliated by raising tariffs which reduced world trade by 30%. Imports were cut by 66%, and U.S. exports were reduced 65%. Unemployment increased again because of the Tarrif Act and the government failed in its first attempt to stem the depression.

For those who question whether the Federal Reserve caused the Great Depression, Milton Friedman, recipient of the Nobel Prize in economics, stated for 40 years that the Federal Reserve caused the

Great Depression. While working for the government in the mid-1930s, Friedman also said that the government intervention with the New Deal was "the wrong cure for the wrong disease." Former chairman of the Federal Reserve, Ben Bernanke, agreed with Friedman in a speech at Friedman's retirement party.

The generally accepted cause of the Great Depression is that stock-market speculation caused the depression, and that President Roosevelt's New Deal fixed it. As Friedman explained in his writings, nothing could be further from the truth. In addition to investors jumping from hotel windows, the unemployed rode freight trains looking for work. Many farmers traveled west to look for work on the farms in California. During their trip, some stayed in shantytowns, called "Hooverville" by Democrats, mocking former President Hoover, a Republican. The shantytowns were similar to refugee camps and were policed by local politicians. Soup lines were started throughout the country, and unemployed workers sold apples on street corners. The eleven years of the Great Depression were terrible, and Americans suffered more than can be imagined. Unfortunately, politicians ignored the fact that the government caused the debacle.

In addition to the historic drop in the economy and the terrible plight of people across the country, the Great Depression changed the automobile industry from a healthy, growing business that employed thousands of workers, to a group of near-bankrupt companies. In 1932, the combined losses of auto companies totaled $191 million ($3 billion today). The three-billion-dollar loss might not seem high in today's economy when the national debt is nearly $20 trillion, but annual vehicle sales were one third of today's volume at that time.

The Big Three survived the depression, but all suffered a loss of volume, and worker layoffs were necessary for the companies to survive. General Motors, with Alfred Sloan's expert leadership, survived the depression without a loss year, which was a near miracle. Ford remained in business, but lost money because of the fixed costs accumulated with the 1927 launch of the Model A, and the investment in the huge Rouge manufacturing complex. Chrysler gained market share from Ford, and took second place in sales in 1937. CEO Walter Chrysler also did an outstanding job of managing his company through the economic disaster.

The Great Depression was such a terrible time that it is impossible for the young people of today to understand the suffering of Americans during this period. The fact that our government caused the debacle is tragic, and even worse was that Washington politicians were unable to determine the cause. President Roosevelt has been given credit for steering the country through the terrible times, but if an analysis is made of his New Deal, the results show that the 42 government agencies created did little to fix the problem. The White House and Congress blaming employers and business monopolies for the Great Depression was an excuse to hide the real cause. Politicians refused to accept responsibility at that time, and still ignore the fact that the Federal Government caused the depression.

Prohibition began in 1920 and lasted until 1933. The feelings toward alcohol were so strong that when Prohibition was passed, some towns actually sold their jails thinking that alcohol was the root cause of all crime. The "speakeasy" got its name because patrons had to whisper their name to enter illegal taverns. The average worker earned $1000 a year, or $0.50 an hour, while Al Capone made $60 million. However, over 800 gangsters were killed in the city of Chicago alone during the Prohibition era.

Six years into the depression, Congress found a scapegoat – employers. The government badly needed an excuse for the economic disaster and blamed business. The National Labor Relations Act (Wagner Act) was passed in 1935. The Wagner Act blamed the depression on employers, and the solution recommended was union organization.

The opening statement of the Wagner Act was "to protect the rights of employees, to encourage collective bargaining, and to curtail certain management practices which can harm the general welfare of employees, and damage the economy." Under "findings and policies" in the Wagner Act, paragraph two stated, "the inequality of bargaining power between employees, who do not possesss freedom of contract, and employers who are organized as a corporation, tends to aggravate recurrent business depressions." President Roosevelt blamed "business monopolies" for the depression in his many radio speeches. The Tariff Act had failed miserably, and there was nothing in the Washington house of cards to fix the problem, so Congress needed a scapegoat, and business became the target.

The UAW was formed in 1935, and took advantage of the Wagner Act. The first recorded labor strike occurred in 1677, and involved violence. The UAW developed a new tactic called the sit-down strike, and was successful in organizing the Big Three. The sit-down strike involved workers sitting down at their workstations and occupying the plant. The government demanded a stop to strikes during World War II, but as soon as the war ended, massive strikes were the order of the day. The UAW called a 113-day strike against General Motors three months after V-J Day. The union strike effort resumed.

The public had enough and demanded that Congress put controls on unions. Congress responded with the Taft-Hartley Act in 1947. The legislation was the first revision to the 1935 National Labor Relations Act and included several revisions to put an end to union unfair labor practices. In reality, the Taft-Hartley Act was ineffective in stemming union activity. One of the provisions of the act was forbidding unions to contribute to political campaigns. However, the provision is evidently not enforced, because unions have continued to be among the largest contributors to political campaigns.

The attempts by the government to control the economy resulted in the Great Depression, and the legislation attempting to correct the economic catastrophe failed. Most legislators are attorneys and trained in the law. However, politicians proved that a law degree provided little problem-solving ability since they failed to determine the cause of the Great Depression. Engineers are trained to solve problems, and one of the techniques used is to determine "what changed." If politicians had used this basic approach to problem solving they possibly could have found the root cause of the Great Depression was the interest rate increase by the Federal Reserve. Evidently, politicians should be engineers rather than attorneys.

The auto industry grew to be the largest industry in the country, but government legislation and regulations hindered industry growth similar to the Red Flag Act in England a century earlier. Beginning with the National Labor Relations Act in 1935, continuing with legislation controlling emissions, safety, and fuel economy, and finally, with the bankruptcies of Chrysler and General Motors, the Federal Government has taken control of the automobile industry.

The government legislation to solve the nations's problems has somehow missed the mark. To fix the Great Depression, Congress passed the National Labor Relations Act that blamed employers for the Great Depression and recommended unions as the solution. The auto fuel-economy legislation was intended to make the nation independent of OPEC and foreign oil imports by increasing fuel economy in vehicles. Unfortunately, neither accomplished the objectives. A realistic energy policy would have eliminated the foreign oil import problem, and the elimination of the Federal Reserve would have helped the economy. The automobile emission legislation was an attempt to reduce smog and has been partially successful; the smog problem still exists in Los Angeles at certain times. The safety legislation has achieved its objective.

Smog is an air pollutant that affects the eyes and causes breathing problems. It was originally identified in London as early as 1300. The term "peasouper" was used to define the London fog, or smog. King Edward I of England actually banned coal fires in London for a short time to reduce smog in 1306. People in London had to dress warmly in 1306. Smog was recognized to be a problem in the U.S. in the early 1950s, particularly in the Los Angeles area.

Despite the long history of smog, scientists had not identified its elements before government officials were writing legislation to control the pollutant. The first legislation by the state of California mandated the installation of "blow by" devices on vehicles sold in California in 1963. The device returned unburned gases to the combustion chamber. Research had shown that "blow by" gases amounted to 25% of hydrocarbon emissions. The Federal Government passed the Clean Air Act in 1963 to establish smog controls, and the Motor Vehicle Air Pollution Act of 1965 established national standards for automotive emissions. The Clean Air Act was amended in 1970 to include stationary pollution sources.

The research to determine the make-up of smog was incomplete in the 1960s, but scientists identified hydrocarbons and carbon monoxide as two elements of smog. Legislation was enacted to control the emission of both elements, and automotive engineers worked around the clock to redesign engines to meet the new emission standards. Engines had been designed for performance and fuel economy, but the new emission laws required that hydrocarbons and carbon monoxide be included in engine calibration. The control of the two new elements required new engine calibration, and engine engineers worked overtime to recalibrate engines to reduce hydrocarbon and carbon monoxide emissions. The hydrocarbon and carbon monoxide elements were in opposition to fuel economy and performance engine curves.

Legislation established limits on the pollutants, and had firmly established limits on vehicle sales if vehicles failed to meet the new standards. After working to reduce hydrocarbons and carbon monoxide, and still include the performance and fuel economy objectives, the Big Three produced engines that met the new government pollution standards. The next surprise was that scientists discovered that nitrogen oxides (NO and NOx) were key elements of smog, and legislators quickly added these elements to the law. Unfortunately, engine engineers discovered that nitrous-oxide control required a completely different curve for engine calibration, and the previous design and development work had to be reengineered. The government rush to issue legislation cost time and money in engine design and development.

The Big Three petitioned the government to allow the auto companies to work together to solve the new engine design and development problems, as the Japanese were doing. Not only did the Japanese government allow its car companies to work together, the government formed a consortium to develop engine solutions for emissions. The U.S. government refused to allow the Big Three to work together under the threat of anti-trust. As a result, engineers actually were afraid of going to jail if technical information was shared with other companies. The Japanese auto companies, working together, were able to meet the new emission standards faster, and at less cost.

The rush to pass legislation before scientific data identified the elements of smog gave politicians the publicity they wanted, but actually delayed the implementation of engine changes because of the continual changes in the smog control laws. The Federal Government could have, and should have, helped the process by allowing Big Three engineers to work together to develop new engine technology. Politicians are primarily interested in reelection, and because of this, could not vote against the emission laws if they wanted to keep their seats.

The auto fuel-economy legislation was passed after the OPEC oil crisis of 1973. OPEC decided to penalize the United States for its support of Israel in the Gulf War by creating an oil embargo. Gasoline prices doubled, and long lines at gas stations were a normal occurrence. The U.S. vehicle market changed almost overnight. Prior to OPEC, car buyers had to wait twelve weeks for the delivery of large cars. Immediately after OPEC, dealer lots were filled with large cars, since buyers were flocking to small, fuel-efficient vehicles. The Big Three had not developed competitive small cars, and Japanese import sales soared.

The government had the opportunity to open up oil exploration and drilling to make the country independent of foreign oil, but the environmental lobby was too powerful. The government buckled to the lobby and shifted the responsibility to the automobile industry by passing legislation to increase vehicle fuel economy. The auto engineers met the new fuel economy standards, but the dependence on foreign oil increased. The number of vehicles on the road, and the number of drivers, increase every year, so there was no way that increasing vehicle fuel economy was going to make the country independent of foreign oil. Politicians included environmental issues in their fuel economy equation, but omitted the fact that additional vehicles and drivers would affect the outcome.

The 1979 Iranian oil crisis created the same oil shortage, gas-price increases, and fear on the part of Americans, and again the government reacted by increasing vehicle fuel-economy requirements, with identical results – oil imports increased. An even larger share of the U.S. vehicle market went to the Japanese. The amount of foreign oil imported increased by 15% despite the fuel-economy increase in vehicles.

The government simply refuses to allow oil exploration and drilling to make the country independent of foreign oil. Oil companies have developed a new fracking process for obtaining oil from shale oil deposits, but the environmental lobby has petitioned the government to stop the new process. A country can be environmentally friendly, and still drill for oil. Norway is known for its social benefits and being environmentally friendly, but it uses offshore drilling rigs in its famous fiords to produce oil. Norway exports oil and is a rich country. For example, the Norwegian government pays for the college education of its citizens. The bottom line is that the U.S. government is responsible for higher gas prices because the environmental lobby controls Congress, and additional drilling for oil is prohibited.

Safety became an issue when there were a number of deaths attributed to vehicles in 1960. In 1966, Congress enacted the Highway Safety Act, and the National Traffic and Motor Vehicle Safety Act. This legislation authorized the federal government to establish vehicle-safety standards. Some of the vehicle-safety requirements added by the government included headrests, shatter-resistant windshields, seat belts, additional lights, energy-absorbing steering wheels, and 5-mph crash-resistant bumpers. These safety features added significant cost to vehicles, but safety reduced fatalities.

Despite the government claim that the auto industry had failed to provide safety features in vehicles, the Nash Rambler had provided seat belts in 1950, but customers disconnected the belts because they were uncomfortable. In the 1950s, Ford introduced safety features including seat belts, and padded instrument panels, but customers ignored the safety items and refused to buy them. Seat belt legislation varies by state, but in 1981, years after seat belts were standard equipment in vehicles, only 11% of drivers used seat belts. It wasn't until states required seat belts with the penalty of a traffic ticket that the public began to use seat belts.

The government involvement in safety is understandable, but the efforts to control the economy have been disastrous. The Federal Reserve has proven to be incapable of managing the economy, assuming that the Great Depression is part of its report card. The founding fathers of the country had no plans for the Federal Government to control housing, but the 2008 Great Housing Recession was caused by government interference in the housing market. Home equity had always been a safe investment, and even remained constant throughout the Great Depression and other recessions caused by the government. The government interference in the housing market changed all that.

The 2008 Great Housing Recession caused homeowners to lose 50% of their home equity. In many cases, the investment in homes was the largest part of the net worth of families, but the housing recession reduced that safe investment. In prior recessions, investors in the stock market suffered the losses, but in the 2008 recession, homeowners were also big losers, and eight years later, they have not completely recovered their equity.

The government interference in the housing market involved legislation to increase home ownership for minorities and low-income families. Congress passed legislation to stimulate home mortgages for people unable to afford a home, and the White House added executive orders that relaxed mortgage rules. These changes stimulated the housing market, resulting in a housing boom in 2001-2006. Many of the new low-income homeowners could not make the mortgage payments, and their homes went into foreclosure. There were fifteen million home foreclosures by 2015. The government *plan* actually reduced home ownership.

The large number of foreclosures ended the housing bubble and the subprime mortgage security fiasco. Wall Street had overinvested in the subprime mortgages, and had billions of worthless mortgages on their balance sheets. For the first time, Wall Street was facing bankruptcy.

The government drive for affordable housing for minorities had created the worst economic crisis since the 1930s. When Lehman Brothers filed for bankruptcy on September 15, 2008, the bottom fell out of the economy, and the nation was in another depression, according to Ben Bernanke, chair of the Federal Reserve.

2008 Great Housing Recession

The economic growth since the 2008 recession has been less than 2%; far less than the 5% growth in past post-recession periods. The government legislation eliminated the controls in home mortgages, and created a housing balloon that burst in 2007, resulting in the 2008 Great Housing Recession. The Wall Street subprime mortgage security crisis caused the bankruptcies in the financial community.

There were actually two elements in the 2008 Great Housing Recession. The first was congressional legislation to increase home ownership for minorities and low-income families, and the second was the subprime mortgage debacle. The legislation caused the housing boom, and the subprime mortgage securities caused the Wall Street crisis. Wall Street had failed, possibly deliberately, to include the risk of foreclosures in the mortgage bond prospectus, and investors did not know what they were buying. The subprime mortgage securities became a worldwide product with sales throughout the world.

Legislation That Caused the 2008 Housing Recession

- Community Reinvestment Act – promoted mortgages for minorities and low-income applicants.
- Adjustable Rate Mortgage Act – lowered initial mortgage payments – over 90% of toxic mortgages were adjustable rate loans.
- Housing and Community Development Act – reduced discriminatory credit practices, and encouraged banks to increase loans to minorities and low-income families.
- Housing Enterprises Financial Act – gave HUD authority to administer government targets for low-income mortgages.
- National home ownership strategy relaxed credit standards.
- President Clinton directed HUD to require banks to give at least 50% of loans to minorities and low-income families.
- Repeal of Glass-Steagall Act of 1933.
- Commodity Modernization Act – exempted derivatives from regulations and supervision.
- Federal Reserve lowered interest rates from 5.25% to 0.25%% in less than a year.
- SEC relaxed capital reserve requirements.

The above legislation was a recipe for economic disaster. The government drive for home loans for minorities and low-income families went beyond practical limits, and the repeal of the Glass-Steagall act in 1999 was a major change in the control of Wall Street banks. Under the Glass-Steagall Act, investment banks were privately held companies and could not buy commercial banks. Investments were made with their own money. This changed in 1999; investment banks were allowed to buy conventional banks and become public corporations, investing stockholder money rather than their own. Within a few years, Wall Street banks had over $5 trillion of debt – stockholder debt.

The reduction in interest rates by the Federal Reserve fueled the housing boom. The interest-rate reduction from 5.25% to 0.25% was historic, and the reduction in interest rates occurred in less than one year, an amazing cut that had never happened before.

Although the author did not use the book *Reckless Endangerment* by Gretchen Morgenson in the research, the book mirrors the premise that the Federal Government caused the 2008 Great Housing Recession. The treatise also makes a case that the responsible government officials should be held accountable. For those who question that the government caused the 2008 financial debacle, *Reckless Endangerment* would be interesting reading.

Wall Street investment banks took advantage of the boom in housing and mortgages, and created mortgage bonds that included thousands of toxic mortgages. The bond prospectus conviently ignored the risk of the toxic subprime mortgage securities, and investors were unaware of the toxic mortgage risk. Wall Street earned huge profits and bonuses during this period, and this is the same group of firms and executives that were bailed out by the government with trillions of taxpayer money.

The housing bubble peaked in 2006, however, in early 2007 investment banks finally realized the extent of the toxic mortgages on their balance sheets, and attempted to sell the bonds. However, the market had already determined that the mortgage bonds had no value, and nobody was buying. This necessitated huge write-offs and Wall Street investment banks were near bankruptcy.

The government evidently saw the economic disaster coming because the Federal Reserve bailed out Wall Street's Bear Stearns with $30 billion of taxpayer money in March 2008. However, the company was beyond saving, and was sold to J.P. Morgan Chase on May 29, 2008. This was the first *too big to fail* attempt by the government, and it failed. Further attempts would also fail; the Treasury and Federal Reserve used $14 trillion of taxpayer money in the attempt to save Wall Street, banks, and mortgage firms.

Another bailout attempt that has been ignored was the $138 billion given to J.P. Morgan Chase in a failed attempt to save Lehman Brothers. The Treasury, under Secretary Henry Paulson, was determined to bailout Wall Street with the too big to fail idea.

The first bailout money given to Wall Street, AIG, and the GSEs included $30 billion to Bear Stearns, $138 billion to Lehman Brothers, $180 billion to AIG, and $400 billion to Fannie Mae and Freddie Mac. The total was more than 10 times the amount of TARP funds granted to Chrysler and General Motors to pay their bills during the Congressional Hearings and the Rattner's study.

The government paid out trillions to the parties guilty of developing the toxic mortgage debacle, and the top executives who took millions in bonuses. The auto companies were the victims of the government-caused economic calamity, but were refused bailout funds.

The stock market peaked in October 2007 with the Dow reaching 14,000, but 17 months later it bottomed at 6600, a drop of 53%. The economy declined for four consecutive quarters, with one quarter dropping 9%. The subprime mortgage recession resulted from the government attempts to increase home mortgages for low-income families, and the attempt just went too far. The government had no business interfering in the housing market.

On September 15, 2008, Lehman Brothers filed for bankruptcy precipitating the Great Housing Recession. The subprime mortgage recession of 2008 was the worst financial event since the Great Depression of 1929. In a document filed on August 22, 2014 with the U.S. Court of Federal Claims as part of the AIG lawsuit, Ben Bernanke was quoted as saying; "September and October of 2008 was the worst financial crisis in global history, including the Great Depression." Unemployment jumped from 5% to over 10%, the stock market fell 50%, auto sales dropped 40%, and homeowners lost 50% of their home equity. The drop in vehicle sales created a depression in the automobile industry.

The job market has yet to recover. The reported unemployment rate of 5% is faulty since the real number is twice that. Unemployment data is an inaccurate government statistic because it is based on a monthly "survey" of 60,000 households, and people who have stopped looking for work are not included in the estimate. Over 9 million unemployed workers are not included in the government unemployment statistics. Unfortunately, the Federal Reserve uses the inaccurate data to make its decisions on the economy.

The Big Three had excess capacity because foreign competition had taken over 50% of the U.S. market. Many manufacturing and assembly plants should have been closed, but the UAW jobs bank restricted management's ability to close plants. The workers laid off in a plant closure simply moved into the jobs bank, and received 95% of their pay and 100% of their benefits. The jobs bank was costing the Big Three over a billion dollars a year in out-of-pocket costs, and this number did not include the fixed costs of the excess plants.

Working capital became a serious problem with the 40% drop in vehicle sales – the companies could not pay their bills. Ford had mortgaged their entire company in 2006, and borrowed $23.6 billion from the banks for restructuring and used the loan for working capital. Chrysler and GM were unable to obtain bank loans in 2008 because the banks were in bankruptcy.

The housing recession was in full force. The Federal Government bailouts of Wall Street, AIG, Fannie Mae, and Freddie Mac required the government to raise the debt ceiling to over $10 trillion in 2009. Unfortunately, the Obama administration continued to spend, and the debt is now close to $20 trillion.

Congress passed the Emergency Economic Stabilization Act on October 3, 2008 in an attempt to avoid another depression. The legislation created the $700 billion TARP fund for troubled assets.

Chrysler and General Motors were out of working capital in late 2008 due to the decline in vehicle sales, and were close to bankruptcy. Ford was still using the $23 billion bank loan for working capital, but the other two members of the Big Three were in deep trouble. Since banks were also near bankruptcy, the government was the only source of funds.

The TARP fund was approved and available, but Secretary of the Treasury Paulson was the TARP fund czar. Since the government had bailed out Wall Street, AIG, and the GSEs, the Big Three CEOs petitioned the Treasury for a $35 billion loan for working capital to keep the companies going while restructuring their business models.

The auto execs supplied Paulson with complete financials and business plans for restructuring, and met with Paulson and his auto experts. Despite the working-capital crisis, Paulson did not intend to give money to automotive, and refused to grant any of the TARP fund to the auto companies. Not only did Paulson fail to help the auto companies, he wasted over a month with meetings. As a former CEO of Goldman Sachs, he gave bailout funds to Wall Street, but passed the auto-industry problem to Congress. Michigan legislators accused Paulson of bias in his handling of the TARP fund, and the accusation turned out to be accurate.

The Treasury and the Federal Reserve started bailing out Wall Street, the GSEs, and financial institutions in March 2008, and taxpayer money was used for the bailout. There were 888 banks, including foreign banks, 172 mortgage companies, Wall Street, AIG, Fannie Mae, and Freddie Mac, receiving the bailout funds, but Paulson refused funds for automotive. Of the $79.2 billion eventually loaned to Chrysler and GM, $60 billion was working capital for the companies to pay their workers and suppliers during the eight-months of government studies. The government ignored the need for working capital to keep Chrysler and General Motors open during the ridiculous studies.

While the government was the perpetrator of the subprime mortgage recession, the group receiving the bailout funds was the enabler. The "too-big-to-fail" theory was used for Wall Street, but not for automotive. The number of people employed in the automotive businesses total three million, which would appear to qualify for the "too-big-to-fail" justification criteria. When Paulson rejected the bailout funds for the automotive industry, he obviously excluded the auto business from his criteria that justified a bailout. Paulson bailed out 1065 financial institutions, but was perfectly willing to allow the auto industry to go into bankruptcy.

The Japanese government would have approved a bailout of its auto companies in an instant, and its support of the automotive business is one of the reasons that Japan produces more vehicles than America. There would have been no eight-month delay in awarding government aid to to the Japanese auto manufacturers.

By bucking the decision to Congress, Paulson was "washing his hands" of the auto problem. His meetings with the auto executives were contentious, with the politicians refusing to accept the argument that the cause of the working capital problem was the 40% drop in vehicle sales, and the housing recession had caused the decline in sales. Paulson had his blinders on and could only see the Wall Street problem.

Since the government was the only available option for working capital, the auto companies next appealed to Congress. The Congressional Hearings began in November 2008, and continued into December. The politicians refused to analyze the financial data, and concentrated on public humiliation of the automobile executives. One of the first questions asked was why the Big Three CEOs flew to Washington in their company aircraft. This topic seemed to go on for weeks, and the media kept it going. The working capital problem received no attention. The hearings turned into a kangaroo court with legislators spending their time criticizing the auto executives.

After nearly two months of Congressional Hearings, the House passed a $14 billion loan for Chrysler and GM. However, Republicans in the Senate demanded that the UAW reduce wages and benefits to meet the Japanese levels, and the UAW refused. Senate Democrats supported the union, and the vote was 52-35 against an auto bailout on December 12, 2008. Congress actually voted against an auto bailout. The negative vote has received little media attention, and the public is unaware that Congress voted against a bailout of automotive. Congress made the decision to allow Chrysler and General Motors to go into bankruptcy – not a bailout.

The three million workers in the auto businesses were anxiously awaiting the decision for a bailout, but the Treasury and Congress failed to grant any of the TARP fund to Chrysler or General Motors. Over 1065 financial institutions were allowed to restructure with bailout funds, but not the auto companies.

President Bush provided a $17.4 billion loan to Chrysler and GM on December 19, 2008 to permit the companies to pay their bills until newly elected President Obama assumed office. Even though President Bush favored the bailout of the auto companies, his turning the situation over to the new president was a mistake. Obama had a history of avoiding decisions, and was loyal to the union since the UAW had donated large funds to his campaign. Chrysler and General Motors would have been much better off if the companies had decided to file for bankruptcy after the Senate voted against a bailout. The companies would have proceeded through a normal bankruptcy rather than the Obama controlled bankruptcy in 2009. The law in a normal bankruptcy treats creditors equally, so the UAW would not have been given priority, as was done in the Obama bankruptcy. Unfortunately, Chrysler and GM management trusted the government, and expected a bailout since the financial community had received trillions in taxpayer money during Paulson's bailout lottery.

One of the first problems Obama faced as president was the auto problem. The nation had been waiting nearly four months for a government decision to bailout the auto firms. Instead of making a decision to allocate TARP funds for a bailout, President Obama decided to delay a decision by starting another automotive *study*. The Treasury and Federal Reserve had used trillions of taxpayer money bailing out Wall Street, and President Obama was concerned that negative public opinion would result if he forced the auto companies into bankruptcy. Another study would delay a decision, and allow the auto furor die down. Another study was certainly not required since the Treasury and Congress had *studied* the automobile industry for nearly four months.

Steven Rattner was given the job as task-force leader of "Team Auto." Michigan legislators objected to Rattner because of his lack of experience in manufacturing and the automotive business, but the president ignored the objection. A team appointed to develop a solution for Chrysler and General Motors should have included auto people who knew the business. However, Rattner recruited Wall Street people who knew nothing of the business and had never been near an auto plant. Some did not even own a car.

The Rattner auto task force began by interviewing Chrysler and General Motors executives in Detroit. By mid-February, another $21.6 billion was necessary to keep the two auto companies open. Including President Bush's loan of $17.4 billion, $39 billion had been used by this time for working capital to pay Chrysler and GM's bills while the government was *studying* the auto issue. The $39 billion was not bailout money.

In March 2009, Rattner fired CEO Rick Wagoner of General Motors. Rattner did not have the authority to fire the CEO of the largest automobile company in America, but he did just that. The GM board of directors objected, but President Obama supported Rattner. This was the first time in history that a president had fired a CEO of a public or private company.

The result of the Obama-Rattner task force study was the bankruptcy of Chrysler and GM, and the five-month study by the task force cost the nation $60 billion for working capital to keep Chrysler and GM's doors open. The $60 billion was 75% of the $79 billion loaned to GM and Chrysler. It seems ridiculous that the auto companies were forced into a government "study," and then required to pay the government for the working capital necessary to pay their bills during the five-month study. The entire eight-month process was indicative of the anti-business behavior of the government.

Chrysler exited bankruptcy on June 10, 2009 as a subsidiary of Fiat. The court gave 55% of Chrysler to the UAW VEBA, 20% to the government, and 20% to a foreign auto company, Fiat. The Chrysler bondholders, holding $7 billion in secured bonds and $2 billion in unsecured bonds received nothing. The UAW was owed $8 billion in *unsecured* pension and health care, and received 55% of the company along with a $4.6 billion promissory note with 9% interest. The bankruptcy law requiring that bondholders receive first payment was ignored.

The bankruptcy court also dictated that 25% of the Chrysler dealers be eliminated. Of the 789 dealers cancelled, all but one was a donor to the Republican Party. Politics were in play again. The cancelled dealers were refused vehicles even though they had new orders, and the Chrysler dealers were given only two weeks to close their franchisees. Even though many Chrysler dealers were family-owned enterprises, and had been with Chrysler for decades, they lost their businesses. Fiat did not pay anything for 20% of the third largest car company in the nation. Rattner literally gave Chrysler to Fiat.

Rattner forced Chrysler into bankruptcy, and then gave the company to the UAW and Fiat. Fiat lost $1.4 billion in 2012 and Chrysler bailed them out with a $1.7 billion profit. Fiat was the only car company bailed out by the Obama-Rattner team.

General Motors came out of bankruptcy court on July 10, 2009, with the name "General Motors Company," as opposed to General Motors Corporation. The General Motors Company consisted of Chevrolet, Buick, Cadillac, and GMC, with the balance of the brands and 2000 dealers eliminated. The court gave 60.8% of GM to the U.S. government, 11.7% to the Canadian government, and 17.5% to the UAW VEBA. The GM bondholders lost 90% of their $30 billion secured investment while the union kept its pay, pension, and health-care benefits, another under-reported fact.

General Motors Company became "Government Motors," with over 70% of the company owned by the U.S. and Canadian governments. Rick Wagoner and Fritz Henderson were fired, and the government appointed a new CEO, Ed Whitacre. Whitacre flew home to Texas every weekend, evidently thinking the CEO position was a part-time job. The government also appointed seven consultants to high-level executive positions.

In hindsight, the companies should have made the decision to go into Chapter 11 when Congress voted against a bailout. The outcome would have certainly been better than Chrysler being owned by Fiat, and GM owned by the government. Normal bankruptcy law would have allowed both companies to renegotiate their union contracts and obtain lower wages and benefits.

The management of Chrysler and General Motors failed to prepare for bankruptcy thinking that the government would bail them out. Neither company believed the government would drive them into bankruptcy. This error ended up causing the eight-month government delay problem. GM and Chrysler management failed to understand, or accept, the government's animosity toward the auto companies, and that that the Obama administration was determined to favor the UAW. The politicians had no intention of bailing out the car companies. Unfortunately, the *too big to fail* idea only applied to the financial community; the automobile industry was not included

The Obama admistration violated bankruptcy law in the Chrysler and GM bankruptcies. The law demands that a secured creditor be paid first. Chrysler and GM bondholders held $40 billion of secured debt, but received hardly anything. The government gave the union first priority for unsecured pension and health-care.

The eight-month delay by the government was appalling. A brief summary of the delay in decision-making is shown below.

GOVERNMENT DECISION DELAYS

- Secretary Paulson of the Treasury held meetings in October 2008 but refused the request of General Motors and Chrysler for loans from the TARP fund. The government had given trillions to Wall Street, AIG, mortgage companies, Fannie Mae and Freddie Mac, but refused any help for automotive.
- Congress held two months of Congressional Hearings in November and December of 2008, criticizing the Big Three, but refused to grant any money from the TARP fund for automotive. The Senate voted 52-35 against an auto bailout. The decision was to allow the auto companies to go into bankruptcy.
- The auto bailout issue reached newly elected President Obama's desk in January 2009, but the president rejected the use of TARP funds for a bailout. President Obama made a political decision to "study" the auto problem to allow public opinion to die down. The Obama-Rattner task-force study took five months. Chrysler and GM were forced into bankruptcy – there was no bailout.

The misfortune was that it was necessary to provide Chrysler and General Motors working capital to pay their employees and suppliers during the Rattner study. The firms could not pay their bills. The five-month "Team Auto" study cost taxpayers $60 billion for working capital; 75% of the $79.2 billion attributed to the reported "bailout" cost.

The only recipients of a bailout were the UAW and Fiat. The UAW had donated funds for President Obama's election campaign, and the president was determined to pay them back. The abuse of the bankruptcy law was a travesty, and should have been opposed in a lawsuit by the bondholders. The fact that the Obama administration misused bankruptcy law has received no media attention and the public is unaware of the sham.

The government attempt to increase home ownership for low-income families and minorities actually reduced home ownedrship because of the 15 million foreclosures. Legislation allowed families who could not afford to own a home to obtain mortgages, but unfortunately, the loans resulted in toxic mortgages and foreclosures when the new homeowners could not make the house payments. The government failed to recognize that foreclosures would occur, and had no back-up plan. The regulatory agencies also failed to control lending and mortgage fraud.

The government actions during the recession were entirely political, and the abuse of bankruptcy law was tragic. The government preferential treatment of the union has received no media attention, so the public knows nothing about the allocation of assets by the bankruptcy court. The common thinking is that the automobile industry was bailed out, and many believe that the bailout was wrong. The term bankruptcy is never used, and if the average person were asked what happened, the response would be that the government favored the auto companies at the expense of taxpayers. The fact that the union was granted priority over stockholders and bondholders is not remembered. The gift of Chrysler to Fiat is not recognized, and that Fiat moved Chrysler headquarters to London receives no attention. The government has done a great job in hiding the actual proceedings of the bankruptcy court. Federal officials have also ignored that legislation to give home loans to people unable to afford homes was the root cause of the financial debacle that cost taxpayers $14 trillion.

SEVEN

OUTLOOK

The U.S. economy continues to struggle nearly eight years after the supposed end of the 2008 Great Housing Recession. The National Bureau of Economic Research, the government agency responsible for estimating the start and end of recessions, determined that the recession started in December 2007 and ended in June 2009. Even if the bureau is correct in its 18-month estimate, the Great Housing Recession was the longest since the Great Depression of the 1930s, and the recovery has been the slowest and the weakest. Gross Domestic Product was less than 2% between 2009 and 2016, while the average GDP for recovery periods after prior recessions was 5% to 10%. This alarming stastatistic clearly shows how bad the economy has been in the past eight years. GDP measures the size of the economy, and is the most accurate indicator, since it includes the total dollar value of all goods and services produced. The government has ignored the lack of GDP growth while claiming the economy was great.

The media have ignored the lack of GDP growth, and have ignored the decline in home equity caused by the 2008 recession. For the first time in history, homeowners lost nearly 50% of their net worth in this normally "safe" investment. In prior recessions, the losses were in the stock market, but not in home equity. The 2008 housuing recession hit the middle class hard.

The manufacturing sector has declined, and unemployment is still high. The government-reported unemployment rate of 5% is double the rate in prior recoveries, and does not include the millions who have stopped looking for a job. Half of the 2012 college graduates were unable to find a job, and many of those who did find work were working part time jobs like Starbucks and McDonalds that do not require a college degree.

The outlook for the U.S. economy is, at best, questionable. The Great Housing Recession of 2008 was the deepest recession since the Great Depression of the 1930s, and the government caused both disasters. The recovery from the 2008 recession has been so tepid that many believe the country is still in a recession.

THE GOVERNMENT

The outlook for the government is more of the same. The Federal Reserve has caused half the recessions since World War II; the Federal Government needs a new business model, but continues with age-old fomulas.

Legislation to increase home ownership for minorities and low-income families created the housing bubble that burst in 2007. The requirements for down payments and income verification were eliminated, and anybody could obtain a mortgage with a signature. The new homeowners could not make mortgage payments, and fifteen million foreclosures resulted. The government plan (?) for affordable housing for the poor actually reduced home ownership because of the 15 million foreclosures.

Just as the auto industry went into bankruptcy during the Great Depression because of the 75% drop in vehicle sales, the industry was in bankruptcy again in 2008 when vehicles sales declined 40%. The auto business was the victim of the government caused housing recession. Similar to politicians in the 1930s blaming the Great Depression on business, Congress blamed the 2008 auto decline on poor business management.

The government aided the unions with the 1935 National Labor Relations Act that recommended unions as the solution for recessions, and helped the UAW in the 2009 bankruptcy by favoring the union over bondholders.

The government has controlled the automobile industry with legislation and regulations since the 1920s, and the attempts to manage the economy have been disasterous. The government needs a new game plan, but until term limits are imposed on politicians, there is no chance for a change.

The government hostility toward the auto industry was apparent during the 2008 Congressional Hearings; the hearings were similar to a kangaroo court with the Big Three CEOs on trial. The eight-month delay in decision making on the auto bailout was a classic. After three months of Treasury meetings and Congressional Hearings, the Senate voted 52-35 against a bailout.

The Obama-Rattner task force was a total failure. Chrysler and General Motors were driven into bankruptcy, there was no bailout. The government too big to fail program rewarded Wall Street and financial institutions; there were 1065 financial firms bailed out, but Main Street was driven into bankruptcy. Only Washington politicians can cause bankruptcy and call it a bailout.

The outlook for the government is to continue with anti-business and anti-auto industry legislation that will result in a continued decline in market share by the U.S. automakers. The government must change its attitude, but the prospect of a change does not appear to be likely.

UAW

The outlook for the UAW is also "more of the same." The inability of union management to adapt to the changing labor environment is baffling. The old days of labor violence and long strikes are gone, and younger workers just want a job. The 1950s security of a UAW auto job no longer exists due to the loss of market share to foreign competition. The UAW has lost 70% of its membership over the last 50 years, yet union management still does not recognize that their enemy is foreign competition, not Big Three management. UAW management hubris has caused the loss of membership.

The UAW has maintained an adversarial attitude toward auto management since the union was founded in 1935, and the anti-management posture permeates the organization. This negative attitude has caused UAW workers to slash tires to cause vehicle recalls, and put pop cans inside door panels to cause rattles. The pattern-bargaining tactic continues to favor the union in contract negotiations.

The labor cost of $78 an hour is double that of foreign competitors located in the nation. Unfortunately, the UAW contract gains in wages and benefits have driven labor costs to the level where the U.S. carmakers became non-competitive. UAW management killed the goose that laid the golden egg.

UAW management's inability to recognize that a change is necessary in labor-management relations, and their continuous drive against management, will cause further conflict. The union continues to lose members, and since Michigan is now a right-to-work state, UAW members can elect to drop out of the union. The right-to-work law could cause a further drop in UAW membership.

The outlook for the UAW is more of the same; continued conflict with management, continued use of patern bargaining, and continued loss of union membership.

GENERAL MOTORS

After losing $70 billion between 2005 and 2008, an average of $17.5 billion a year, General Motors has reported profits in the post-bankruptcy period. However, massive quality recalls have put a dent in profits as well as the quality reputation.

The bankruptcy court gave over 70% of GM to the U.S. and Canadian governments, 17.5% to the UAW VEBA, and GM bondholders received only 10% of their $30 billion investment. The UAW maintained their wages and fringes. General Motors exited bankruptcy on July 10, 2009, and the U.S. government took complete control of the company.

The government immediately began to make people changes. After firing two GM CEOs in an eight-month period, the government appointed two new CEOs (Whitacre and Akerson) in a four-year period. The government also brought in a number of Wall Street types in key positions.

There were five CEOs of GM between March 2009 and January 2014. Five CEOs in a four-and-one-half-year period was certainly a record. During these changes, employees tend to go into a "foxhole" mentality. To avoid making waves, individuals pull their helmets over their ears, and sink into their "foxholes" to avoid layoffs. GM had been going through reorganizations since Roger Smith took over in 1981, and the people changes continue.

General Motors announced the recall of 29 million vehicles in 2014, shortly after the government sold its last remaining shares of the company. Delphi, the former GM subsidiary, designed and built an ignition switch that moved to the off, or accessory, position, and caused the engine to stop running. When the engine stops, all power in the vehicle is lost. The power brakes and power steering fail to work, and the airbags fail to deploy in an accident. A number of accidents and fatalities involving ignition switches have been reported and a massive recall is in progress.

Documents submitted to the government showed that General Motors recognized the switch problem in 2002, twelve years prior to the recall announcement. The documents also reported that there were nearly 500 dealer repairs on the switches, and GM failed to recall the vehicles because the recall cost exceeded the warranty savings. The government "experts" managed GM for nearly five years, and many of the vehicles with safety and quality problems were produced during that period. The government *auto experts* obviously failed to handle the issue.

General Motors market share has dropped from 50% to 17.1% in the last 50 years, and the decline has been a disaster. Gains in market share are difficult under normal conditions, but almost impossible to attain in a company recovering from bankruptcy.

The outlook for General Motors is continual organization changes that will cause inefficiency and morale issues. The recalls and safety issues will plague the company for years, and potential General Motors customers may refuse to buy a GM vehicle because of the negative press. The bankruptcy days were difficult, but GM is not out of trouble. General Motors will continue in business, but has lost its leadership.

FIAT CHRYSLER (FCA)

The outlook for FCA is bleak. The company has suffered with low volume since losing market share due to the 1949 104-day strike. The result of the strike was a huge profit loss, and a major loss of market share. The loss of market share was a disaster that pushed the company into third place in vehicle sales, and the lower volume was close to its break-even point. Because of the lower volume and revenue, Chrysler only made money in the good times. When recessions caused auto sales to decline, Chrysler lost money. The lower revenue also created a cash problem, and limited funds for the annual model change.

UAW pattern bargaining changed Chrysler from a successful company to a business that struggled to stay alive. The lower volume eventually caused near-fatal results when the 1979 recession caused a bankruptcy situation. Lee Iacocca brought Chrysler back, but the company still had the volume problem. After bankruptcy in 2009, Chrysler was profitable, but the parent company, Fiat continued to lose money.

Fiat has never been successful in the U.S. market, and part of the reason was its lack of quality. The nickname "Fix It Again Tony" came about because of its quality problems. Fiat lost $1.4 billion in 2012, and was bailed out by Chrysler's profits.

Twenty years ago, Chrysler reported profits of $3.7 billion, had 15% of the American market, and was the low-cost producer in the Big Three. Lee Iacocca and his team had turned the company around, and Chrysler was again a viable company. Eaton forced Chrysler into the Daimler-Benz takeover in May 1998, and the infamous "merger of equals" resulted in Daimler replacing eleven Chrysler executives in a two-year period. The Daimler Chrysler venture failed, and Daimler sold Chrysler to Cerberus in 2007.

Sixteen months later, the 2008 Great Housing Recession hit, and vehicle sales declined. Due to the drop in revenue, Chrysler ran out of cash to pay its bills. With the banks in bankruptcy, the government was the only source of cash.

The Treasury and Congress spent nearly four months studying the auto business, and voted against a bailout. The Rattner *study* lasted five months, so the government wasted eight months reviewing the auto issue. Chrysler was driven into bankruptcy by the Obama-Rattner task force on April 30, 2009, and the bankruptcy court gave Chrysler to the UAW and Fiat.

The outlook for Chrysler is grim. If Fiat is unable to obtain profitability, the company may be forced to sell Chrysler to avoid bankruptcy. The gloomy forecast for Chrysler is unfortunate, but realistic.

FORD

The outlook for the Ford Motor Company is questionable. Alan Mulally turned the firm around after losses of $12.6 in 2006; the company's market share had dropped to 18.5%. Bill Ford's tenure as CEO saw the company go from record profits and gains in market share, to record losses and a loss of market share every year. The company also had quality problems and recalls. The market-share loss dropped Ford's volume below its break-even level, and the firm was near bankruptcy. Ford obtained a $23.6 billion bank loan in 2006 for restructuring, and the loan turned out to be the savior for Ford during the 2008 recession. Ford was able to use the cash for working capital to avoid bankruptcy.

The age-old problem of not having models in the mid-market segment still exists. The Mercury brand failed to compete, was cancelled, and has not been replaced. The infamous Edsel was also intended for the mid-market segment, but the brand was rejected by buyers and cancelled after two years. The Ford brand competes in the lower end of the market, and the Lincoln brand attempts to compete in the high end, but there is nothing between the two brands. This has been a factor limiting Ford's attempt to increase volume since the days of the Model T, and is still a problem for the company. The inability to develop mid-market brands that sell is a puzzler. The company has the talent and resources to develop new vehicles, but has not been able to launch a mid-market brand that attracts customers. The lack of products in the mid-market segment will limit its growth. The Lincoln brand is last in sales in the luxury market segment, and is a problem despite continual styling changes.

Alan Mulaly did an outstanding job in turning Ford around, but he retired in 2014. Mark Fields took over as CEO, but was fired by the Ford family in 2017 despite record profits. The outlook for Ford is to remain second in the marketplace.

OUTLOOK FOR THE U.S. AUTOMOBILE INDUSTRY

It is a sad state of affairs when the American public believes the U.S. automobile industry should go away. A recent CNN poll shows that over 60% of Americans believe the government should not have bailed out the auto companies. The government and mainstream media have convinced the nation that Uncle Sam did a heroic job in bailing out the automobile business, but Chrysler and General Motors were forced into bankruptcy, which is just the opposite from a bailout. However, based on the Senate vote of 52-35 against a bailout, the public is mirroring their elected politicians' position. Similar to the CNN poll, the Senate vote was exactly 60% against a bailout.

The UAW pattern bargaining tactic has increased wages and benefits to $78 per hour, which is three times the amount paid to the average private sector worker, and twice that of foreign competitors in the nation. In addition to wages and fringes, the labor contracts included benefits such as the jobs bank that paid workers not to work. Unfortunately, the labor costs exceeded that of foreign auto companies, and resulted in a $4000 per vehicle cost penalty for U.S. automakers. The UAW killed the goose that laid the golden egg.

With the OPEC oil embargo of 1973, the U.S. automobile market changed to small, fuel-efficient vehicles, and the Big Three attempts at small cars failed. The excessive labor costs prevented profits in small cars, and U.S. carmakers continued to focus on large vehicles since they were more profitable. The Big Three led in the light truck, van, and SUV markets, but failed to meet the competition in the small-car segment. During the 1970s when OPEC was raising the price of oil, small cars dominated the market because of fuel economy. In the past 40 years, foreign competition has increased their market share, and U.S. automakers have less than 50% of the market.

The loss of market share by the U.S. carmakers resulted in a loss of manufacturing capability and a loss of manufacturing jobs. The government continues with its anti-business and anti-automotive policies despite the decline of manufacturing. The UAW continues with its anti-management behavior in spite of losing 75% of its membership during the past 35 years. The car companies are still run by finance people who fail to consider customers in their cost-control decisions; Big Three management must reduce the dominance of finance in decision-making since market share dictates sales and profits.

The government remains a problem. If the government could adopt the Japanese system of working with business, the nation could be a primary producer of manufactured products in the world. However, politicians are firmly entrenched in their anti-business posture. If the UAW could be a partner with management, instead of an adversary, the U.S. auto companies would be more competitive, and return to being the best in the world; but this behavioral change is not likely to happen. The world has changed, but the major players in the U.S. auto market haven't changed.

China is by far the leading producer of vehicles in the world with 22 million units produced in 2013, which is 25% of the world's production. The U.S. is second with 11 million units and 12.5% of the world market. However, U.S. production was 12.8 million units in 2000, and the Chinese production was only two million. China has increased auto production by 1100% in the past 13 years, while the U.S. production has declined. Japan's production has remained at 10 million units during this period, and UK production has been a constant 1.5 million. If the U.S. is to remain a leading vehicle producer, the major players, management, the UAW, and the government, must adapt to the world market changes. This is an absolute necessity, but is unlikely to happen under current conditions.

If the UAW is unable to change, and continues with its pattern bargaining tactics in contract negotiations, the U.S. carmakers will continue to have higher labor and fringe costs that will result in further losses of volume to foreign companies. The volume loss with cause more automotive and supplier plants to close, and result in more UAW job losses, and increased unemployment.

The government is hopeless and will continue with its anti-business behavior. Politicians criticize auto management, and continue to pass legislation and regulations that hamper business. The process limits auto production, entrepreneurs, and small business owners who create most jobs.

The failure of U.S. carmakers to develop competitive small cars has been a problem for years. Since small vehicles make up 40% of the nation's market, the lack of U.S. competitive products has caused the loss of market share. Volume is the key element in the capital-intensive business, and the loss of market share has caused huge losses of volume and profits. U.S. manufacturers focus on SUVs and light trucks because the products are highly profitable, but have lost the small-car volume. The loss of the small car market has been a disaster for the Big Three, and resulted in a 30% overcapacity problem. The jobs bank has gone away, so the firms can finally eliminate unused manufacturing plants. Labor costs are a big problem, but management must find a way to be competitive.

The U.S. auto companies have the technology and engineering capability to develop small vehicles, and must target this market segment to increase volume. The introductions of the Chevrolet Cruze, Ford's new Focus, and Chrysler's new Dodge Dart have helped the U.S. automakers increase their share of the small car market from 20% in 2009 to 30% in 2014, so there has been improvement. The improvement must continue because foreign competition still controls the small car market segment. The inability of the Big Three to develop competitive small cars has been costly.

The U.S. auto industry will survive, and General Motors and Ford will be profitable; Fiat Chrysler is questionable because of Fiat's losses. The future of Fiat Chrysler will depend on Fiat's ability to improve in Europe. If U.S. companies fail to attack the small-car market with competitive vehicles, foreign competition will continue to increase market share. When recessions hit, customers flock to the small-car market segment to obtain better gas mileage, and small vehicles take an increasing share of the market.

Gasoline prices will increase unless the government develops an energy policy that allows drilling for oil. The OPEC increases in oil prices and the drive for environmental objectives caused gasoline prices to increase. The nation has sufficient oil reserves to be independent of OPEC, and must limit oil imports to reduce oil and gasoline prices. The lack of an energy policy has increased foreign oil imports, caused gasoline prices to increase, and the small-car market to be the major section of the auto market.

U.S. automakers must adapt to the market change to small vehicles if volume is to increase. If the carmakers can focus on the small-car market segment, the companies can increase market share and return to the *good old days* when America dominated the automotive world, and make America great again.

DATA SOURCES

Sources of data included research of congressional legislation, the Treasury Department Center for Public Integrity, and publications on the 2008 recessiion, all of which are public domain. All images shown are public domain.

Made in the USA
Columbia, SC
28 June 2017